Table of Contents

Unit 1: Changing and Growing

Unit 2: Reformers, Newcomers, and Innovators

Unit 3: Politics, Power, and the People

Unit 4: Making Things Better

Unit 5: Taking a Position

Unit 6: Entering a New Century

Unit 7: A Fascinating Era

MS American History Since 1865

Student Guide

Second Edition

Illustrations Credits
All illustrations © K12 Inc. unless otherwise noted

About K12 Inc.
K12 Inc., a technology-based education company, is the nation's leading provider of proprietary curriculum and online education programs to students in grades K–12. K¹² provides its curriculum and academic services to online schools, traditional classrooms, blended school programs, and directly to families. K12 Inc. also operates the K¹² International Academy, an accredited, diploma-granting online private school serving students worldwide. K¹²'s mission is to provide any child the curriculum and tools to maximize success in life, regardless of geographic, financial, or demographic circumstances. K12 Inc. is accredited by CITA. More information can be found at www.K12.com.

978-1-60153-495-8

Printed by LSC Communications, Harrisonburg, VA, USA, April 2018

Unit 10: Recovery, Reaction, Reform

Unit 11: A Turbulent Time

Unit 12: Not So Long Ago

Unit 13: Into the Twenty-First Century

Student Guides and Worksheets

Student Guide

Unit 1: Changing and Growing
Lesson 1: Welcome to American History

The country changed dramatically in the late nineteenth century. Homesteaders and the transcontinental railroad opened the West. Cowboys rode the plains. Native Americans, however, lost their lands and had to change their way of life. As immigrants swelled the nation's cities, reformers and writers challenged the corrupt people who twisted the law to their own advantage.

Our story will be told in a series of books called *A History of US (Concise Edition)*. You'll start with *Volume C (1865-1932)*. In it you'll meet characters like Mark Twain, P.T. Barnum, Chief Joseph, and Jacob Riis.

Lesson Objectives

- Locate selected information in *A History of US (Concise Edition)* in order to gain familiarity with the text.
- Discuss the purposes of studying history.

PREPARE

Approximate lesson time is 60 minutes.

Advance Preparation

- It's important that you read the course introduction for MS American History Since 1865 before starting this lesson. You can find it in the OLS Help section.

Materials

For the Student

A History of US (Concise Edition), Volume C (1865-1932) by Joy Hakim

History Journal

Getting Started

Why Study History?

LEARN

Activity 1: A History of US *(Offline)*

Instructions

A. Introducing Your History Book

The book you are about to begin is full of stories. It has pictures and drawings and even some cartoons. But it is different from many storybooks because its stories are all true. The author, Joy Hakim, is a wonderful storyteller. Every one of her stories has something to do with you. How can that be? You will find an explanation later. For now, do the following:

- Look at the cover of *A History of US (Concise Edition), Volume C (1865-1932)*. This is the third book in a series called *A History of US (Concise Edition)*. There are 4 books in all, but you'll only use Volume C and Volume D in this course.
- Print the Getting Started sheet.
- Answer the first nine questions.

You did some detective work to answer those questions. Historians do a lot of detective work to find facts. Then they think about what they find. The thinking you just did about the picture is called document analysis. You'll do more of that later, but for now, let's get back to detective work.

- Complete the sheet.
- Compare your answers to those in the Answer Key.
- Put the sheet in your History Journal. It will be page 1.

Do you know what a primary source is? Primary means that it is original; it's a record created at the time and place something happened. A document is anything that is on paper (or something like paper). It could be any firsthand record—a will, a letter, a painting, or a photograph. Even an audio recording or film shot when something happened is a primary source. Other things may be considered primary sources, as long as they are from the time and place of the event.

You will see many primary sources in *A History of US (Concise Edition)* . You'll also find definitions, explanations, and extra information on many pages. Look at those before or after you read the text, or you'll miss things you'll want to know.

Now it's time to get started. Do you know why people study history? There are many reasons. Ms. Hakim will tell you why she thinks history is important. See if you agree.

Activity 2: Why Study History? *(Offline)*

Instructions

B. Read and Discuss

Stories of Reconstruction, of immigrants seeking freedom, of inventions that changed our world, of wars, and of going to the moon are all part of your story. America's story is fascinating--and it's not over yet. But that's not the only reason to study it. The Why Study History sheet explains.

- Read the Why Study History sheet.
- In your History Journal, list five reasons for studying American history and then compare your answers to those in the Lesson Answer Key.
- Discuss with an adult the quotations in the margins and your reasons for studying history.

ASSESS

Lesson Assessment: Welcome to American History (*Online*)

You will complete an online assessment covering the main goals of this lesson. Your assessment will be scored by the computer.

LEARN

Activity 3. Optional: Welcome to American History *(Online)*

Instructions

Ms. Hakim's books inspired a television series aired on PBS. They also produced an excellent companion website. This site has lots of audio, photos, documents, games, quizzes, and resources that support your textbook. In this optional activity, you can explore this site and see how you can use it to enrich your learning in *A History of US.*

Freedom: A History of US: http://www.pbs.org/wnet/historyofus/

Name Date

Getting Started

You'll need to become a detective to find the right answers for all these questions. Get ready to search for the answers. They are all in *A History of US (Concise Edition), Volume C (1865–1932)*.

1. Go to the title page (page iii). Who is the author of *A History of US (Concise Edition), Volume C?*

2. Go to the next page. Who are the editors of the K[12] Concise Edition?

3. Look at the front cover. What time period is covered in this book?

4. This is Volume C in a series. Look at the back cover. How many volumes are in this series?

5. Look at the Table of Contents. This book is divided into parts. How many parts does this book have? How many chapters are in this book?

6. Each chapter has a good story. But for now, turn to page 331. What begins on this page?

7. On what page would you find the beginning of the Atlas?

8. There is a section on primary sources. Where can you find these primary sources?

9. Use the index to help you find the pages on which you would find information about Joseph McCoy.

10. Go to page 13. Calamity Jane was a great storyteller. What was her real name?

____

11. A word is defined on page 24. What is it?

____

12. There is a map on page 30. What does this map show?

____

13. Go to pages 53 and 56. You'll see that the green boxes have additional information known as featured articles. What or who is being featured in these green boxes?

____

14. Political cartoons are located throughout the book. Look at the political cartoon on page 174. What is the message in this political cartoon?

____

15. What is the information in the yellow box on page 245?

____

16. What information do you learn by studying the graph on page 268?

____

Name Date

Why Study History?

What's the point of studying history? Who cares what happened long ago? After all, aren't the people in history books dead?

Those are good questions. They bother a lot of people. They bother some people so much that they never study history. That's too bad, because those people miss out on something very important: their own story.

History is the story of US. It tells who we are and where we have been. Sometimes it is so surprising it jolts your mind. Here are a few answers to the questions about studying history:

History is full of stories—true stories—the best ever. Those stories have real heroes and real villains. When you read history, you are reading about real-life adventures.

History is a mystery. No one knows what happened in the past—at least we don't know the whole story. We weren't there. Have you ever put a jigsaw puzzle together? That's what learning history is like. You gather pieces of information and try to discover how they fit. Suddenly, when you have enough pieces in place, you begin to see the big picture. That's exciting, and so is studying history, because new pieces of the puzzle keep fitting in.

When we read about *the mistakes people made in the past,* we can try not to make them ourselves. Nations and people who don't study history sometimes repeat mistakes.

History is especially important for Americans. In many nations—Japan or Sweden, for instance—most citizens share a common background. They have a similar look. They may worship in the same church. That isn't true of us. Some of us were once Chinese, or Italian, or Turkish, or Ethiopian. Americans don't all look alike. Sometimes we don't think alike. But as Americans we do share something. It is our history. We Americans share a common heritage. If you are an American, then the Indians, the Vikings, the Pilgrims, and the slaves are all your ancestors. You will want to know their stories.

Learning about our country's history will make you understand *what it means to be an American.*

History, after all, is the memory of a nation.
—John F. Kennedy
35th President of the United States

History is more or less bunk.
(And, at another time):
The farther you look back, the farther you can see ahead.
—Henry Ford
Founder, Ford Motor Company

The first law for the historian is that he shall never dare utter an untruth. The second is that he shall suppress nothing that is true.
—Cicero
Ancient Roman Statesman

And being an American is a privilege. People all over the world wish that they, too, could be American. Why? Because we are a nation that is trying to be fair to all our citizens. That is unusual.

Which brings me to this book's theme. It is this: *I believe the United States of America is the most remarkable nation that has ever existed. No other nation, in the history of the world, has ever provided so much freedom, so much justice, and so much opportunity to so many people.*

That is a big statement. You don't have to agree with it. Arguing with a book's theme is okay.

Some people will tell you of evil forces in the United States. They will tell of past horrors like slavery and war. They will tell of poverty and injustice today. They will be telling the truth.

The United States isn't perfect. Far from it. Being fair to everyone in a large nation is very difficult. (Do you treat everyone you know equally? How about people you don't like?) The U.S. government has made some terrible mistakes. But usually this nation can, and does, correct its mistakes. That is because we are a democracy: power belongs to the people, not the rulers. We are also a nation governed by law. Everyone—the president, congressmen, congresswomen, and you—lives by the same laws.

Our top—or supreme—law is the Constitution. Even bad presidents and congresses obey the Constitution. They have to. They can be impeached—which means "brought to trial"—if they don't.

Our Constitution is part of what makes us so unusual. The Constitution of the United States was the first written constitution—in all of world history—to attempt to treat each citizen equally. It begins with the words *"We the People..."* You are part of "the People."

The Bill of Rights (another name for the first 10 amendments to the Constitution) guarantees rights you wouldn't want to be without. It protects your right to worship as you wish, and it gives you the right to speak out and say or write what you want. You can criticize the government and not worry about being thrown into jail. That isn't true in some countries.

It is one thing to write like a poet, and another thing to write like a historian. The poet can tell or sing of things not as they were but as they ought to have been, whereas the historian must describe them, not as they ought to have been, but as they were, without exaggerating or hiding the truth in any way.

—Miguel de Cervantes

From his novel, *Don Quixote*. Cervantes died in 1616, the same year as Shakespeare.

A man without history is like a tree without roots.

—Marcus Garvey

Founder in 1917 of Universal Negro Improvement Association

What experience and history teach is this—that people and governments never have learned anything from history, or acted on principles deduced from it.

—G. W. F. Hegel

19th Century German Philosopher

When you say the Pledge of Allegiance, do you ever think about the meaning of the words *with liberty and justice for all?*

Liberty is freedom, and you know what that is. But think what it might be like to live in a country where you are not free. In some countries you are told what work you must do and where you must live.

Justice is fairness. Having the same law for everyone is fair.

The last words in the Pledge of Allegiance are for all. This is a nation that tries to offer opportunity for all. In the United States you are free to do anything that anyone else can do. You can run for president, be an artist, write books, or build houses.

The more you study history, the more you will realize that all nations are not the same. Some are better than others.

Does that seem like an unfair thing to say? Maybe, but I believe it.

I don't believe that people in one nation are better than those in another. Every nation has a mixture of good and bad people.

So why, if people are the same, are nations different?

Ideas have a lot to do with it. Nations stand on their ideas. We're lucky. The architects who designed this nation had sound ideas. They were looking for liberty, justice, and opportunity when they came here. They made sure the United States provided them.

Then they did something never done before: they created a people's government. Some men and women in other parts of the world thought that was impossible. After all, it was an untried idea. But America's citizens proved that government by the people can work. How we did that is a fascinating story.

That's the story of the US—the people of the United States—the story you're about to read. It's a history of the men and women and boys and girls who came to a strange land and made it their own. It's a story with heroes, and villains, and big ideas.

We're going to continue that story with Americans on the Move. Enjoy it—there is much to tell.

Where there is history children have transferred to them the advantages of old men; where history is absent, old men are children.
—Juan Vives
Spanish Philosopher, Born 1492

History never repeats itself; at best it sometimes rhymes.
—Mark Twain
Author of *The Adventures of Tom Sawyer*

The famous people quoted here don't agree about the importance or even the meaning of history. It would be boring if they did. But who should you agree with? And how do you come up with opinions of your own? Reading and listening will give you information to form your own ideas. Keeping an open mind will help make those opinions sound.

Student Guide
Lesson 2: Westward Ho!

"In God we trusted, in Kansas we busted," read the signs on the covered wagons heading back East from the Great Plains. With the end of Civil War, thousands of people surged westward, hoping to establish homesteads. But farming the prairie was nothing like farming in the East. About a third of the homesteaders gave up and went back home. Those who survived the danger and hardships turned the plains into "the nation's breadbasket."

Lesson Objectives

- Describe the obstacles settlers encountered as they moved west.
- Identify the products produced on the Great Plains and their markets.
- Recognize that in the late 1800s, new cities sprang up and existing cities, such as Chicago, grew larger.
- Define *prairie,* describe the prairie, and use maps to locate the prairies of the United States.

PREPARE

Approximate lesson time is 60 minutes.

Materials

For the Student

Viewing the Prairie

A History of US (Concise Edition), Volume C (1865-1932) by Joy Hakim

History Journal

Keywords and Pronunciation

Cheyenne (shiy-AN)

Sioux (soo)

LEARN

Activity 1: Across the Great Prairie *(Offline)*

Instructions

A. Focus on Geography

Before settlers arrived, the American prairie was a sea of grasses, wildflowers, and wildlife that spanned more than 69 million acres. When farmers began to till the soil they changed the landscape forever. Today, less than 5.5 million acres of prairie remain (that's about the size of the state of Massachusetts!). Find out more about the prairie:

View pictures of the United States prairie region in the Prairie Slideshow. Then analyze the Prairie Map. Look at how much area the prairie covers. Note where different grass types grew and where most crops and livestock are raised today.

B. Use What You Know

Print the Viewing the Prairie sheet. Use the book *(Chapter 1, pages 2-7)*, the online map, and slideshow to help you answer the questions. When you are finished, compare your answers to those in the Lesson Answer Key.

C. Read On *(Chapter 2, pages 8–13)*

Read about the life of a cowboy on the plains and how the railroad and barbed-wire fences changed that life, and prepare to answer the following questions:

1. What were the factors that made cattle raising profitable?
2. Describe the life of a cowboy.
3. Describe the diversity of the cowboy population. How did this diversity contrast with that of the homesteader population? (Review page 11 if you need help.)

In your History Journal, define range. When you have finished, check your definition against the definition in the Keywords section of the next lesson.

ASSESS

Lesson Assessment: Westward Ho! (*Online*)

You will complete an online assessment covering the main goals of this lesson. Your assessment will be scored by the computer.

LEARN

Activity 2. Optional: Westward Ho! *(Online)*

Name Date

Viewing the Prairie

Use your book *(Chapter 1, pages 2-7)*, the online map, and the Prairie slideshow to answer the following questions.

1. Define prairie.

2. On the map *(page 2)*, color in the prairies of the United States. Include tall grass, mixed grass, and short grass areas.

3. What were the primary products produced on the Great Plains?

4. What were some obstacles settlers encountered as they moved west?

5. In what ways did westward movement affect the growth of cities?

Viewing the Prairie

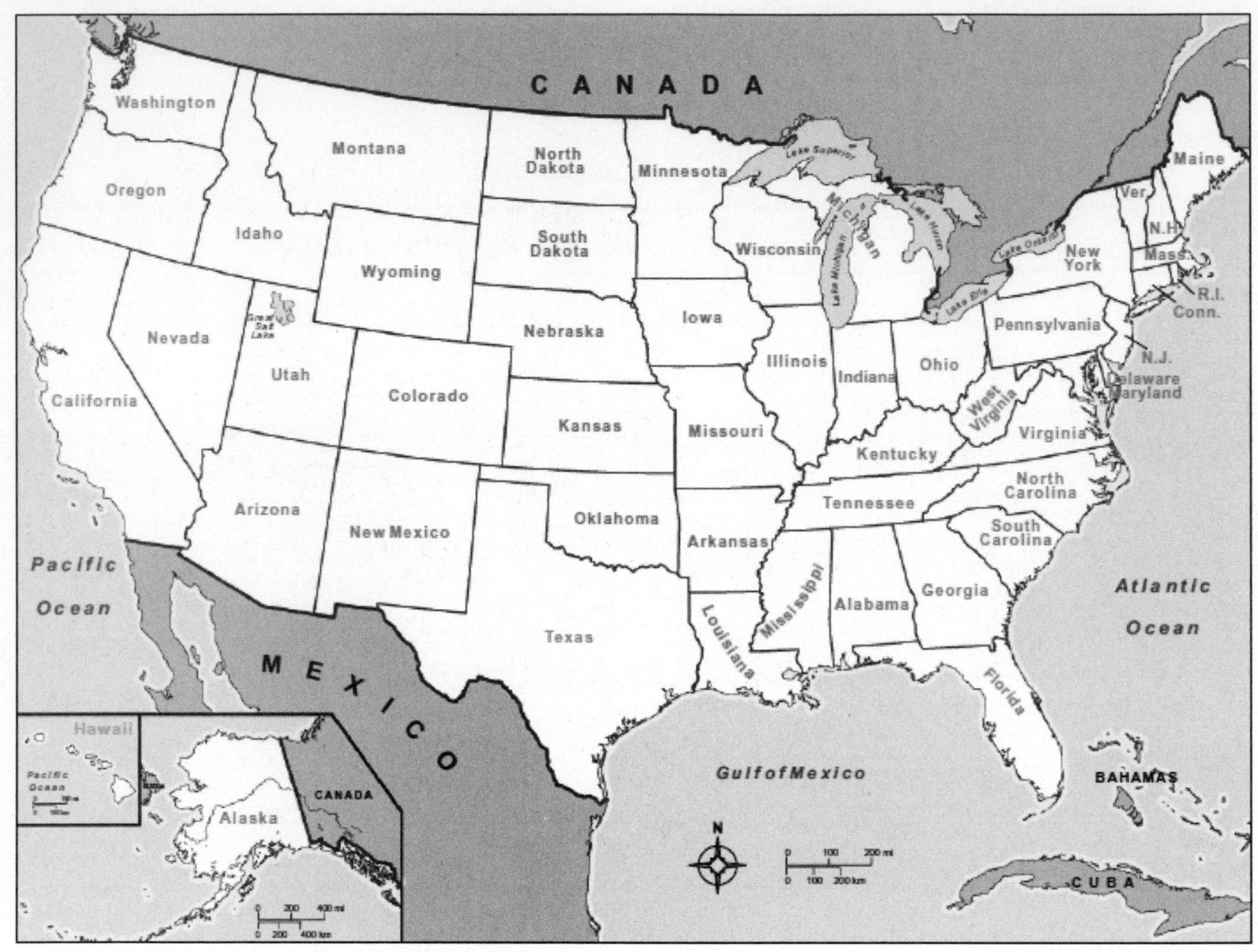

Student Guide
Lesson 3: A Cowboy's Life

The Great Plains briefly belonged to the Texas longhorns and cattle herders who rode the open range. They were the "knights of the prairie"—the skilled and strong-willed men (and women) who pushed the cattle across the great American prairie.

Lesson Objectives

- Explain the developments that made the cattle business profitable.
- Describe the life of a cowboy.
- Recognize the democratic aspects and diversity of the cowboy population.

PREPARE

Approximate lesson time is 60 minutes.

Materials

For the Student

A History of US (Concise Edition), Volume C (1865-1932) by Joy Hakim

History Journal

Keywords and Pronunciation

range : open land for grazing cattle

LEARN

Activity 1: Knights of the Prairie *(Offline)*

Instructions

A. Check Your Reading *(Chapter 2, pages 8–13)*

Review the reading by answering the following questions. Compare your answers to those in the Lesson Answer Key.

1. What factors made the cattle business profitable?
2. Describe the life of a cowboy.
3. Describe the diversity of the cowboy population. How did this diversity contrast with that of the homesteader population? (Review page 11 if you need help.)

Check your definition for the term *range* against the definition in the Keywords section of this lesson.

B. Use What You Know

Imagine you are a member of a homesteading family. Your uncle, who is a cattle driver on his way up the Chisholm Trail, comes to visit and shares many interesting stories with you. Write two diary entries describing his experiences.

Include both the hardships and rewards of working the open range. Don't forget to describe his trail mates (the other cowboys with him) and his impressions of the changes happening on the prairie.

C. Read On *(Chapter 3, pages 14–18)*
As you read, consider the following:

1. When was the transcontinental railroad built and where did it run?
2. Who directed the construction of the railroad, and what groups of people built it?
3. What problems did the builders encounter?
4. When and where was the railroad completed?

ASSESS

Lesson Assessment: A Cowboy's Life (*Online*)

You will complete an online assessment covering the main goals of this lesson. Your assessment will be scored by the computer.

LEARN

Activity 2. Optional: A Cowboy's Life *(Online)*

Student Guide
Lesson 4: Rails

On May 10, 1869, work crews of the Central Pacific and the Union Pacific railroads met at Promontory Point, Utah. After enduring nearly seven years of brutal weather, avalanches, and Indian attacks, their monumental task was complete. As bands played and telegraph wires hummed with the news, the term *United* States began to take on new meaning. Even the builders of the railroads had not forseen the changes that would take place as East met West in the nation's first transcontinental railroad.

Lesson Objectives

- Describe the difficulties of building a transcontinental railroad.
- Explain that Chinese and Irish immigrants and African Americans did most of the work on the railroad.
- Identify the legal and illegal means used to finance railroad construction.
- Recognize that one long-term effect of the railroad was the creation of a system of time zones.

PREPARE

Approximate lesson time is 60 minutes.

Materials

For the Student

- Map of U.S. Time Zones
- Transcontinental Railroad: The Movie!
- A History of US (Concise Edition), Volume C (1865-1932) by Joy Hakim
- History Journal

LEARN

Activity 1: Rails Across the Country *(Offline)*

Instructions

A. Check Your Reading *(Chapter 3, pages 14–18)*

Review your reading by completing the Transcontinental Railroad—the Movie sheet.

B. Focus on Geography

Up until 1883, communities in the United States set their own local time. People set their clocks by the sun. When the sun was at its highest point, it was noon in that community. But as railroads expanded and people began to travel more and travel faster, this inexact method of measuring time began causing problems.

Describe some problems you think this would have caused.

____

____

____

One problem this caused was that it was difficult to establish train schedules that made sense. To help railroads create practical train schedules, the United States and Canada set up time zones. The time zones they created in 1883 are still in use today.

Pretend you're a railroad executive in 1883, and write a brief statement explaining to the public why the railroads have set up these time zones and what the benefits of the time zones will be.

____

____

____

____

____

Use the map of U.S. Time Zones to help you answer the following questions:

1. Which time zone do you live in?____________________
2. Which time zone are the following cities in?
   Portland, Oregon _________________
   Savannah, Georgia ________________
   Dallas, Texas ____________________
   Salt Lake City, Utah ______________
3. What time is it in Chicago if it's 3:00 p.m. in Los Angeles? ____________
4. What time is it in Denver if it's 5:30 a.m. in Miami? ________________
5. If you flew from San Francisco to New York, what would you need to do to your watch when you arrived in New York? (Assume you haven't touched it since you left San Francisco.)

   ____
6. Which states are divided into more than one time zone?

   ____

Check your answers with those in the Lesson Answer Key. When you have finished, place this sheet in your History Journal.

ASSESS

Lesson Assessment: Rails (*Online*)

You will complete an online assessment covering the main goals of this lesson. Your assessment will be scored by the computer.

Name Date

Transcontinental Railroad – the Movie!

Imagine you have been commissioned to write the screenplay for a movie about the building of the Transcontinental Railroad. Use the following to help organize the information you'll need for the screenplay.

Setting: Where does your movie take place? When does it take place?

Characters: Who are the main characters in your movie? You can include individuals and groups of people.

Plot: What is your movie about? Describe what it's about in one or two sentences.

Problem(s): What problems will your characters face?

Resolution: How will your movie end?

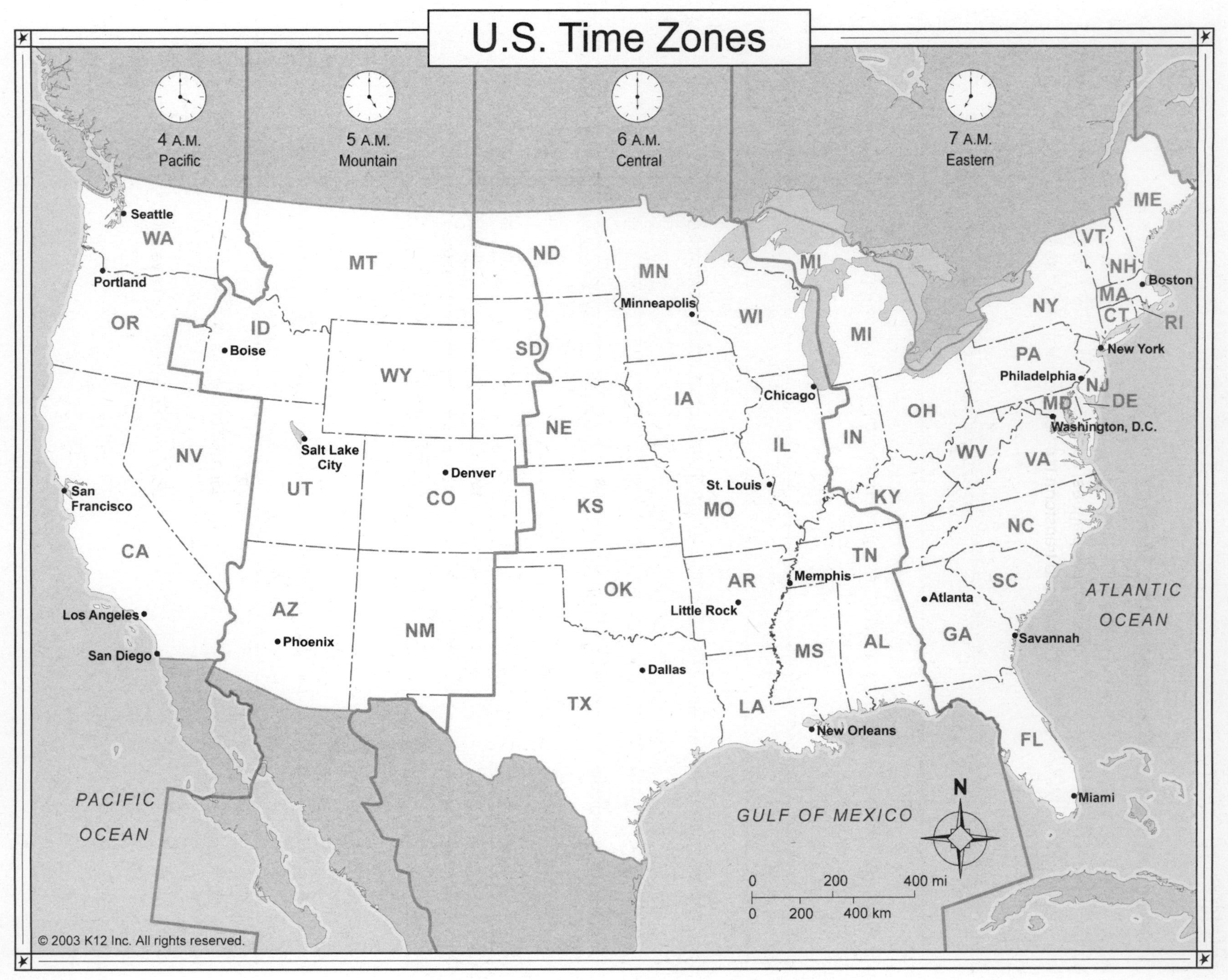
U.S. Time Zones
4 A.M.
Pacific
5 A.M.
Mountain
6 A.M.
Central
7 A.M.
Eastern
Seattle
WA
Portland
OR
ID
Boise
MT
WY
ND
SD
MN
Minneapolis
WI
MI
MI
NY
VT
NH
ME
Boston
MA
CT
RI
New York
PA
Philadelphia
NJ
DE
MD
Washington, D.C.
NV
Salt Lake City
UT
Denver
CO
San Francisco
CA
NE
IA
Chicago
IL
IN
OH
WV
VA
KS
St. Louis
MO
KY
NC
TN
AR
Memphis
OK
Little Rock
SC
Atlanta
GA
Savannah
Los Angeles
AZ
NM
Phoenix
San Diego
MS
AL
Dallas
TX
LA
New Orleans
FL
Miami
ATLANTIC OCEAN
PACIFIC OCEAN
GULF OF MEXICO
N
0 200 400 mi
0 200 400 km
© 2003 K12 Inc. All rights reserved.

Student Guide
Lesson 5: Homesteading

When the Homestead Act opened the plains, settlers moved westward to find their own land. To carve out homesteads, farmers fought drought, grasshopper plagues, and the tangled roots of the grass itself. They used inventions like barbed wire and windmills to transform the "Great American Desert" into a thriving agricultural region.

Use the Magnifier to examine the poster *Millions of Acres* and see the promises that lured the homesteaders west.

Lesson Objectives

- Explain why people moved westward to settle the Great Plains.
- Describe the hardships farmers faced on the plains.
- Identify the solutions farmers came up with to meet the challenges of life on the plains.

PREPARE

Approximate lesson time is 60 minutes.

Materials

For the Student

Settling the Plains: Challenges and Solutions

A History of US (Concise Edition), Volume C (1865-1932) by Joy Hakim

History Journal

Keywords and Pronunciation

barbed wire : twisted wire with sharp barbs used to build fences to control cattle and mark property lines
Great American Desert : a term the early pioneers and Forty-Niners used to describe the Plains States
Homestead Act : a law passed in 1862 that offered settlers 160 acres of land for $10

LEARN

Activity 1: Home on the Range *(Offline)*

Instructions

A. Read *(Chapter 4, pages 19–22; Chapter 5, pages 23–26)*
As you read complete the Settling the Plains: Challenges and Solutions sheet.

Write a brief definition for each of these words in your History Journal. When you have finished, check your definitions with those in the Keywords.
barbed wire
Great American Desert
Homestead Act

Use the online flash cards, Homesteading Challenges, to review some nineteenth-century inventions that changed the plains forever. If needed, use information from the Flash Cards to complete the Settling the Plains: Challenges and Solutions sheet.

B. Use What You Know

Imagine you are part of a homesteading family. Write three diary entries detailing different aspects of your life. Describe:

- Why your family decided to travel west, and your first impressions of the prairie
- Your family's experiences finding and establishing a homestead farm
- The problems you and your family face living on the prairie, and their solutions

---

ASSESS

Lesson Assessment: Homesteading (*Online*)

You will complete an online assessment covering the main goals of this lesson. Your assessment will be scored by the computer.

Name ______________________________ Date ______________________________

Settling the Plains: Challenges and Solutions

List the challenges that homesteaders faced in settling the plains, and the solutions they found to overcome them.

Challenges	Solutions
Shortage of water	Windmills could pump water from deep wells.

1. In what ways were the changes to the plains an agricultural revolution?

____

____

____

____

2. Who was harmed by the farming revolution of the late 1800s?

____

Student Guide
Lesson 6: Losing a Way of Life

As more and more settlers flooded onto the Great Plains, Native Americans struggled desperately to maintain their way of life. "We had buffalo for food, and their hides for clothing and for our tepees," said Crazy Horse, a Sioux chief. "All we wanted was peace and to be left alone." But as the two very different cultures came face to face, a bitter conflict arose that would end up destroying a centuries-old way of life.

Lesson Objectives

- Explain that Native Americans and homesteaders had incompatible ways of life.
- Identify the settlers' primary views on how to solve the Indian conflicts.

PREPARE

Approximate lesson time is 60 minutes.

Materials

For the Student

A History of US (Concise Edition), Volume C (1865-1932) by Joy Hakim

History Journal

Keywords and Pronunciation

Sioux (soo)

LEARN

Activity 1: Western Indian Conflicts *(Offline)*

Instructions

A. Read *(Chapter 6, pages 27–34)*

Before you read, think about the definition of the word incompatible--not able to work, live, or exist together in agreement or harmony. It is clear that the Native Americans and homesteaders had incompatible ways of life. While you read, think about these questions:

1. In what ways were the lives of Native Americans and homesteaders incompatible?
2. Why couldn't the two groups live together on the same land?
3. What were the settlers' main solutions for resolving the Indian conflicts?

B. Focus on Geography

In 1600, Native Americans controlled all of the land that is now the United States. By 1850 they had lost half of the land. In the following 40 years they would lose most of the rest.

Study the map on page 30, Indian Lands Lost, 1850–1890, to see how much land Native Americans lost between 1850 and 1890. Answer the following questions and compare your answers with the answers in the Lesson Answer Key.

1. About what percentage of land did Native Americans lose in the years between 1850 and 1890?
2. Why was it hard for Native Americans and new Americans to share the land?
3. How did the new Americans attempt to solve the Native-American conflicts? How are their solutions reflected on the map?

C. Use What You Know

Political cartoons can express things that regular art or photos cannot. They always state an opinion or make a point. Draw a political cartoon that shows either some causes of the Indian conflicts, or the attitudes of the settlers and soldiers toward the Indians. Draw it from the perspective of either Native Americans or settlers. In other words, how would an Indian or a settler see the issues?

Possible items to include in your cartoon are hunters, farmers, ranchers, soldiers, buffalo, railroads, fences, a reservation, or an Indian academy. You can add speech callout balloons and a title to help make your point.

ASSESS

Lesson Assessment: Losing a Way of Life (*Online*)

You will complete an online assessment covering the main goals of this lesson. Your assessment will be scored by the computer.

Student Guide
Lesson 7: Sorrow

Fleeing from the U.S. Army, the courageous Nez Perce leader, Chief Joseph, led his people in a desperate journey toward Canada and freedom. Even to this day, his eloquent plea for freedom and justice speaks for peoples of all races and backgrounds.

Lesson Objectives

- Identify the Nez Perce Indians and their leader, Chief Joseph.
- Analyze Chief Joseph's speech.

PREPARE

Approximate lesson time is 60 minutes.

Materials

For the Student

Document Analysis: Chief Joseph's Speech

A History of US (Concise Edition), Volume C (1865-1932) by Joy Hakim

History Journal

Keywords and Pronunciation

Nez Perce (nez puhrs)

LEARN

Activity 1: The Nez Perce Flight for Freedom *(Offline)*

Instructions

A. Read *(Chapter 7, pages 35–38)*

B. Use What You Know

You can learn a lot by studying, or analyzing, documents such as speeches. Document analysis is a skill that historians use to learn about the past.

Primary source documents are documents created by people who actually saw or participated in an event and recorded that event soon afterward. When you are considering the value of a primary source document, these are some important facts to know:

- The type of document
- The name and position (title) of the person who produced the document
- The date
- The audience

In 1877, Chief Joseph surrendered and made his "I will fight no more forever" speech. Two years later, he gave a public speech in Washington, D.C. The last three quotes (indented italicized text) on page 38 of *A History of US (Concise Edition),* Volume C, are excerpts from that speech.

Read the excerpts and then answer the questions on the Document Analysis: Chief Joseph's Speech sheet.

ASSESS

Lesson Assessment: Sorrow (*Online*)

You will complete an online assessment covering the main goals of this lesson. Your assessment will be scored by the computer.

LEARN

Activity 2. Optional: Sorrow *(Online)*

Name Date

Document Analysis: Chief Joseph's Speech

Read the last three excerpts from Chief Joseph's speech in Washington, D.C., on page 38 in *A History of US (Concise Edition), Volume C*. Then answer these questions.

1. What type of document is this? ______

2. Is this a primary source document? ______

3. Who was the speaker? ______

4. What was the speaker's position or title? ______

5. For whom was the speech given? ______

6. List three things the speaker said that you think are important.

7. Why do you think this speech was made? ______

8. What evidence in the speech tells you about life in the Americas at the time that it was made? ______

9. Write a question to the speaker that the speech leaves unanswered.

Student Guide
Lesson 8: Unit Review

You have finished the unit! It's time to review what you've learned and prepare for the Unit Assessment.

Lesson Objectives

- Demonstrate mastery of important knowledge and skills in this unit.

PREPARE

Approximate lesson time is 60 minutes.

Materials

For the Student

A History of US (Concise Edition), Volume C (1865-1932) by Joy Hakim

History Journal

LEARN
Activity 1: A Look Back *(Offline)*
Instructions
A. History Journal Review

Review what you've learned in this unit by going through your History Journal. You should:

- Look at activity sheets you've completed for this unit.
- Review unit Keywords and definitions.
- Read through any writing assignments you did during the unit.
- Review the assessments you took.

Don't rush through; take your time. Your History Journal is a great resource for a unit review.

B. Online Review

Review the following in this unit:

- Prairie Map
- Time Line: 1865–1890
- Flash Cards: Railroads
- Flash Cards: Homesteading Challenges

Student Guide
Lesson 9: Unit Assessment

You've finished the unit! Now it's time to take the Unit Assessment.

Lesson Objectives

- Identify the Nez Perce Indians and their leader, Chief Joseph.
- Describe the era of the long cattle drive, including cowboy life, and the reasons for the end of that era.
- Identify the challenges and impacts of building a transcontinental railroad.
- Recognize the major causes and results of conflict between Native Americans and settlers.
- Describe the Great Plains and the advantages and disadvantages of farming there in the late 1800s.
- Discuss reasons for studying history.
- Explain the relationship between new technology and inventions and the settlement of the Great Plains.
- Explain the relationship between new technology and inventions and the settlement of the Great Plains.
- Summarize the major reasons for westward expansion in the late 1800s.
- Use maps to gain familiarity with the American prairie.
- Explain the relationship between new technology and inventions and the settlement of the Great Plains.

PREPARE

Approximate lesson time is 60 minutes.

ASSESS

Unit Assessment: Changing and Growing, Part 1 *(Online)*

Complete the computer-scored portion of the Unit Assessment. When you have finished, complete the teacher-scored portion of the assessment and submit it to your teacher.

Unit Assessment: Changing and Growing, Part 2 *(Offline)*

Complete the teacher-scored portion of the Unit Assessment and submit it to your teacher.

Student Guide

Unit 2: Reformers, Newcomers, and Innovators
Lesson 1: Corruption and Reform

There was plenty that was right with America in the late 1800s, but there were problems, too. What could be done about corrupt city governments, or overcrowded, filthy tenements? Who could find ways to help thousands of eager immigrants become Americans? How would women gain the right to vote? Were there ways to improve daily life or make the earth a little safer? Americans used ingenuity and hard work to tackle these issues. Some especially brave and resourceful individuals stepped forward to make the country a better place for everyone.

In the late 1800s, a few powerful men controlled many of the nation's large cities. In New York, William Marcy Tweed built a political machine that ruled the city by intimidating and bribing officials, but did little to solve the problems of pollution and traffic congestion. Find out how a clever political cartoonist played a key role in bringing down the corrupt "Boss" Tweed.

Click Student Activity and take a look at New York City in the late 1800s.

Lesson Objectives

- Recognize the reasons for pollution in cities during the late 1800s.
- Identify Boss Tweed as the leader of a political machine that ran New York by using bribery and intimidation.
- Identify Thomas Nast as the political cartoonist who helped bring down Tweed.

PREPARE

Approximate lesson time is 60 minutes.

Materials

For the Student

Thomas Nast: Political Cartoonist

A History of US (Concise Edition), Volume C (1865-1932) by Joy Hakim

History Journal

Keywords and Pronunciation

constituents : the people a politician represents
fraud : dishonesty or cheating
political machine : an unofficial government that exists alongside a real government

Instructions

A. Read ***(Chapter 8, pages 39–45)***
As you read, write the definitions for the following terms in your History Journal. When you have finished, compare your definitions with those in the Keywords section of this lesson.

constituents
fraud
political machine

B. Use What You Know
Complete the Thomas Nast: Political Cartoonist sheet. When you have finished, compare your answers with those in the Lesson Answer Key.

ASSESS

Lesson Assessment: Corruption and Reform (*Online*)

You will complete an online assessment covering the main goals of this lesson. Your assessment will be scored by the computer.

LEARN

Activity 2. Optional: Corruption and Reform *(Online)*

Name ______________________ Date ______________________

Thomas Nast: Political Cartoonist

Many people think Thomas Nast was one of the most important American political cartoonists who ever lived. His cartoons appeared in many national publications, and thousands of people saw them. Nast commented on issues he felt Americans should be concerned about. Like all political cartoonists, he used humor to get his point across. His symbols and caricatures (drawings of people with exaggerated features) attracted attention and helped explain important ideas.

The cartoon below is Nast's drawing of William Marcy "Boss" Tweed. Nast was determined to put a stop to Tweed's corrupt politics, so he set out to show the people what a wicked man Tweed was. Study the image and its caption and figure out what Nast was trying to say about Tweed. **Remember, to understand a political cartoon you must first consider what the symbols represent, and then try to make sense of the overall meaning.**

"Well, what are you going to do about it?"

1. Who was Boss Tweed, and why did Nast dislike him? ______________________

____

2. What does the money bag symbolize? ______________________

3. Looking at how the different parts of the cartoon work together (including the caption), what do you think Nast was trying to say in this cartoon?

____

4. Why was Tweed more concerned about these negative cartoons than he was about the nasty articles and editorials published in the same newspapers?

____

5. Imagine that you are a citizen of New York City in the 1870s. In your History Journal, write a letter to the editor of the newspaper in which this cartoon appeared. In your letter, answer the question posed in the caption. Do you support or oppose Tweed and his political machine?

Adapted from *A History of US*

Student Guide
Lesson 2: Mark His Words

The United States was changing fast! In the late 1800s, sleepy towns began transforming into booming industrial centers. The great American writer Mark Twain captured the country's enterprising spirit in his stories. But Twain was also concerned that Americans were being corrupted by wealth and greed. Can you guess why he named this period the Gilded Age?

Lesson Objectives

- Identify Mark Twain as the pen name of Samuel Clemens, the author of *The Adventures of Tom Sawyer, Adventures of Huckleberry Finn,* and other novels.
- Explain the term *Gilded Age* and describe Twain's dissatisfaction with the country during that period.

PREPARE

Approximate lesson time is 60 minutes.

Materials

For the Student

Words Tell the Story

A History of US (Concise Edition), Volume C (1865-1932) by Joy Hakim

History Journal

LEARN

Activity 1: Glitter and Gold *(Offline)*

Instructions

A. Read (*Chapter 9, pages 46–49*)

As you read, complete the Words Tell the Story sheet. When you have finished, compare your answers with those in the Lesson Answer Key.

B. Use What You Know

Read the online Flash Cards: Schemers and Dreamers

ASSESS

Lesson Assessment: Mark His Words (*Online*)

You will complete an online assessment covering the main goals of this lesson. Your assessment will be scored by the computer.

LEARN

Activity 2. Optional: Mark His Words *(Online)*

Name Date

Words Tell the Story

Samuel Clemens knew this fact–words are a powerful force. One of America's most celebrated authors, Clemens viewed the Gilded Age as a time of "ridiculous excess." He painted word pictures about this time of excess.

Directions: Based on your reading, use the Word Bank to choose words or phrases that describe Samuel Clemens (Mark Twain), and those that describe the Gilded Age. Then, add a few words of your own.

Word Bank

urban areas rumpled segregated humorous
writer with a message honest glitter dreamer adventurous
child labor gaudiness youthful years after the Civil War

Samuel Clemens (Mark Twain)	The Gilded Age

Student Guide
Lesson 3: New Arrivals

Can you imagine leaving your home and friends and moving to a place where no one speaks your language? In the late nineteenth century, millions of people did just that. After the Civil War, huge numbers of immigrants began arriving in the United States. Most had traveled thousands of miles on crowded ships. They all shared one dream–to start a new life in a free country.

Click Newcomers to view an image of immigrants arriving in New York.

Lesson Objectives

- Identify the two largest immigrant groups of the nineteenth century as Irish and German.
- Explain why people immigrated to the United States in the nineteenth century.
- Summarize the difficulties immigrants faced in leaving their homes and making a new life in America.
- Identify Jacob Riis as a Danish immigrant who photographed immigrant life to make people aware of the problems immigrants faced.

PREPARE

Approximate lesson time is 60 minutes.

Materials

For the Student

Immigration from 1860-1900

A History of US (Concise Edition), Volume C (1865-1932) by Joy Hakim

History Journal

LEARN
Activity 1: Why Did They Come? *(Offline)*
Instructions

A. Read (*Chapter 10, pages 50-57*)

As you read, answer the following questions. Write the answers in your History Journal. You will use your answers to assess how well you understood the lesson. Compare your answers with those in the Lesson Answer Key. You may also want to discuss some of the answers with an adult.

1. What were the two largest groups of immigrants during the late nineteenth century?
2. Why did immigrants come to the United States during the second half of the nineteenth century?
3. What difficulties did immigrants face in leaving their homes and making a new life in the United States?
4. Who was Jacob Riis?

B. Use What You Know

Complete the Immigration from 1860-1900 sheet. Compare your answers with those in the Lesson Answer Key.

ASSESS

Lesson Assessment: New Arrivals *(Online)*

You will complete an online assessment covering the main points of this lesson. Your assessment will be scored by the computer.

Name ________________________________ Date ________________________________

Immigration from 1860–1900

During the late 1800s, a flood of immigrants from all over the world came to the United States. Look at the map and answer the questions.

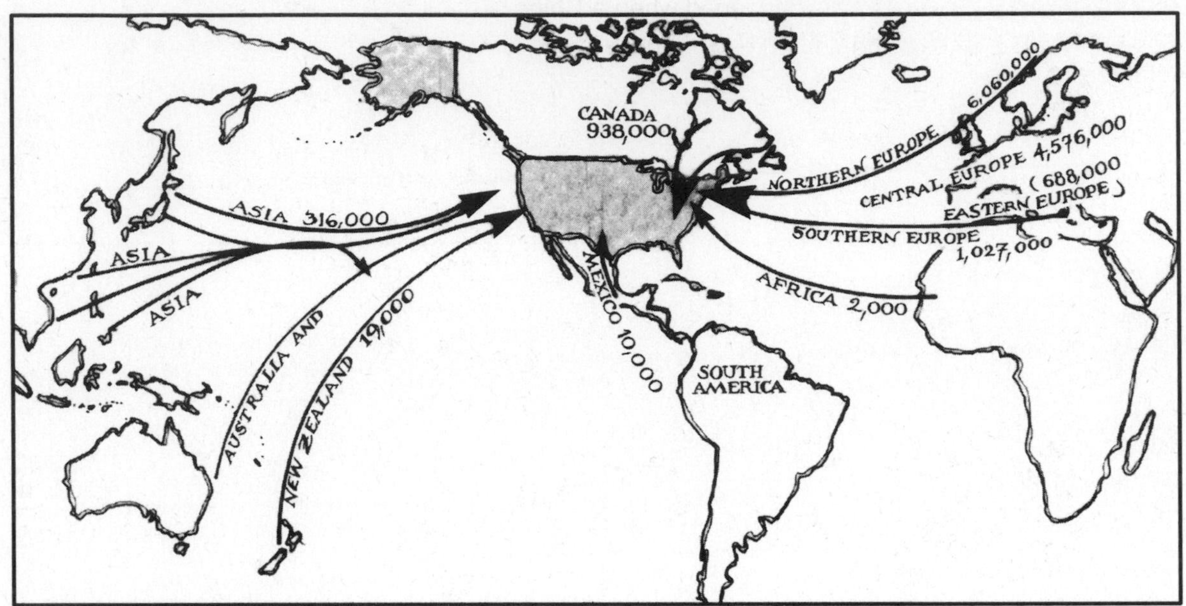

1. What type of information does this map provide? ________________________________

____

2. What region did the most immigrants come from? Where did the fewest come from? List the regions in order from those with the most immigrants to those with the least:

________ # of immigrants ________ ________ # of immigrants ________

________ # of immigrants ________ ________ # of immigrants ________

________ # of immigrants ________ ________ # of immigrants ________

________ # of immigrants ________ ________ # of immigrants ________

________ # of immigrants ________ ________ # of immigrants ________

3. How many people immigrated to the United States between 1860 and 1900? ________

4. In 1882, there were just over 50 million people in the United States. Compare this to the total number of immigrants. Based on this comparison, what general statement can you make about the population of the United States at the end of the century?

____

____

Adapted from *A History of US*

Student Guide
Lesson 4: Barring the Doors

Some Americans did not welcome newcomers to the United States. The unhappy Americans feared the immigrants would work for lower wages and take away their jobs. They greeted the new immigrants with racism and discrimination. Find out what happened when a Chinese man challenged an act of discrimination in California and took his case all the way to the Supreme Court.

Lesson Objectives

- Identify the major reasons for the move to restrict immigration.
- Give examples of prejudiced-based groups and actions intended to limit immigration.

PREPARE

Approximate lesson time is 60 minutes.

Materials

For the Student

The Supreme Court Decides

A History of US (Concise Edition), Volume C (1865-1932) by Joy Hakim

History Journal

Keywords and Pronunciation

alien : a person who is not a citizen of the country he is living in
civil case : a court case to settle an argument when no law has been broken
criminal case : a court case involving a violation of the law
prejudice : dislike of another ethnic group, gender, race, or religion

---

LEARN

Activity 1: Searching for Liberty *(Offline)*

Instructions

A. Read *(Chapter 11, pages 58-62; Chapter 12, pages 63-67)*

New immigrants faced racism, prejudice, and discrimination in the United States. Find out what happened to one immigrant who refused to accept discrimination and took his case to the Supreme Court.

As you read, write a brief definition for each of the following terms in your History Journal. When you have finished, compare your definitions with those in the Keywords section of this lesson.

alien
civil case
criminal case
prejudice

Answer the following questions in your History Journal. When you have finished, compare your answers to those in the Lesson Answer Key.

1. Why did some people want to restrict immigration?
2. Name at least three groups that were prejudiced against others.
3. What was the Chinese Exclusion Act?
4. What is the difference between civil cases and criminal cases? What type of case is *Yick Wo* v. *Hopkins*?
5. Why was the *Yick Wo* case so important?
6. Why did Sheriff Hopkins and the states that supported him lose the case?

B. Focus on Civics

Lee Yick was a Chinese immigrant who was willing to fight for his rights. But what were his rights? He wasn't a citizen. Did he have the same rights as an American citizen? Who decides?

Complete The Supreme Court Decides sheet. When you have finished, compare your answers to those in the Lesson Answer Key.

ASSESS

Lesson Assessment: Barring the Doors (*Online*)

You will complete an online assessment covering the main objectives of this lesson. Your assessment will be scored by the computer.

Name Date

The Supreme Court Decides

In the case of *Yick Wo v. Hopkins*, the Supreme Court struck down the San Francisco law, stating that it violated the 14th Amendment of the U.S. Constitution. Read the 14th Amendment carefully, and circle crucial words that are difficult or uncommon. Then compare the 14th Amendment with your edits to the one on page 2, and answer the questions on page 3.

14th Amendment

Section 1

All persons born or naturalized in the United States, and subject to the jurisdiction thereof, are citizens of the United States and of the State wherein they reside. No State shall make or enforce any law which shall abridge the privileges or immunities of citizens of the United States; nor shall any State deprive any person of life, liberty, or property, without due process of law; nor deny to any person within its jurisdiction the equal protection of the laws.

14th Amendment

Section 1

All persons born or naturalized in the United States, and subject to the jurisdiction thereof, are citizens of the United States and of the State wherein they reside. No State shall make or enforce any law which shall abridge the privileges or immunities of citizens of the United States; nor shall any State deprive any person of life, liberty, or property, without due process of law; nor deny to any person within its jurisdiction the equal protection of the laws.

Terminology

naturalized: made a citizen
abridge: reduce
privileges: rights
jurisdiction: authority
immunities: protections
deprive: take away
subject: under the rule of
due process of law: to act fairly, according to established legal procedures

The Supreme Court Decides

1. Who is a citizen of the United States?

2. What laws are states not allowed to make?

3. How must states apply or enforce their laws?

Student Guide
Lesson 5: Wyoming Wins

Wyoming was the first U.S. territory to grant women the right to vote and to hold office. When Wyoming applied for statehood, some U.S. politicians threatened to deny it statehood because the women in Wyoming had the right to vote. But the Wyoming legislature declared: "We may stay out of the Union for 100 years, but we will come in with our women."

Lesson Objectives

- Define *suffrage.*
- Describe the conflicts involved in Wyoming's decision to grant women the vote.

PREPARE

Approximate lesson time is 60 minutes.

Materials

For the Student

A History of US (Concise Edition), Volume C (1865-1932) by Joy Hakim

History Journal

Keywords and Pronunciation

suffrage (SUH-frihj) : the right to vote

LEARN

Activity 1: Women's "Firsts" *(Offline)*

Instructions

A. Read (*Chapter 13, pages 68–70*)

Some people believed that suffrage was a basic right of American citizenship. But were women American citizens? Should they have the right to vote? One woman in the Wyoming Territory believed they should, and she did something about it.

Read about one woman's remarkable tea party and the role it played in winning women the right to vote. As you read answer the following questions. When you have finished, compare your answers to those in the Lesson Answer Key.

1. What does *suffrage* mean?
2. What role did Esther Morris play in the suffrage movement?
3. What were some of the conflicts Wyoming faced in its decision to grant women the right to vote?

B. Use What You Know

Wyoming was the first U.S. territory to grant women suffrage. There were other political "firsts" for women in the western United States. For example, Jeanette Rankin from Montana was the first woman elected to the U.S. Congress. Make a poster listing some of these political firsts for women.

Use page 70 in your *A History of US (Concise Edition)*, Volume C as the main source for your information. For additional firsts for women in the United States, visit this website: http://www.museumoftheamericanwest.org/explore/exhibits/suffrage/index.html

C. Read On *(Chapter 14, pages 71–77)*
Learn how Susan B. Anthony challenged the law about the definition of the word *citizen* as stated in the 15th Amendment. Reformers like Susan B. Anthony, Elizabeth Cady Stanton, and others thought that a woman without a vote was not a full citizen. Who was a citizen? As you learned earlier, in Wyoming women were citizens—they could vote. But in the East, women never voted. Were they citizens? If they were citizens, then could they vote?

Prepare to answer the following questions:

1. What did Susan B. Anthony and Elizabeth Cady Stanton think about women's suffrage and citizenship?
2. Women in the nineteenth century had the responsibilities but not the rights of citizenship. Give two examples.
3. What question was raised in the trial of Susan B. Anthony?
4. What new issue did the trial raise?
5. Describe the results of Anthony's trial.

You'll see the term *temperance* as you read. Write a brief definition of it in your History Journal and then compare it with the definition in the Keywords section of the Don't Citizens Vote? lesson.

ASSESS

Lesson Assessment: Wyoming Wins (*Online*)

You will complete an online assessment covering the main goals of this lesson. Your assessment will be scored by the computer.

Student Guide
Lesson 6: Don't Citizens Vote?

How would you feel if you were arrested just for trying to vote? That's exactly what happened to Susan B. Anthony in 1872. In those days, women could be taxed but they couldn't vote. They could be arrested, but they couldn't serve on a jury. Susan B. Anthony and other reformers fought for decades so American women could have the same rights as men. What freedoms, protections, and rights do you enjoy today?

Lesson Objectives

- Identify Susan B. Anthony and Elizabeth Cady Stanton as leaders in the women's rights movement of the nineteenth century.
- Explain the legal circumstances of women in the nineteenth century.
- Describe at least two results of Susan B. Anthony's trial.

PREPARE

Approximate lesson time is 60 minutes.

Materials

For the Student

Voting: A Right and a Responsibility

A History of US (Concise Edition), Volume C (1865-1932) by Joy Hakim

History Journal

Keywords and Pronunciation

temperance : avoiding intoxicating liquor

LEARN

Activity 1: Susan B. Anthony Goes on Trial *(Offline)*

Instructions

A. Check Your Reading (*Chapter 14, pages 71–77*)

Discuss:

1. What did Susan B. Anthony and Elizabeth Cady Stanton think about women's suffrage and citizenship?
2. Women in the nineteenth century had the responsibilities but not the rights of citizenship. Give two examples.
3. What question was raised in the trial of Susan B. Anthony?
4. What new issue did the trial raise?
5. Describe the results of Anthony's trial.

Check your definition of the term *temperance* against the definition in the Keywords section of this lesson.

B. Focus on Civics

Read and complete the Voting: A Right and a Responsibility sheet. When you have finished, compare your answers with those in the Lesson Answer Key.

ASSESS

Lesson Assessment: Don't Citizens Vote? (*Online*)

You will complete an online assessment covering the main goals of this lesson. Your assessment will be scored by the computer.

LEARN

Activity 2. Optional: Don't Citizens Vote? *(Online)*

Name Date

Voting: A Right and a Responsibility

As citizens of the United States, we all have certain rights. We have the right to free speech—that is, we can say whatever is on our mind without fear of being sent to jail for saying it. We have the right to express our thoughts, beliefs, and opinions in writing. We have the right to worship God in whatever way we want. As U.S. citizens, we have the right to gather peacefully in groups, and the right to publicly protest problems we think need to be solved. If accused of a crime, we have the right to a trial by jury. These are just a few of the rights we enjoy as U.S. citizens.

But there's a lot more to being a U.S. citizen—particularly a good citizen—than having rights. U.S. citizens have certain responsibilities. In fact, democracy could not exist if citizens did not fulfill their responsibilities.

What are some responsibilities of U.S. citizens? Loyalty, or allegiance, to the United States is one. Obeying the law is another. So is respecting the rights of others. U.S. citizens must serve on a jury if they are called upon, even if it means stopping work and attending the trial for as long as it lasts. During times of war, men who are physically able must serve in the armed forces if the government asks them to do so. U.S. citizens have the responsibility to pay their taxes honestly and on time. To be responsible members of their community, citizens can also do volunteer work, participate in town meetings, and pitch in to solve community problems.

U.S. citizens have another very important right and responsibility—the right and responsibility to vote.

Why is it important to vote? As Abraham Lincoln said, the United States has a government "of the people, by the people, and for the people." Voting is the basis of American democracy. It gives people a voice in the government. It is by far the most powerful way people can express their opinions on local or national issues. As U.S. citizens, we can choose who will represent us in Washington, the state house, or city hall. We can vote officials in or out of office. Everybody's vote is equal. Democracy can flourish only when citizens go to the polls to vote.

People who don't vote lose their voice in the government. And people who don't know what they're voting for may well be throwing their vote away. Before going to the polls on election day, each citizen should take the time to learn about the issues and candidates. That's another important responsibility that comes with U.S. citizenship—being an *informed* voter.

Any citizen who is 18 or older can register to vote. Usually a citizen must live in a state for a certain period of time before he can register to vote in that state. When someone registers to vote, his name is added to the list of people who are qualified to vote. In most localities, officials check each person's name against the list of registered voters before that person can vote on election day.

Each state has the power to decide which residents of the state can vote. Some voting rights, however, are guaranteed by the Constitution. States cannot:

- Deny people 18 years and older the right to vote
- Keep people from voting because of their race, color, or gender
- Make people pay money to vote (pay a poll tax)
- Deny people the right to vote in national elections for president or vice president

States can deny the right to vote to citizens who have been convicted of a serious crime or who are not able to make rational decisions. But states cannot require citizens to pass a reading or writing test before granting them the right to vote.

Susan B. Anthony, Elizabeth Cady Stanton, and other women reformers knew that a woman without a vote was not a full citizen. In the early years of our country, women had very few legal rights. Not only were they denied the right to vote, they could not testify in court, serve on a jury, sue anyone, or be guaranteed equal pay for equal work. Everything a married woman had—her children, her property, and all the money she earned—belonged to her husband.

Today, the Constitution guarantees all U.S. citizens (including women) certain freedoms, protections, and legal rights.

Voting: A Right and a Responsibility

Now that you know more about the rights and responsibilities of U.S. citizens, answer the following questions:

1. List at least four rights of U.S. citizens.

2. In the United States, each state has the power to decide who can or cannot vote. List at least three factors a state cannot use as reasons to deny a citizen the right to vote. Then list at least two factors a state *can* use as reasons to deny a citizen the right to vote.

   A state cannot:

   A state can deny the right to vote to citizens who:

3. Citizens of the United States have certain civic duties or responsibilities. List at least three of their duties and responsibilities.

Read the following paragraphs and answer the questions.

Mia Jackson was born in the United States. Her parents are African-American citizens of the United States. She is 25 years old has lived in the United States all her life. She has a very good job and a steady income. A few years ago, Mia was involved in a traffic accident. The police gave her a traffic ticket. The other driver also sued her for damages in a civil case.

This year is an election year for governor in the state where Mia lives. She has never voted and is not registered to vote.

4. Based on the reading, does Mia have the right to register and vote?

____

5. Can the state where she lives deny her the right to vote?

____

Student Guide
Lesson 7: Finding and Organizing Information, Part 1

The first step in writing an essay is to identify a topic. We've taken that step for you. Here's your topic: major innovations of the late nineteenth and early twentieth centuries and their impact on life in the United States. Once you have a topic, you need to do some research. In this lesson, you'll find information about some important innovators and their innovations in the late nineteenth and early twentieth centuries.

Lesson Objectives

- Identify major innovators of the late nineteenth and early twentieth centuries and their innovations.
- Identify major inventors and inventions of the transportation and communications revolution and the results of their accomplishments.

PREPARE

Approximate lesson time is 60 minutes.

Materials

For the Student

Innovations Change America

A History of US (Concise Edition), Volume C (1865-1932) by Joy Hakim

History Journal

LEARN

Activity 1: Finding and Organizing Information *(Offline)*

Instructions

Begin work in the Innovations Change America sheet. You'll also need to have Volume C of *A History of US (Concise Edition)*.

After you have completed the activity, take the online Lesson Assessment.

ASSESS

Lesson Assessment: Finding and Organizing Information, Part 1 (*Online*)

You will complete an online assessment covering the main goals of this lesson. Your assessment will be scored by the computer.

Name Date

Innovations Change America

An *innovation* is simply a new way of doing something. An innovator, sometimes called an inventor, is someone who comes up with a new way of doing something or a new invention.

1. Scan the following chapters. Do not read the entire chapters; skim through them to find the most important information.

   In Volume C:

   - Chapter 15, pages 78–82
   - Chapter 16, pages 83–87
   - Chapter 44, pages 222–224
   - Chapter 45, pages 225–228

Use the chart on the next page to guide your reading and help organize the information.

2. As you read, complete as much of the chart on the next page as you can. Some innovators will have more than one innovation/invention. As you scan the chapters, add any interesting details and facts that you discover about the innovators and their innovations. Also add information about the impact these innovations had on life in the United States.

   An example of how an innovation affected life in the United States is Henry Ford's use of the assembly line to make automobiles quickly and inexpensively. His innovation eventually spread to other areas of manufacturing. Then, more and more people could afford to buy all kinds of consumer goods.

3. In the Finding and Organizing Information, Part 2 lesson, you'll do some additional research to complete the sheet. This activity will help you organize your ideas in preparation for writing an essay in the Writing the Essay lesson.

Innovation(s)	Innovator	Details/Facts	Impact on Life in the U.S.
telephone			
	Edison		
	Ford		
airplane			

Student Guide
Lesson 8: Finding and Organizing Information, Part 2

You have a topic for your essay and you've gathered some information. Now it's time to dig a little deeper—to find out more about major innovations of the late nineteenth and early twentieth centuries. The Innovations Change America chart will help you organize your information and ideas as you get ready to write an essay.

Lesson Objectives

- Describe three innovations of the late nineteenth and early twentieth centuries and their impact on American life.

PREPARE

Approximate lesson time is 60 minutes.

LEARN

Activity 1: Finding and Organizing Information *(Online)*

Instructions

Look at the Innovations Change America sheet from the Finding and Organizing Information, Part 1 lesson. Choose three innovations to research in greater depth. Use one or more of the following search engines to learn more about the innovations and their impact on life in the United States. Be sure to look for interesting details about each invention and add them to your chart.

Search engines:

- Yahoo Kids
- Ask Jeeves - Kids
- Google Kids

You can also use *The New Book of Knowledge*, Grolier's online encyclopedia.

Student Guide
Lesson 9: Writing the Essay

You have researched major innovators of the late nineteenth and early twentieth centuries. You've found information about them and their innovations. You've learned how these innovations influenced life in the United States. And you've organized the information on your Innovations Change America sheet.

Now it's time to take this organized information and write an essay!

Lesson Objectives

- Describe, in a well-developed essay, three innovations of the late nineteenth and early twentieth centuries and their impact on life in the United States.

PREPARE

Approximate lesson time is 60 minutes.

Materials

For the Student

Writing About History

LEARN

Activity 1: Writing the Essay *(Online)*

Instructions

Follow the steps in the Writing About History sheet and write a five-paragraph essay in response to an essay question.

When you have finished, an adult will assess your essay.

ASSESS

Lesson Assessment: Writing an Essay (*Offline*)

You will complete an offline assessment covering some of the main points of this lesson. Your assessment will be scored by the teacher.

Name ____________________ Date ____________________

Writing About History

Background Information: Advances in technology during the late nineteenth and early twentieth centuries changed the lives of people in the United States. These changes took place in many areas including communication, transportation, manufacturing, and consumer goods.

Essay Question: What were three important innovations of the late nineteenth and early twentieth centuries, and how did each innovation change life in the United States?

Step 1: Read and Analyze the Question

- Read the question.
- Highlight important words in the question.
- What does the question ask you to do? (Circle one or more items below.)

  1. Compare and contrast
  2. Explain
  3. Describe
  4. Agree or disagree with a statement
  5. Prove something

- Rewrite the question as a sentence that shows you understand what the essay question is asking you to do. Start with "I will ______."

I will ____

____

____

____

____

____

- Show your sentence to an adult and discuss your understanding of the question.

Step 2: Record and Organize What You Know

The Innovations Change America sheet has helped you record and organize information. If you haven't completed the chart for at least three innovations, add new information now. For example, did you add that Ford's assembly line made it possible for factories to produce consumer goods more cheaply so more people could afford the goods?

Step 3: Write a Thesis Statement

Go back and read the essay question. Also read the sentence you wrote showing you understand the question. What is your short answer to the question?

1. Write your answer in one or two clear sentences.
2. Mention the three innovations and state that they changed life in the United States.
3. Write in a general way. Do not use specific information. You will add specifics later.
4. Use third person—don't use the words "I," "you," or "we."

Answer:

____

____

____

You've just written a thesis statement! A thesis is the main idea of an essay. Your short answer to the essay question is the thesis of your essay.

Step 4: Prepare an Outline

The Innovations Change America sheet organized information on a chart. Now you will organize this information the way you will use it in your essay in outline form. Use the blank outline on pages 4-6 to complete Step 4. Your essay will follow this format:

Paragraph 1 – Introduction that includes the thesis statement
Paragraph 2 – Innovation 1 and its impact
Paragraph 3 – Innovation 2 and its impact
Paragraph 4 – Innovation 3 and its impact
Paragraph 5 – Conclusion that summarizes the main ideas and restates the thesis

- Introduction: Your thesis statement will be the introduction to your essay. Write your thesis statement next to Roman numeral I on the outline.

- **Main Topic:** Your outline will contain three main topics—the three inventions you chose to write about. Main topics in an outline are listed next to Roman numerals. The first main topic in your outline is the first innovation you chose. Write a topic sentence about the innovation next to Roman numeral II on your outline. If you chose the electric lightbulb, for example, your topic sentence might say something like "Thomas Edison's most important invention was the electric lightbulb, and it changed life in the United States."
- **Subtopics:** Now decide what pieces of information you will use to support your first main topic, and what order that information should be in. In an outline, these pieces of information are called subtopics, and they are listed next to capital letters (A., B., C.) You may not need all the capital letters on the outline, or you may add more if you need them. Add the subtopics to your outline under the first main topic. You must list at least two subtopics under each main topic. If you chose the electric lightbulb, one subtopic might be "Thomas Edison's lightbulb was the first lightbulb that could be made inexpensively."
- **Specific Facts:** Now add some specific facts about the subtopics. For example, "Before Edison developed his lightbulb, people had to limit their activities after dark." In an outline, specific facts are listed next to Arabic numerals (1., 2., 3.). List at least two facts under each subtopic.
- Finally, check the Innovations Change America chart. You will probably not use all the information you recorded, but be sure you have not left out anything you think is important to answer the question. Remember, your essay will follow the outline exactly. When you have completed the section for the first main topic, follow the same procedure for the other two main topics.
- **Conclusion:** Your essay will contain a concluding paragraph that summarizes the main ideas and restates the thesis. Jot down a few ideas for the conclusion next to Roman numeral V on the outline.

OUTLINE

I. Introduction: Thesis Statement

____

____

____

____

II. First Main Topic: Innovation 1

Topic Sentence:

____

____

____

____

A. ______________________________

1. ______________________________

2. ______________________________

B. ______________________________

1. ______________________________

2. ______________________________

C. ______________________________

1. ______________________________

2. ______________________________

D. ______________________________

1. ______________________________

2. ______________________________

III. Second Main Topic: Innovation 2

Topic Sentence:

____

____

____

____

A. ______________________________

1. ______________________________

2. ______________________________

B. ______________________________

1. ______________________________

2. ______________________________

C. ______________________________

1. ______________________________

2. ______________________________

D. ______________________________

1. ______________________________

2. ______________________________

IV. Third Main Topic: Innovation 3

Topic Sentence:

____

____

____

____

A. ______________________________

1. ______________________________

2. ______________________________

B. ______________________________

1. ______________________________

2. ______________________________

C. ______________________________

1. ______________________________

2. ______________________________

D. ______________________________

1. ______________________________

2. ______________________________

V. Conclusion:

____

____

____

____

Step 5: Write Your Essay

Now it's time to write the essay. Follow your outline exactly. Keep your Innovations Change America chart where you can refer to it.

- Write the first paragraph of the essay—the Introduction—which includes your thesis statement. You may add some general information before or after your thesis statement if you wish.
- Write the second paragraph:

1. Use the first main topic sentence, Roman numeral II in your outline, to state the main idea of the paragraph.
2. Explain the topic sentence using the information listed in the subtopics and specifics in that section of the outline.
3. Write a concluding sentence that connects back to the thesis statement.

- Write the other paragraphs of your essay using the same procedure.
- Write a concluding paragraph three or four sentences long that summarizes the main ideas of your essay and restates your thesis in some way.

Step 6: Revise and Refine

- Read back through the whole essay. Did you answer the essay question? Did you state all your ideas clearly? If not, reword or rewrite any sections that need to be revised.
- Check that your essay follows the correct format:

Paragraph 1 – Introduction that includes the thesis statement
Paragraph 2 – Innovation 1 and its impact
Paragraph 3 – Innovation 2 and its impact
Paragraph 4 – Innovation 3 and its impact
Paragraph 5 – Conclusion that summarizes the main ideas and restates the thesis

- Correct any spelling, grammar, or punctuation mistakes you see. Reading the essay aloud will help you spot errors.
- Share your essay with an adult.

Student Guide
Lesson 10: (Optional) Your Choice

You may use today's lesson time to do one or more of the following:

- Complete work in progress.
- Locate the U.S. Map Puzzle 50 States in the game or print the outline map and see how many of the 50 states you can identify.
- Go on to the next lesson.

Please mark this lesson complete in order to proceed to the next lesson in the course.

Lesson Objectives

- Explore knowledge and skills taught in this course.

PREPARE

Approximate lesson time is 60 minutes.

Materials

For the Student

Map of the United States

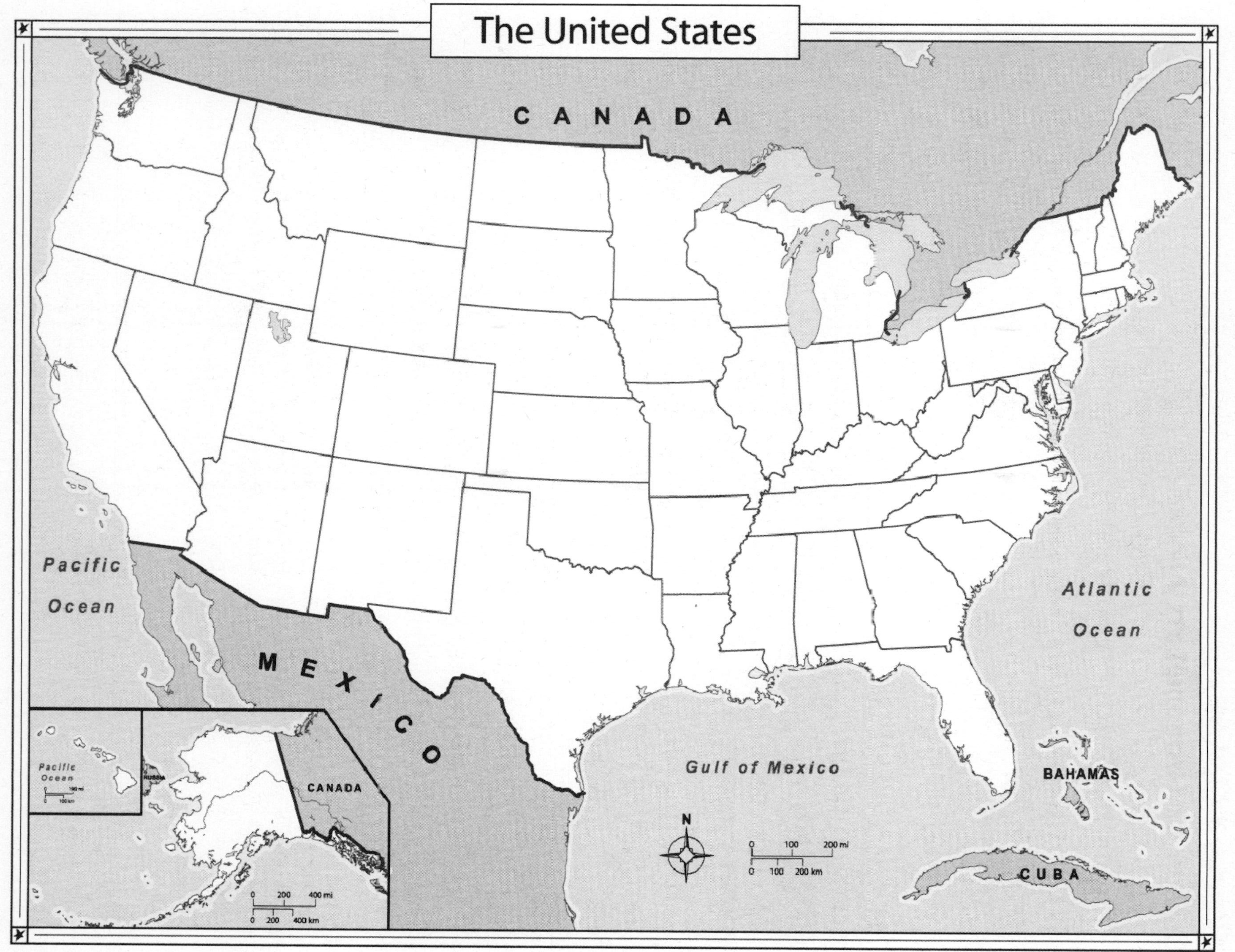
The United States
CANADA
Pacific Ocean
MEXICO
Atlantic Ocean
Gulf of Mexico
BAHAMAS
CUBA
N
0 100 200 mi
0 100 200 km
CANADA
Pacific Ocean
0 200 400 mi
0 200 400 km

Student Guide
Lesson 11: Separate but Unequal

After the Civil War, the country was in turmoil. During Reconstruction, blacks in the South gained new freedoms and privileges, such as the right to go to school, to vote, and to hold public office. But when Reconstruction ended, whites plotted to strip away those rights. Did they succeed?

Lesson Objectives

- Define *segregation* and *Jim Crow.*
- Describe the ways in which race relations in the North and South changed after Reconstruction.
- Chart the path of Southern race relations from antebellum slavery to the Jim Crow era.
- Explain the importance of *Plessy v. Ferguson,* its relationship to the 14th Amendment, and its impact on segregation.

PREPARE

Approximate lesson time is 60 minutes.

Advance Preparation

- Unit 2, Lesson 11, Separate but Unequal, discusses violence against blacks in the South after Reconstruction ended. You may want to preview the lesson before you assign it to your student. Be prepared to spend extra time discussing this topic with your student.

Materials

For the Student

One Step Up, Two Steps Back

A History of US (Concise Edition), Volume C (1865-1932) by Joy Hakim

History Journal

Post-Reconstruction Violence

Keywords and Pronunciation

Plessy v. Ferguson : an 1896 Supreme Court case in which the court ruled that segregation (Jim Crow) laws were constitutional

Jim Crow : a common name for segregation laws, some of which forbade intermarriage and ordered business owners and public institutions to keep black and white patrons separated

segregation : the practice of separating racial, ethnic, or religious groups from one another, especially in public places

LEARN

Activity 1: No Rights, No Respect *(Offline)*

Instructions

A. Read *(Chapter 17, pages 88–92)*

Review the reading by answering the following questions. Compare your answers to those in the Lesson Answer Key.

1. What is segregation?
2. What is Jim Crow?
3. Briefly describe how race relations in the North and South changed after Reconstruction.
4. What was the issue in the case of Plessy v. Ferguson? What did the court rule?

B. Use What You Know

Putting It Together

Analyze the events affecting the civil rights of blacks from slavery to the Jim Crow era by completing the One Step Up, Two Steps Back sheet.

Forming an Opinion

In the case of *Plessy v. Ferguson,* the court ruled that segregation was constitutional. Only Justice Harlan dissented (disagreed). He seemed to foresee the problems that would arise from the "separate but equal" doctrine. In your History Journal, argue Judge Harlan's position and explain why he was correct.

Activity 2: Focus on Geography *(Online)*

Between 1882 and 1958, every state in the Union except Rhode Island, Connecticut, New Hampshire, and Massachusetts reported mob murders--executions without trials.

Complete the Post-Reconstruction Violence sheet as you continue with the lesson.

ASSESS

Lesson Assessment: Separate but Unequal *(Online)*

You will complete an online assessment covering the main points of this lesson. Your assessment will be scored by the computer.

LEARN

Activity 3. Optional: Separate but Unequal *(Online)*

Name ______________________________ Date ______________________________

One Step Up, Two Steps Back

Many events affected the lives of African Americans and their rights following the Civil War. Use your memory, History Journal, and textbook to identify the events that advanced (+) or obstructed (–) the struggle for equality.

______ **A.** The 13th Amendment is passed.

______ **B.** Black codes are enacted.

______ **C.** Congress passes the first Civil Rights Act.

______ **D.** The KKK is founded.

______ **E.** Congress establishes the Freedmen's Bureau.

______ **F.** The poll tax is introduced.

______ **G.** The 14th Amendment is passed.

______ **H.** The 15th Amendment is passed.

______ **I.** The last former Confederate state is readmitted to the Union.

______ **J.** Rutherford B. Hayes becomes president.

______ **K.** Booker T. Washington founds Tuskegee Institute.

______ **L.** The Supreme Court hands down a decision in *Plessy v. Ferguson*.

Name Date

Post-Reconstruction Violence

Create a color-coded map that shows the number of mob murders in each area. Select a color to represent each number range in the table. Shade in the map with the appropriate colors. Then use your map to answer the questions.

Mob Murders – 1882 to 1958		
Number of Murders	**States**	**Color**
1–9	NY, PA, NJ, DE	
10–49	WV, MD, OH, IL	
50–199	MO, VA, NC, SC	
200–399	FL, AL, TN, KY, AR, LA	
400 or more	TX, MS, GA	
Source: Historical Atlas of the United States (National Geographic)		

Post-Reconstruction Violence

1. In what region of the country were African Americans most likely to face violent treatment?

   ____

2. Were African Americans safe in the North?

   ____

3. What regions of the country experienced the fewest incidents of mob violence?

   ____

Student Guide
Lesson 12: Courage

Ida B. Wells shouldered responsibility at an early age. Only 16 when her parents died, she took on the difficult job of raising her six brothers and sisters. By the time she was in her twenties she was championing the African-American struggle for equality.

Lesson Objectives

- Identify Ida B. Wells.
- Recognize methods that whites used to keep blacks from exercising their rights.
- Describe the ways in which Ida B. Wells fought lynching and other forms of discrimination.

PREPARE

Approximate lesson time is 60 minutes.

Advance Preparation

- Unit 2, Lesson 12, Courage, discusses violence against blacks in the South after Reconstruction ended. You may want to preview the lesson before you assign it to your student. Be prepared to spend extra time discussing this topic with your student.

Materials

For the Student

A History of US (Concise Edition), Volume C (1865-1932) by Joy Hakim

History Journal

Keywords and Pronunciation

lynching : kidnapping and execution of a person by a mob

vigilante (vih-juh-LAN-tee) : one who takes or advocates the taking of law enforcement into one's own hands

---

LEARN

Activity 1: Her Pen Was Her Sword *(Offline)*

Instructions

A. Read *(Chapter 18, pages 93–98)*

Review the reading by answering the following questions. Compare your answers to those in the Lesson Answer Key.

1. Who was Ida B. Wells?
2. What methods were used to keep blacks from exercising their constitutional rights?
3. Describe three ways in which Ms. Wells fought lynching and other forms of discrimination.

B. Profile of Courage

People sometimes make excuses for why they don't vote, such as "My one vote doesn't count." "I really can't accomplish anything by myself." "No one will take me seriously." "If I stand up for what I believe, people may make fun of me." Ida B. Wells did not believe in those excuses.

- Read more on Ida B. Wells by visiting the National Park Service website. Go online and click the Profile of Courage: Ida B. Wells link.
- Consider the impact of a single life—her life—on the fight against racial violence by answering the following questions:
    1. What if Ida Wells had moved to the smoking car when the conductor told him to? How would that have been an easier choice?
    2. What if she had decided to keep her opinions to herself and not write articles for the paper? How would her life have been different? What changes may not have happened in the United States?

- Write a well-developed paragraph explaining why it was important that Wells took a stand, even though she often acted alone.
    1. What prepared Wells to become a crusader for justice?
    2. Did her actions improve life for others?
    3. Think of ways you could assume the role of a crusader, and include them in your answer.

C. Discuss

Discuss with an adult the wrongs of vigilante justice and alternatives to vigilante justice. Points of discussion may include:

vigilante (vih-juh-LAN-tee) justice

- Denies Sixth Amendment rights—the right to a trial by an impartial jury, right to a lawyer, right to confront witnesses against and obtain witnesses in defense
- Impedes the principle of innocent until proven guilty
- Disregards the rule of law
- Violates the safeguards provided by the separation of powers

Alternative points of discussion:

- Citizen's arrest
- Use of 911 emergency number
- Exposure in the media
- Initiating political and or social change

ASSESS

Lesson Assessment: Courage *(Online)*

You will complete an online assessment covering the main points of this lesson. Your assessment will be scored by the computer.

Student Guide

Lesson 13: Differing Views

It was a time when most African Americans in the South could barely scratch out a living from the land. Booker T. Washington valued economic freedom more than all other freedoms, and he tried to teach blacks how to achieve it. Northern-born W.E.B. DuBois had very different ideas. He demanded nothing less than full equality for African Americans.

Lesson Objectives

- Identify Booker T. Washington.
- Identify W.E.B. DuBois.
- Compare and contrast the goals and methods of Washington and DuBois.

PREPARE

Approximate lesson time is 60 minutes.

Materials

For the Student

Profile

A History of US (Concise Edition), Volume C (1865-1932) by Joy Hakim

History Journal

Keywords and Pronunciation

anti-Semitism (AN-tee-SEH-muh-tih-zuhm) : hostility toward or discrimination against Jews as a religious, ethnic, or racial group

NAACP : the National Association for the Advancement of Colored People, an organization of blacks and whites formed to fight racial injustice

W.E.B. DuBois (dyoo-BOYS)

LEARN

Activity 1: Two Very Different Leaders *(Offline)*

Instructions

A. Read *(Chapter 19, pages 99–102; Chapter 20, pages 103–106)*

As you read, define the following words in your History Journal. When you have finished, compare your definitions to those in the Keywords section.

anti-Semitism (AN-tee-SEH-muh-tih-zuhm)
NAACP

B. Use What You Know

Review the life, achievements, and ideals of Washington and DuBois by completing Two Very Different Leaders online activity.

C. Profile

Washington and DuBois were pioneers in education for black people. Both men had the same goal—equality of blacks and whites—but they had very different ideas about how to achieve that goal.

Decide whose view you most agree with—Washington's or DuBois's. Write a Profile for the man you chose. (You may use previously printed Profiles in your History Journal for reference.) Then, write a paragraph explaining why you would have supported this man's approach if you had lived during that time.

ASSESS

Lesson Assessment: Differing Views *(Online)*

You will complete an online assessment covering the main points of this lesson. Your assessment will be scored by the computer.

Name Date

Profile of __________

Place Picture Here

Student Guide
Lesson 14: Unit Review

You have finished the unit! It's time to review what you've learned. You will take the Unit Assessment in the next lesson.

Lesson Objectives

- Demonstrate mastery of important knowledge and skills in this unit.
- Demonstrate mastery of important knowledge and skills taught in this unit.

PREPARE

Approximate lesson time is 60 minutes.

Materials

For the Student

A History of US (Concise Edition), Volume C (1865-1932) by Joy Hakim

History Journal

LEARN

Activity 1: A Look Back *(Online)*

Instructions

A. History Journal Review

Review what you've learned in this unit by going through your History Journal. You should:

- Look at activity sheets you've completed for this unit.
- Review unit Keywords and definitions.
- Read through any writing assignments you did during the unit.
- Review the assessments you took.

Don't rush through; take your time. Your History Journal is a great resource for a unit review.

B. Online Review

Review the following online:

- Flash Cards
- Time Line
- Leaps and Bounds
- Two Very Different Leaders

Student Guide
Lesson 15: Unit Assessment

You've finished the unit! Now it's time to take the Unit Assessment.

Lesson Objectives

- Identify Boss Tweed as the leader of a political machine that ran New York by using bribery and intimidation.
- Identify Thomas Nast as the political cartoonist who helped bring down Tweed.
- Identify Mark Twain as the pen name of Samuel Clemens, the author of *The Adventures of Tom Sawyer, Adventures of Huckleberry Finn,* and other novels.
- Identify Jacob Riis as a Danish immigrant who photographed immigrant life to make people aware of the problems immigrants faced.
- Recognize major immigrant groups of the late 1800s and their challenges, opportunities, and contributions.
- Identify individuals, groups, or movements that helped or hindered the growth of civil rights and opportunity in the late 1800s.
- Recognize the growing role of the courts in expanding or restricting civil rights in the late 1800s.
- Give examples of the cultural response to the changes of the late 1800s.
- Define *segregation* and *Jim Crow.*
- Describe the ways in which race relations in the North and South changed after Reconstruction.
- Chart the path of Southern race relations from antebellum slavery to the Jim Crow era.
- Explain the importance of *Plessy v. Ferguson,* its relationship to the 14th Amendment, and its impact on segregation.
- Recognize methods that whites used to keep blacks from exercising their rights.
- Describe the ways in which Ida B. Wells fought lynching and other forms of discrimination.
- Identify Booker T. Washington.
- Identify W.E.B. DuBois.
- Compare and contrast the goals and methods of Washington and DuBois.
- Explain the relationship between new technology and inventions and the settlement of the Great Plains.|
- Explain why people immigrated to the United States in the nineteenth century.
- Summarize the difficulties immigrants faced in leaving their homes and making a new life in America.

PREPARE

Approximate lesson time is 60 minutes.

Unit Assessment: Reformers, Newcomers, and Innovators, Part 1 *(Online)*

Complete the computer-scored portion of the Unit Assessment. When you have finished, complete the teacher-scored portion of the assessment and submit it to your teacher.

Unit Assessment: Reformers, Newcomers, and Innovators, Part 2 *(Offline)*

Complete the teacher-scored portion of the Unit Assessment and submit it to your teacher.

Student Guide

Unit 3: Politics, Power, and the People
Lesson 1: Getting and Giving

The late 1800s was a time of extremes known as the Gilded Age. Entrepreneurs introduced new ways of doing business that led to fantastic wealth for owners, terrible poverty for workers, and monopolies that eliminated competition. Cities grew and changed, the economy rose and fell, and farmers struggled to maintain a way of life. Through it all, Lady Liberty held her lamp high for thousands of immigrants who chose to become Americans.

Andrew Carnegie's life is the classic story of rags to riches. Born into a poor family in Scotland, Carnegie became one of the richest men in the world. Unfortunately, he gained his wealth at the expense of thousands of poorly paid workers who labored in his mills. Near the end of his life, however, he gave away almost all his wealth in an attempt to make the world a better place.

Lesson Objectives

- Describe how Andrew Carnegie rose from poverty to become one of the world's richest men.
- Describe the Homestead Strike.
- Explain the importance of the Bessemer process in making steel.
- Identify examples of Carnegie's steps to improve society.
- Summarize Hakim's reasons for calling the late 1800s an age of extremes.

PREPARE

Approximate lesson time is 60 minutes.

Materials

For the Student

A History of US (Concise Edition), Volume C (1865-1932) by Joy Hakim

History Journal

Keywords and Pronunciation

Bessemer process : a method of making high-quality steel at a reasonable price
capital : wealth used for investment to make more wealth
strike : work stoppage to demand better wages or working conditions

LEARN

Activity 1: Carnegie Changes Everything *(Offline)*

Instructions

A. Read: *(Chapter 21, pages 108–110; Chapter 22, pages 111–115)*

Answer the following questions and compare your answers to those in the Lesson Answer Key.

1. Why does Joy Hakim call the late 1800s an age of extremes?
2. Describe how Andrew Carnegie's life changed from beginning to end.
3. What influences did Andrew Carnegie's father, mother, and uncle have on him?
4. How did Carnegie get rich?
5. What happened to most of Carnegie's wealth?
6. Describe the Homestead Strike.
7. What is the Bessemer process and why was it an important development?
8. What steps did Carnegie take to improve society?

B. Use What You Know

Identify Carnegie's good and bad traits and practices by completing the Knowing Carnegie online activity.

C. Read On *(Chapter 23, pages 116–119; Chapter 24, pages 120–121)*

Carnegie wasn't the only man in the United States who made money from money. Read about J. P. Morgan and John D. Rockefeller to see how they redefined capitalism.

ASSESS

Lesson Assessment: Getting and Giving *(Online)*

You will complete an online assessment covering the main points of this lesson. Your assessment will be scored by the computer.

LEARN

Activity 2. Optional: Getting and Giving *(Online)*

Student Guide
Lesson 2: Mountains of Money

For John D. Rockefeller, the pursuit of happiness meant the pursuit of money. The less he paid his workers, the richer he became. Still, he gave away half his fortune before he died. Similarly, J. P. Morgan commanded an empire so powerful that it once even bailed out the financially troubled U.S. Treasury. Another time]he saved the country from economic ruin by persuading a few wealthy men to rescue a failing trust company.

Lesson Objectives

- Demonstrate mastery of skills from a previous lesson.
- Identify J. P. Morgan.
- Identify Andrew Carnegie.
- Identify John D. Rockefeller.
- Compare and contrast Rockefeller and Morgan in terms of their rise to power, business practices, and use of wealth.

PREPARE

Approximate lesson time is 60 minutes.

Materials

For the Student

A History of US (Concise Edition), Volume C (1865-1932) by Joy Hakim

History Journal

LEARN

Activity 1: Wealth Beyond Reason *(Offline)*

Instructions

A. Check Your Reading *(Chapter 23, pages 116–119; Chapter 24, pages 120–121)*

Review the reading by answering the following questions. Compare your answers with those in the Lesson Answer Key.

1. How did John D. Rockefeller earn his wealth?
2. How did Rockefeller take control of the industry?
3. What were the two conflicting sides of Rockefeller's personality?
4. How did J.P. Morgan earn his wealth?
5. What were some ways Morgan used his wealth to influence government?

B. Read On *(Chapter 25, pages 122–125)*
Many Americans regarded men like John D. Rockefeller as "captains of industry," but as time went on, more and more people began to think of them as "robber barons." Wielding enormous economic and political power, they could manipulate prices and influence government actions.
As you read, prepare to answer the following questions:

1. Describe the advantages and disadvantages of a monopoly.
2. How did monopolies conflict with the idea of "government by the people"?
3. How does competition work for the benefit of the consumer?
4. How did the Sherman Antitrust Act attempt to reform business practices?
5. What do tariffs do to prices? How do they affect the consumer?

Be prepared to define these words:

- command economy
- corporation
- hybrid economy
- market economy
- monopoly
- Sherman Antitrust Act
- tariff
- traditional economy
- trust

You can check the definitions in the Keywords section of the next lesson.

ASSESS

Lesson Assessment: Mountains of Money (*Online*)

You will complete an online assessment covering the main goals of this lesson. Your assessment will be scored by the computer.

LEARN

Activity 2. Optional: Mountains of Money *(Online)*

Student Guide
Lesson 3: How Much Is Too Much?

Big business was out of control. Rockefeller's Standard Oil trust owned 90 percent of the oil industry, and had wiped out most of its competitors. But capitalism and free enterprise were the backbone of the American economy. How could the federal government regulate big businesses without crushing the spirit of capitalism? And who was strong enough to enforce the regulation?

Lesson Objectives

- Recognize and define *monopoly, trust, command economy, market economy, hybrid economy, corporation,* and *tariff.*
- Describe the kinds of power monopolies have over the economy and the advantages and disadvantages of monopolies.
- Explain the purpose of the Sherman Antitrust Act.

PREPARE

Approximate lesson time is 60 minutes.

Materials

For the Student

A History of US (Concise Edition), Volume C (1865-1932) by Joy Hakim

History Journal

Keywords and Pronunciation

command economy : an economic system in which the government or another central administration regulates supply and prices
corporation : a business owned by many people called stockholders
hybrid economy : an economic system that is a combination of both command and market economies; also called a mixed economy
market economy : a system in which people earn wages and buy the goods and services they choose
monopoly (muh-NAH-puh-lee) : a market that has only one seller of a product for which there are no close substitutes, and the seller can influence the price of the product
Sherman Antitrust Act : an act of Congress (1890) that made monopolies illegal, forbade businesses from limiting competition, and prohibited any contract, conspiracy, or combination of business interests from inhibiting foreign or interstate trade
tariff : a tax on imports or exports
traditional economy : an economic system in which people do the same work their parents did
trust : a form of monopoly in which many different companies in one industry are owned and run by the same people

LEARN

Activity 1: Economix (Offline)

Instructions

A. Check Your Reading *(Chapter 25, pages 122–125)*

Review the reading by answering the following questions. Then compare your answers to the ones in the Lesson Answer Key.

1. Describe the advantages and disadvantages of a monopoly.
2. How did monopolies conflict with the idea of "government by the people"?
3. How does competition work for the benefit of the consumer?
4. How did the Sherman Antitrust Act reform business practices?
5. What do tariffs do to prices? How do they affect the consumer?

Then use the online Economy Flash Cards to review the Keyword definitions.

Activity 2: Focus on Economics (Online)

Instructions

Review each of the online screens until you have mastered the answers. If you need help, click the Get a Clue button several times. Continue playing until you can answer all the questions correctly in one pass.

ASSESS

Lesson Assessment: How Much Is Too Much? *(Online)*

You will complete an online assessment covering the main points of this lesson. Your assessment will be scored by the computer.

Student Guide
Lesson 4: Building Up

Experts said it was impossible. It would be the longest and highest bridge ever built. The foundations for its stone towers would have to be constructed underwater in special chambers filled with compressed air. Completed in 1883, the Brooklyn Bridge still stands as a monument to American creativity. In the late nineteenth century, architects and engineers changed the face of the nation through innovations like steel bridges, skyscrapers, electric lights, and elevators.

Lesson Objectives

- Identify innovations that changed city life in the late 1800s.
- Identify major innovators in the development of modern cities.
- Analyze the growth of urban areas into megalopolises in the United States.

PREPARE

Approximate lesson time is 60 minutes.

Materials

For the Student

- Map of Urban America, 2000
- Profile of an American Innovator
- A History of US (Concise Edition), Volume C (1865-1932) by Joy Hakim
- History Journal

Keywords and Pronunciation

megalopolises (MEH-guh-LAH-puh-luhs-iz) : enormous cities or very thickly populated areas that encompass several cities

---

LEARN

Activity 1: A New Way of Building *(Offline)*

Instructions

A. Read *(Chapter 26, pages 126–130)*

As you read, answer the following question. Then compare your answer with the one in the Lesson Answer Key.

Innovations changed city life in the late 1800s. What were some of the innovations, and who created them?

B. Use What You Know

Choose one of the innovators mentioned in the reading, and research that innovator on the Internet. Then, complete the Profile of an American Innovator sheet, or type the information you found on a piece of paper. Place the completed sheet in your History Journal.

C. Focus on Geography

Megalopolises (MEH-guh-LAH-puh-luhs-iz) are enormous cities or very densely populated areas that include several cities. Architectural and engineering innovations in the late 1800s transformed cities such as New York City and Chicago into megalopolises.

Use the Urban America, 2000, map to answer the following questions. Compare your answers with the ones in the Answer Key.

1. Locate the urban areas on the map. Where are they located? Why?
2. What are the four megalopolises in the United States?
3. Where is the Boswash megalopolis located?
4. Name the major cities in the Boswash megalopolis.
5. Why do you think there are skyscrapers in urban areas and not in rural areas?

Review the online Flash Cards and then take the assessment.

ASSESS

Lesson Assessment: Building Up (*Online*)

You will complete an online assessment covering the main goals of this lesson. Your assessment will be scored by the computer.

LEARN

Activity 2. Optional: Building Up *(Online)*

Name Date

Profile of an American Innovator

Place Picture Here

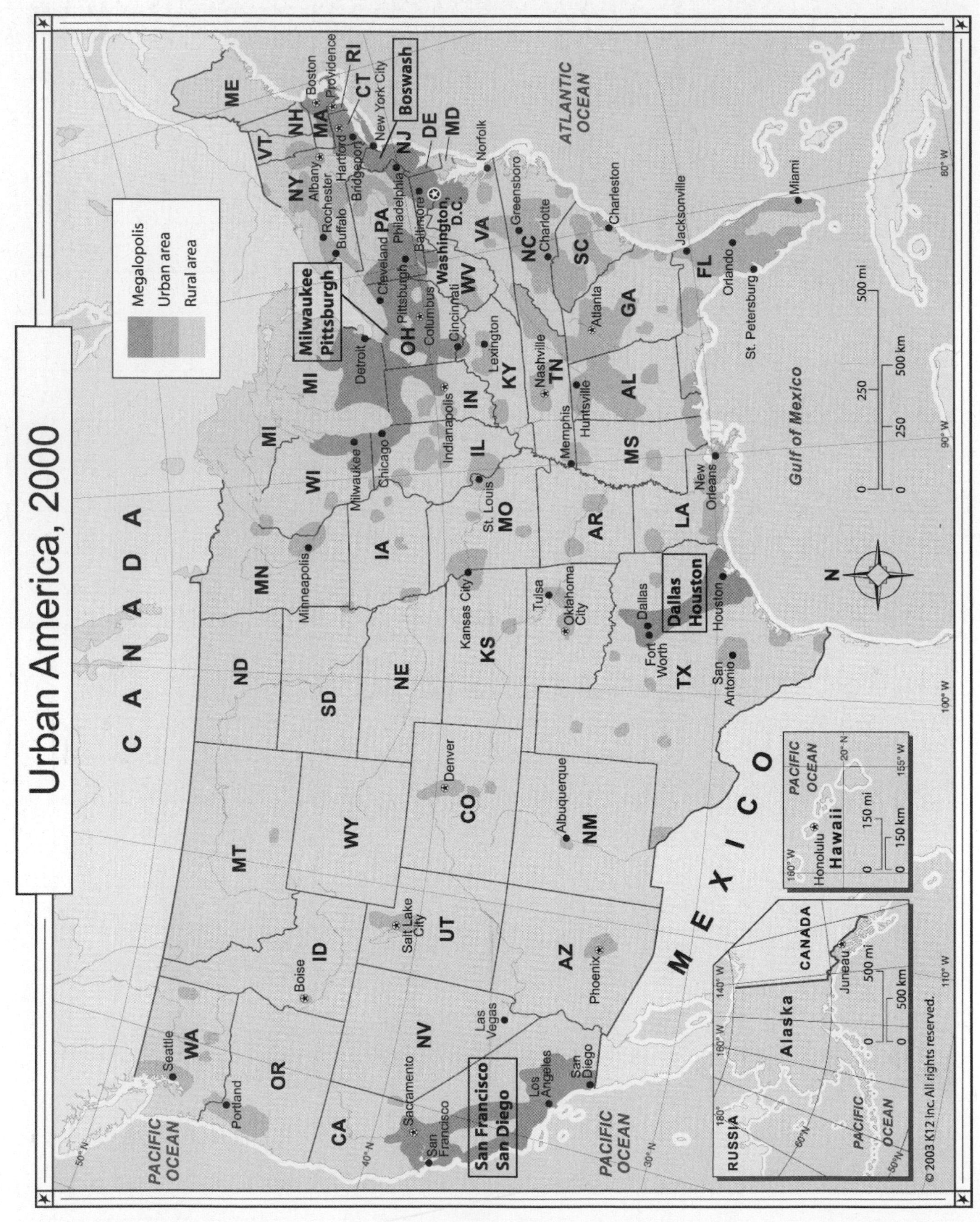
Urban America, 2000
Megalopolis
Urban area
Rural area
C A N A D A
M E X I C O
PACIFIC OCEAN
ATLANTIC OCEAN
Gulf of Mexico
Boswash
Milwaukee Pittsburgh
Dallas Houston
San Francisco San Diego
WA
OR
CA
NV
ID
MT
WY
UT
AZ
CO
NM
ND
SD
NE
KS
TX
MN
IA
MO
AR
LA
WI
IL
MI
IN
KY
TN
MS
AL
OH
WV
VA
NC
SC
GA
FL
PA
NY
VT
NH
ME
MA
CT
RI
NJ
DE
MD
Seattle
Portland
Boise
Sacramento
San Francisco
Las Vegas
Los Angeles
San Diego
Salt Lake City
Phoenix
Denver
Albuquerque
Minneapolis
Kansas City
Tulsa
Oklahoma City
Dallas
Fort Worth
San Antonio
Houston
New Orleans
St. Louis
Milwaukee
Chicago
Indianapolis
Memphis
Huntsville
Nashville
Lexington
Cincinnati
Detroit
Columbus
Cleveland
Pittsburgh
Buffalo
Rochester
Albany
Boston
Providence
Hartford
Bridgeport
New York City
Philadelphia
Baltimore
Washington, D.C.
Norfolk
Greensboro
Charlotte
Charleston
Atlanta
Jacksonville
Orlando
St. Petersburg
Miami
N
0 250 500 mi
0 250 500 km
PACIFIC OCEAN
Honolulu
Hawaii
0 150 mi
0 150 km
RUSSIA
Alaska
CANADA
Juneau
PACIFIC OCEAN
0 500 mi
0 500 km
© 2003 K12 Inc. All rights reserved.

Student Guide
Lesson 5: In Office

In the aftermath of the Civil War, the nation needed a strong leader to help it recover and rebuild. Of the eight men who rose to the presidency between Lincoln's assassination and the turn of the century, only a few would be remembered as good presidents. What qualities do you think a person needs to be a good president?

Lesson Objectives

- Identify the presidents of the nine administrations between 1865 and 1900.
- Explain the role of the electoral college in presidential elections.

PREPARE

Approximate lesson time is 60 minutes.

Materials

For the Student

- All Presidents Are Graduates of This College
- John Quincy Adams Time Line
- Presidential Time Line
- A History of US (Concise Edition), Volume C (1865-1932) by Joy Hakim
- History Journal

LEARN

Activity 1: Nine More—or Was It Eight More? *(Offline)*

Instructions

A. Read *(Chapter 27, pages 131–135)*

Between 1865 and 1901 the United States had nine presidential administrations. Read Chapter 27 to learn how each president's leadership affected the country.

As you read, complete a Presidential Time Line sheet for each president (include two for Cleveland, who served non-consecutive terms): Johnson, Grant, Hayes, Garfield, Arthur, Cleveland, Harrison, Cleveland, and McKinley. You may use the John Quincy Adams Time Line as an example.

Mount the Presidential Time Line sheets on varying colors of construction paper. Then, display the presidents in the order in which they served.

B. Focus on Civics

Read and complete the All Presidents Are Graduates of This College sheet. Compare your answers with the ones in the Lesson Answer Key.

Activity 2: Presidents from 1865 to 1900 *(Online)*

Instructions

Review the presidents by playing the online game, Get a Clue.

ASSESS

Lesson Assessment: In Office (*Online*)

You will complete an online assessment covering the main goals of this lesson. Your assessment will be scored by the computer.

LEARN

Activity 3. Optional: In Office *(Online)*

Name Date

Presidential Time Line:

If you can find a picture of this president, attach it here.

Name:

Years in Office: –

Number of Terms:

Vice president:

First Lady:

President

Name ______________________ Date ______________________

Presidential Time Line: John Quincy Adams

If you can find a picture of this president, attach it here.

Name: John Quincy Adams

Years in Office: 1825–1829

Number of Terms: 1

Vice president: John Calhoun

First Lady: Louisa Catherine Adams

S[illegible]h President

The presidency of John Quincy Adams was not marked by any significant events of national importance. He did propose a high tariff that was signed into law in 1828. The "Tariff of Abominations," as it was called, was imposed on imported manufactured goods. John Quincy Adams is one of only two presidents whose father was also a president.

Name Date

All Presidents Are Graduates of This College

Did you know that a U.S. citizen who goes to the polls to vote for a presidential candidate isn't *really* voting for that candidate? Technically speaking, ordinary American citizens don't elect their president on Election Day. So what are they doing then?

The United States uses an *indirect* method to elect the president and vice president. Each citizen's vote on Election Day helps determine who will be part of a group of people called *electors*. The electors vote for president and vice president a few weeks later. The group of electors is known as the *electoral college*.

Why Do We Use an Electoral College?

The electoral college has been around in one form or another since the founding of the United States. The Founders included it in the Constitution. But why did they decide to use this system?

To understand why, you have to consider what the United States was like when it was young. The country was made up of 13 states all spread out along the Atlantic seaboard. Each state was jealous of the others' power and not really sure the new federal government had the state's interests in mind. And the Founders weren't entirely sure they could trust ordinary citizens to make wise choices in a presidential election. Democracy was still a new system of government in the States, and the Founders didn't know how well it would work. Also, communication at that time was quite poor. There was no TV, radio, or Internet back then, and very few newspapers. How could the average citizen really know what each candidate stood for?

What could the Founders do? They wanted the citizens *and* the states to play an important role in elections, but they needed the process to be calm and deliberate. They felt that the people who elected the president and vice president should be educated and well informed. After much debate they came up with the idea of the electoral college.

How Does the Electoral College Work?

The Constitution gives every state the same number of votes in the electoral college as the number of senators and representatives that state has in Congress. Every state has two senators, but its number of representatives is based on the population of the state. So the larger a state's population, the more electoral votes it has.

The political parties in each state choose people to serve as their electors. We usually think of the United States as having two political parties—Democratic and Republican. But since all political ideas are legal in the United States, there are actually several parties. In recent years, elections have included candidates from the Libertarian Party, the Green Party, the Reform Party, and even the Communist Party. Several weeks before Election Day, each party that has a candidate running for office chooses a set of electors.

On Election Day in November, citizens go to the polls and vote for the candidate of their choice. What they're *really* doing is voting for the set of electors who have pledged to vote for their particular candidate. For example, if you vote for Republican Smith, you're really voting for the Republican electors in your state. If you vote for Democrat Jones, you're really voting for the Democratic electors.

In December after Election Day, the electors who won in each state get together—usually in their state capitol—and vote for their candidates. The votes are then sealed and sent to the U.S. Senate. In early January the electoral votes are opened and read before both houses of Congress. The presidential candidate who gets the most electoral votes is declared the winner, as long as that candidate gets at least half the electoral votes plus one, or an *absolute majority*. Today the electoral college has a total of 538 electoral votes, so a presidential candidate must receive at least 270 electoral votes to be elected. A similar process takes place for electing the vice president.

It could happen, however, that no presidential candidate gets an absolute majority of electoral votes. If this happens the election is "thrown into the House." That means the House of Representatives elects the president from the three candidates who received the most electoral votes. This time, however, each state gets only one vote. If no vice-presidential candidate wins an absolute majority of the electoral votes, the Senate elects the vice president from the two candidates with the most electoral votes.

Popular vs. Electoral Votes

Most of the time, the candidate who gets the most votes from the citizens of a state gets *all* that state's electoral votes. For example, if a state's citizens cast more votes for Republican Smith than any other candidate, only Smith's electors from that state get to vote for president.

But here's the really strange thing about the electoral-college system. A candidate might win the most votes from citizens all over the country (the *popular vote*) but not get the most *electoral* votes. Then the candidate loses the election! How in the world can that happen?

The electoral college system generally gives *all* of a state's electoral votes to the candidate who got the most popular votes in that state. So if a candidate wins a razor-thin majority of the popular votes in a few big states that have large populations, he or she can lose the popular vote and still come out a winner in the electoral college.

Four times in the nation's history a candidate was elected president even though his closest opponent received more popular votes. John Quincy Adams did it in 1824, Rutherford B. Hayes in 1876, Benjamin Harrison in 1888, and George W. Bush in 2000.

Some critics say the electoral college is a dinosaur of an idea. It came out of a different age, they say, and makes the election process too complicated. They suggest getting rid of the system and simply counting the nation's popular vote instead. Defenders of the electoral college say it's still useful because it gives states an important role to play. One thing is certain. Abolishing the electoral college would require an amendment to the Constitution, and the Founders made changing the Constitution a long, difficult task. So for better or worse, the electoral college will likely be part of America's political landscape for years to come.

Answer **TRUE** or **FALSE** to the following statements:

__________ **1.** The Founders of the Constitution did not want the people to select the president because they feared the average citizen might not be an informed voter.

__________ **2.** Election Day for the president and vice president is held in November.

__________ **3.** Each state has the same number of electors.

__________ **4.** It takes 320 electoral votes to win the presidency.

__________ **5.** Today, there are 538 electoral votes in all.

__________ **6.** In December following the presidential election, the electors for each state assemble in their state capitol to cast their ballots for the president and vice president.

__________ **7.** If no candidate gets an absolute majority of electoral votes for president, then the House of Representatives elects the president.

__________ **8.** If no candidate wins a majority of the electoral votes for vice president, the Senate elects the vice president.

__________ **9.** The candidate who gets an absolute majority of the electoral votes is declared the winner.

__________ **10.** Today in most states, the candidate who gets the most popular votes gets all that state's electoral votes.

Answer the following questions:

11. Name two candidates who were elected president even though their closest opponents received more popular votes.

____

____

12. Suppose there was a country that had two states: State A has 100 people and 10 electoral votes, and State B has 90 people and 9 electoral votes. In State A, 51 people vote for Smith, and 49 vote for Jones. In state B, 1 person votes for Smith, and 89 people vote for Jones. So Jones gets 138 votes in all, and Smith gets 52 votes in all. Who wins the election? Explain why.

____

____

____

____

____

____

Student Guide
Lesson 6: A Third Party

During the Gay Nineties, millionaires and wealthy businessmen lived the good life while American farmers went bankrupt trying to pay for land and equipment. Angry with the government for ignoring their needs, the farmers backed a new political party–one that represented the common people.

Lesson Objectives

- Describe the ways in which farming in the United States changed in the late 1800s.
- Identify the mission of the Populist Party as representing the common people.
- Recognize the ways in which the Populist Party proposed to expand the powers of government.
- Analyze land-use maps to gain familiarity with the use of resources in the United States.

PREPARE

Approximate lesson time is 60 minutes.

Materials

For the Student

Land Use in the United States

A History of US (Concise Edition), Volume C (1865-1932) by Joy Hakim

History Journal

Keywords and Pronunciation

currency : paper bills and coins in circulation within an economy
deflation : falling prices due to a decrease in the supply of money
depression : a time of decline in business activity, accompanied by high unemployment and falling prices
inflation : rising prices due to an increase in the supply of money

---

LEARN

Activity 1: The Populist Party *(Offline)*

Instructions

A. Read *(Chapter 28, pages 136–141)*

Read Chapter 28 until you get to the feature titled "Making Money." Answer the following questions and compare your answers with the ones in the Lesson Answer Key.

1. Why is the Populist Party also known as the People's Party?
2. What suggestions did the Populists make for expanding the power of the government?
3. How did conditions change for U.S. farmers after the Civil War?

B. Use What You Know

Many newspapers in large Eastern cities strongly opposed the Populist movement. An editorial in one paper claimed, "No large political movement in America has ever before spawned such hideous and repulsive vipers."

Imagine that you are a Midwestern organizer for the Populist or People's Party. Design a handbill or poster to convince people to join your party.

Before you begin, consider the following:

1. Which group of people did the Populist Party represent?
2. What reforms did the party want for the people?
3. Why did the Populists believe these reforms were good?
4. What were the economic problems of the farmers, and what did other political parties do to address those problems?

C. Focus on Geography
Complete the Land Use in the United States sheet. You'll need to use the online Land Use in the United States interactive map.

D. Read On *(Chapter 28, "Making Money" feature, pages 141–142)*
As you read, list the three most important things you learned in the reading.

Write a brief definition for each of the following terms in your History Journal. When you have finished, compare your definitions with those in the Keywords section of this lesson.
currency
deflation
depression
inflation

ASSESS

Lesson Assessment: A Third Party (*Online*)

You will complete an online assessment covering the main goals of this lesson. Your assessment will be scored by the computer.

Name ______________________ Date ______________________

Land Use in the United States

If you were flying over the United States and looked down from the airplane, you would see the land being used in different ways. You might see land covered with factories, stores, and houses. Other land might be covered with fields with crops or animals. Still other land, like forests and deserts, might look as if people are not using it. Often, however, they are. These are all examples of land use. Land use is a term that refers to how most of the land in an area is used.

Look at the online map. It shows how land was used in the United States in 1900. Click the button for Land Use in the United States, 2000, and you can see how land use has changed over the last 100 years. Go back to the first map, Land Use in the United States, 1900.

1. What color is used to represent land used for crops? ______________________
2. Which region of the country had the most land being used for manufacturing and trade? (Circle one)

   A. the Northeast

   B. the Southwest

   C. the Midwest
3. In which region of the country would you have seen a lot of cattle in 1900?

   ____

Open the map showing land use in the United States in 2000.

4. On the map you can see that manufacturing and trade is concentrated near water. Why?

   ____

To answer the remaining questions you'll need to go back and forth between the two maps.

5. How did land use change in the Great Plains region from 1900 to 2000?

   ____

   ____
6. From 1900 to 2000, land devoted to many categories increased and shifted westward as the country grew and expanded. In which category was the shift most dramatic?

   ____

Student Guide
Lesson 7: Money Matters

In the nineteenth century, how did the United States government back its paper money? Populist leaders wanted to change the system. They pushed for a democratically controlled monetary system because a shortage of money added to the economic woes farmers and poor people faced.

Lesson Objectives

- Explain the role of paper currency and the way the government backs it.
- Define *currency, inflation,* and *deflation.*
- Describe the economic problems of the Gilded Age.
- Recognize the Federal Reserve System as the system that controls our money supply today.

PREPARE

Approximate lesson time is 60 minutes.

Materials

For the Student

A History of US (Concise Edition), Volume C (1865-1932) by Joy Hakim

History Journal

Keywords and Pronunciation

currency : paper bills and coins in circulation within an economy
deflation : falling prices due to a decrease in the supply of money
depression : a time of decline in business activity, accompanied by high unemployment and falling prices
inflation : rising prices due to an increase in the supply of money

---

LEARN

Activity 1: The Ups and Downs *(Online)*

Instructions

Today you'll find out about the ups and downs of the economy and how the business cycle works.

ASSESS

Lesson Assessment: Money Matters (*Online*)

You will complete an online assessment covering the main goals of this lesson. Your assessment will be scored by the computer.

LEARN

Activity 2. Optional: Money Matters *(Online)*

Student Guide
Lesson 8: Money Debates

A short supply of money created a financial panic in 1893. A terrible depression followed the panic. As the United States suffered through the depression, people fiercely debated whether the nation's money should be backed only by gold or by a combination of gold and silver. What was the result of the hottest political debate of the times?

Lesson Objectives

- Explain how the problems of farmers affected the rest of the economy.
- Explain the reasons for, and the results of, the Pullman strike.
- Describe the limited role of the federal government in the economy in the late 1800s.

PREPARE

Approximate lesson time is 60 minutes.

Materials

For the Student

The Election of 1896

A History of US (Concise Edition), Volume C (1865-1932) by Joy Hakim

History Journal

LEARN

Activity 1: Gold or Silver? *(Offline)*

Instructions

A. Read *(Chapter 29, pages 143–145; Chapter 30, pages 146–150)*

As you read, answer the following questions. Your answers will be used to assess how well you understood the lesson. Compare your answers with the ones in the Lesson Answer Key. You may also want to discuss some of the answers with an adult.

1. How did the problems of farmers affect other people in the nation during the late 1800s?
2. What is a tariff? Did high tariffs hurt or help the American economy in the late 1800s?
3. What caused the Pullman strike and what were the results of it?
4. Describe the limited role of the federal government in the economy in the late 1800s.

B. Use What You Know

During 1893 the United States was in a terrible depression. A *depression* is a prolonged recession, or a time when a nation's economy is very slow. The characteristics of a slowed economy are:

- People buy fewer goods and services.
- Factory production decreases and businesses close.
- Factories use fewer raw materials.
- There is more unemployment and less personal income.
- The stock market is unhealthy.

See how the problems of farmers affected other people in the nation during the late 1800s. Complete the Depression Spiral activity online.

C. Read On *(Chapter 31, pages 151–155)*

As you read, complete the Election of 1896 sheet.

ASSESS

Lesson Assessment: Money Debates *(Online)*

You will complete an online assessment covering the main points of this lesson. Your assessment will be scored by the computer.

Name Date

The Election of 1896

Candidates:	**William McKinley**	**William Jennings Bryan**
Political party:		
Type of supporters:		
Issues:		
Campaign process:		
Money spent on campaign:		

1. Explain how the election of 1896 helped determine the nation's direction at the beginning of the twentieth century.

2. What is a special interest? Can you name some special interest groups?

Student Guide
Lesson 9: (Optional) Your Choice

Lesson Objectives
- Explore knowledge and skills taught in this course.

PREPARE

Approximate lesson time is 60 minutes.

Materials

For the Student

Map of the United States

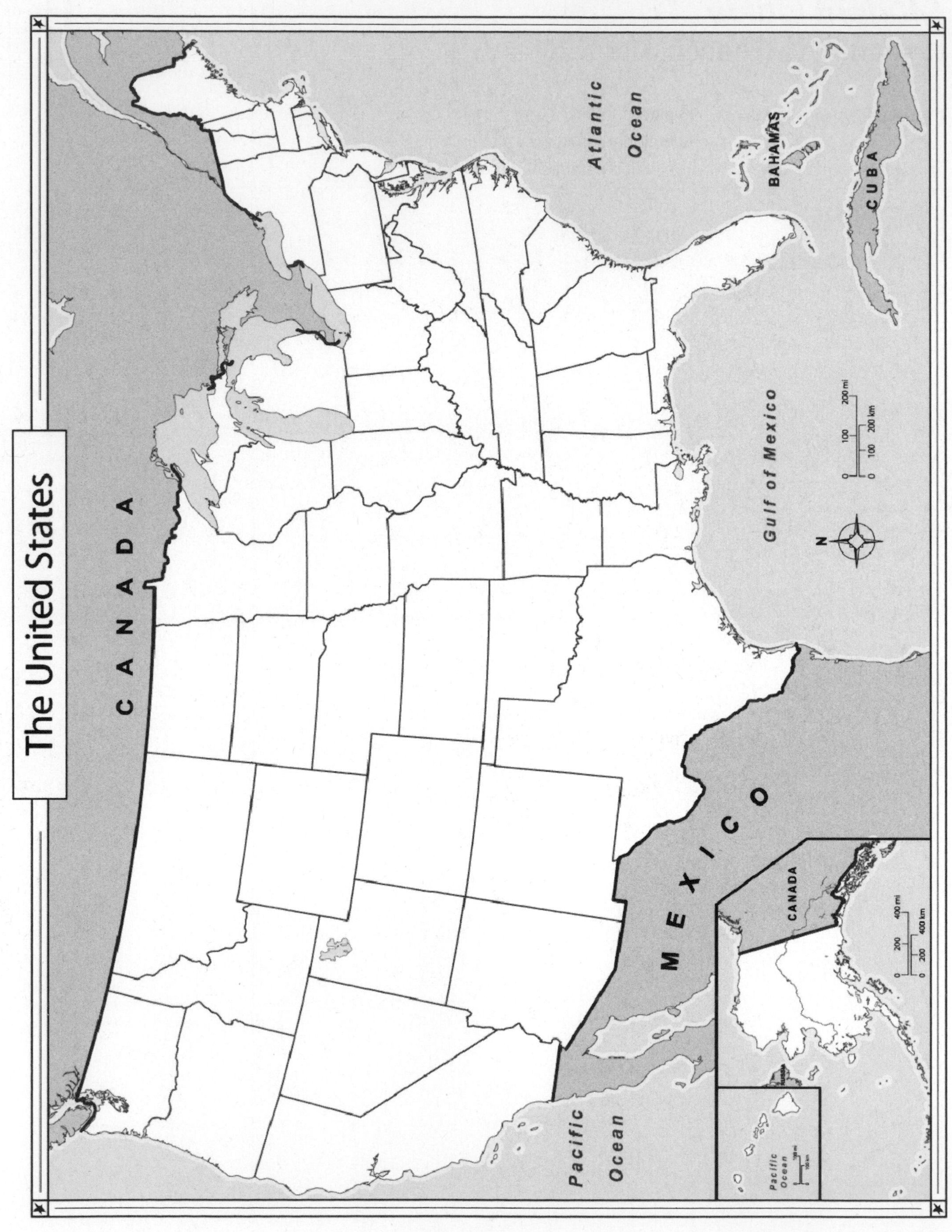
The United States
CANADA
MEXICO
Atlantic Ocean
Pacific Ocean
Gulf of Mexico
BAHAMAS
CUBA
N
0 100 200 mi
0 100 200 km
CANADA
0 200 400 mi
0 200 400 km
Pacific Ocean

Student Guide
Lesson 10: A Grand Campaign

The presidential election of 1896 pitted William Jennings Bryan against William McKinley, but the race involved more than two men and their parties. It was a contest between two very different views of government. The outcome of the election established the direction of the nation in the twentieth century.

Lesson Objectives

- Demonstrate knowledge gained in previous lessons.
- Explain the significance of the election of 1896 in determining the nation's direction at the beginning of the twentieth century.
- Describe the differences between Bryan and McKinley's campaigns.
- Define *special interest.*
- Recognize and define *monopoly, trust, command economy, market economy, hybrid economy, corporation,* and *tariff.*
- Describe the ways in which farming in the United States changed in the late 1800s.
- Identify the mission of the Populist Party as representing the common people.
- Recognize the ways in which the Populist Party proposed to expand the powers of government.
- Define *currency, inflation,* and *deflation.*
- Recognize the Federal Reserve System as the system that controls our money supply today.
- Explain how the problems of farmers affected the rest of the economy.
- Explain the reasons for, and the results of, the Pullman strike.
- Recognize the role of government in the economy through the Federal Reserve System.

PREPARE

Approximate lesson time is 60 minutes.

Materials

For the Student

A History of US (Concise Edition), Volume C (1865-1932) by Joy Hakim

History Journal

LEARN

Activity 1: The Election of 1896 *(Offline)*

Instructions

A. Check Your Reading *(Chapter 31, pages 151–155)*

Compare your answers on the Election of 1896 sheet with the ones in the Lesson Answer Key.

B. Use What You Know

How would you have voted in the 1896 presidential election? Pretend you are an 1896 character—such as a farmer, shopkeeper, reformer, businessman, or railroad owner—writing a letter to the editor of the newspaper. In your History Journal, write a letter attempting to persuade the editor and readers to vote for your candidate. Be sure you explain your reasons for choosing either Bryan or McKinley.

C. Look Back

- Prepare for an assessment by reviewing Chapters 28–31 in *A History of US (Concise Edition)*, Volume C.
- Review your History Journal and online activities for the past four lessons.

ASSESS

Lesson Assessment: A Grand Campaign *(Online)*

You will complete an online assessment covering the main points of this lesson. Your assessment will be scored by the computer.

Student Guide
Lesson 11: All Americans?

The unsettled conditions that shook the nation in the late 1800s helped set off an ugly outburst of racism and bigotry.

Lesson Objectives

- Interpret the words of Emma Lazarus's poem.
- Recognize the weaknesses apparent in American society in the late 1800s.
- Describe the views of nativists and explain why they were incorrect.
- Explain what the Statue of Liberty represents and that it was a gift from the people of France.
- Explain that the Statue of Liberty was a gift from the people of France.

PREPARE

Approximate lesson time is 60 minutes.

Materials

For the Student

A History of US (Concise Edition), Volume C (1865-1932) by Joy Hakim

History Journal

Keywords and Pronunciation

colossus (kuh-LAH-suhs)
nativist : a person who favors native-born citizens and is opposed to immigrants

---

LEARN
Activity 1: They Forgot *(Offline)*
Instructions

A. Read *(Chapter 32, pages 156–160)*
As you read, answer the following questions. When you have finished, compare your answers with the ones in the Lesson Answer Key.

1. The author says, "In America, everyone could see that something was wrong, and not just on the farm." What else was "wrong" in America in the 1890s?

____

____

____

2. How were the nativists' views of new immigrants inaccurate?

Activity 2: Lady Liberty *(Offline)*

Instructions

B. The Statue of Liberty *(Chapter 10, "Lady Liberty" feature, pages 56–57)*

In 1885, the people of France presented the Statue of Liberty to the people of the United States. Today their gift is a worldwide symbol of freedom and opportunity. Read to find out more about how Lady Liberty found her place in New York Harbor.

As you read, answers to the following questions and compare your answers with those in the Lesson Answer Key.

1. What are two things the Statue of Liberty represents?
2. Where and how was the Statue of Liberty conceived?
3. What did Emma Lazarus's poem come to symbolize?
4. Who is the poem talking to—the Old World (Europe) or the New World (America)?
5. What are some descriptive words she uses in the poem to describe the people?
6. What does Lady Liberty want from the Old World?

ASSESS

Lesson Assessment: All Americans? (*Online*)

You will complete an online assessment covering the main objectives of this lesson. Your assessment will be scored by the computer.

Student Guide
Lesson 12: Unit Review

You have finished the unit! It's time to review what you've learned. You will take the Unit Assessment in the next lesson.

Lesson Objectives

- Demonstrate mastery of important knowledge and skills in this unit.

PREPARE

Approximate lesson time is 60 minutes.

Materials

For the Student

A History of US (Concise Edition), Volume C (1865-1932) by Joy Hakim

History Journal

LEARN

Activity 1: A Look Back *(Online)*

Refresh your memory by reviewing your History Journal and the online activities.

A. History Journal Review

When you look over your History Journal, be sure to:

- Look at activity sheets you've completed for this unit.
- Review unit Keywords and definitions.
- Read through any writing assignments you did during the unit.
- Review the assessments you took.

Don't rush through. Take your time.

B. Online Review

Review the following online activities:

- Flash Cards
- Unit Review
- Time Line: 1865-1890

Student Guide
Lesson 13: Unit Assessment

You've finished the unit! Now it's time to take the Unit Assessment for the Politics, Power, and the People unit.

Lesson Objectives

- Identify major business entrepreneurs and the methods they used to build big business and industry in the late 1800s.
- Recognize individuals and innovations that made modern cities possible.
- Recognize the presidents who served between 1877 and 1900 and identify what they are best known for.
- Recognize the role of government in the economy through the Federal Reserve System.
- Describe the kinds of power monopolies have over the economy and the advantages and disadvantages of monopolies.
- Name two things that the Statue of Liberty represents.
- Interpret the words of Emma Lazarus's poem.
- Describe the roles of third parties and special interest money in promoting political ideas and issues.
- Define *monopoly, trust, command economy, market economy, hybrid economy,* and *corporation.*
- Describe the circular relationship among various sectors of the economy.
- Identify groups or individuals who helped or hindered the growth of democracy and opportunity in the late 1800s.
- Recognize the extremes of poverty, wealth, and opportunity in American society in the late 1800s.

PREPARE

Approximate lesson time is 60 minutes.

ASSESS

Unit Assessment: Politics, Power, and the People, Part 1 *(Online)*

Complete the computer-scored portion of the Unit Assessment. When you have finished, complete the teacher-scored portion of the assessment and submit it to your teacher.

Unit Assessment: Politics, Power, and the People, Part 2 *(Offline)*

Complete the teacher-scored portion of the Unit Assessment and submit it to your teacher.

Student Guide

Unit 4: Making Things Better
Lesson 1: Changes at Work

The extremes of the Gilded Age created a need for reform. Americans stepped up to the task of making things better. Workers risked their lives to form unions and demand better conditions and fair wages. Individuals worked to end child labor and help urban immigrants. Journalists exposed the dark side of business and government so the public could demand change. Conservationists warned of the dangers to the environment. People knew they could make the country a better place.

As American businesses grew larger and richer, owners and managers often looked on workers as just another resource to be exploited. Working conditions, pay, and hours did not improve. Workers organized unions to protect their interests. The public was confused about the new labor unions. Many people saw them as radical social organizations, and were afraid.

Lesson Objectives

- Demonstrate mastery of the content of this lesson.
- Describe the changes that took place in worker-owner relationships in nineteenth-century factories.
- Explain the purpose of unions.
- Describe the public reaction to unions.
- Identify the Haymarket Square incident.

PREPARE

Approximate lesson time is 60 minutes.

Materials

For the Student

Life for American Laborers

A History of US (Concise Edition), Volume C (1865-1932) by Joy Hakim

History Journal

Keywords and Pronunciation

anarchism : the rejection of all forms of government based on the belief that government restricts individual freedom; someone who supports anarchism is called an anarchist

socialism : a system in which the government or the whole community owns the major means of production (such as factories)

union : an organization of workers who use their collective strength to bargain for pay and better working conditions

LEARN

Activity 1: The Voice of Labor *(Offline)*

Instructions

A. Read *(Chapter 33, pages 161–166)*

As you read, write definitions for the following terms in your History Journal. When you have finished, compare your definitions with the ones in the Keywords section.

- anarchism
- socialism
- union

Read the online Flash Cards to review the key points of the lesson.

B. Explore

According to the First Amendment, the crowd and the speakers at the Haymarket Rally had the right to assemble peacefully and express their opinions. So why did the police come in and demand that the meeting end? Was it because some people didn't like what was being said?

Re-read the sidebar on page 166. Ms. Hakim presents a tough question that is still being argued today: Should anarchists or neo-Nazis be allowed to speak?

The courts have upheld some limits on free speech. For example, a person cannot yell “Fire!” in a crowded theater if there is no fire. Yelling "fire" could be very dangerous because it could cause people to panic. The courts have also upheld laws against slander—telling deliberate lies about someone to harm that person's reputation. Hearing about unpopular ideas, however, is one way of learning about issues. Remember, hearing an idea is not the same as accepting it.

Should freedom of speech be limited if the ideas are unpopular or in conflict with government positions? What do you think? In your History Journal, write as much as you think is necessary to explain your opinion on this issue.

C. Use What You Know

Complete the Life for American Laborers sheet.

D. Assessment

You will be assessed on your mastery of the Flash Cards. Review them as many times as necessary to be able to answer them all correctly. When you think you're ready, click Shuffle and then answer each of the cards correctly in one pass. When you can do that, go back to report your mastery in the assessment.

ASSESS

Lesson Assessment: Changes at Work *(Online)*

You will complete an online assessment covering the main points of this lesson. Your assessment will be scored by the computer.

Name ______________________ Date ______________________

Life for American Laborers

Life was not easy for turn-of–the-century laborers. They were forced to work long hours in unpleasant conditions. Steelworkers, for example, worked 12 hours a day, six days a week. Textile workers spent 60–80 hours a week on the job. These working-class people did whatever was necessary to make enough money to clothe and feed themselves and their families. The following information gives you a clearer picture of the hardships they endured.

In 1900, the average American worked 6 days a week, 10 hours a day, for 22 cents an hour.

1. How much money did the average American make each day? ________
2. How much money did the average American make each week? ________
3. How much did the average American make in a year? ________
4. If a new bike cost $14.65, how many hours did the average American work to buy one? ________
5. Did a new bike cost more or less than a worker made in one week? ________

Factory workers faced numerous health and safety dangers in the workplace. Working with fast-moving, complex machinery was often the greatest danger. One wrong move and a worker's fi ngers or limbs could get jammed in the moving parts. In addition, workers were often exposed to poisonous materials that, over time, caused sickness and death. If a person became sick or was injured on the job he did not receive any help or pay from his employers. In fact, employers felt very little concern for their workers' safety or well-being. One factory manager said:

> *"I regard my workpeople just as I regard my machinery. So long as they can do my work for what I choose to pay them, I keep them, getting out of them all I can. What they do or how they fare outside my walls I don't know, nor do I consider it my business to know... When my machines get old and useless, I reject them and get new, and these people are part of my machinery."*

6. How would you describe the manager's treatment of his workers?

____

7. If you were one of this man's workers, what would you do to fight for better conditions?

____

____

Student Guide
Lesson 2: Samuel Gompers

In the first half of the nineteenth century, businesses were small and owners and employees worked together. But in the industrial age, factories grew big and impersonal. Owners had most of the power. They could lock workers in or out of the workplace and use their wealth to destroy unions. Courts usually favored owners. The situation changed when unions acquired power and respectability. Then, workers began to reap the benefits of their own productivity. It might not have happened without leaders like Samuel Gompers.

Lesson Objectives

- Describe the Triangle Shirtwaist Factory fire.
- Identify Samuel Gompers.
- Compare and contrast the goals of socialists and anarchists with those of Gompers.
- Recognize the methods employers used against workers and unions.
- Explore the role of unions in the workplace today.

PREPARE

Approximate lesson time is 60 minutes.

Materials

For the Student

A History of US (Concise Edition), Volume C (1865-1932) by Joy Hakim

History Journal

Keywords and Pronunciation

collective bargaining : negotiations between organized workers and their employers

sweatshop : a workplace where workers are forced to work long hours for low pay in hot, cramped, dirty rooms, with no provision for safety, comfort, or refreshment

---

LEARN

Activity 1: Organized Labor Gets a Boost *(Offline)*

Instructions

A. Read: *Chapter 34 (pages 167–171)*

As you read, write definitions for the following terms in your History Journal. When you have finished, compare your definitions with the ones in the Keywords section of this lesson.

sweatshop

collective bargaining

B. Discuss

Unions got off to a rocky start in the nineteenth century, but they have played an important role in the history of the United States. Unions are influential in many industries, including sports and entertainment. Discuss unions today with an adult. Find out:

- If the adult belongs—or has ever belonged—to a union.
- How the adult feels about unions, and why (some people like them, and some people don't).
- What kinds of workers have unions, and what kinds don't.
- About the benefits workers enjoy today as a result of the demands of the labor movement.

C. Use What You Know

Click Radical or Reasonable to compare and contrast the goals of the American Federation of Labor with the goals of the anarchists and socialists.
When you've finished that, click Get a Clue to identify tactics employers used against workers and unions.

D. Explore

Add Samuel Gompers to the Profiles in American History section of your History Journal. You can write your own profile or print a brief biography from a source on the Internet. Be sure to add your thoughts about his influence over time and explain why Gompers should be included in the Profiles collection.You can find an article about him in the Grolier's online encyclopedia, *New Book of Knowledge*.

ASSESS

Lesson Assessment: Samuel Gompers (*Online*)

You will complete an online assessment covering the main objectives of this lesson. Your assessment will be scored by the computer.

LEARN

Activity 2. Optional: Samuel Gompers *(Online)*

Student Guide
Lesson 3: Mother Jones

To help America's workers, Maria Harris Jones went wherever she was needed. She lived with the laborers near the mines and mills. She adopted the workers—and they called her "Mother Jones." She organized workers, especially children, who worked for starvation wages in nightmare conditions in mines, mills, and factories. She focused public attention on the plight of the children and shamed business owners, employers, and government officials into action.

Lesson Objectives

- Identify Mother Jones as a champion of child labor laws.
- Describe the plight of children in factories and mills in the late 1800s and the solutions found to improve their situation.

PREPARE

Approximate lesson time is 60 minutes.

Materials

For the Student

Child Labor Picture Analysis

A History of US (Concise Edition), Volume C (1865-1932) by Joy Hakim

History Journal

Keywords and Pronunciation

muckraker : an investigative journalist who exposes corruption and injustice

---

LEARN

Activity 1: Telling It Like It Is *(Offline)*

Instructions

A. Read *(Chapter 35, pages 172–177)*

As you read, answer the following questions in your History Journal, and then compare your answers to the ones in the Lesson Answer Key.

1. Who was Mother Jones?
2. What were some of the serious issues around children working in factories and mills in the late1800s and what were some of the solutions to those issues?
3. Who were the Wobblies?
4. Why did the Wobblies hate Sam Gompers's American Federation of Labor?

Write a brief definition for *muckraker* in your History Journal. After you have finished, compare your definition with the one in the Keywords section in this lesson.

B. Explore

Add Mother Jones to the Profiles in American History section of your History Journal. You can find a feature on her on the PBS website Freedom: A History of US. You can also find articles about her by using the online Yahooligans search engine. Be sure to add a paragraph describing her influence over time, and explain why she deserves to be added to the Profiles collection.

C. Use What You Know

Review what you've learned about child labor by completing the Get a Clue online activity. Then complete the Child Labor Picture Analysis sheet.

D. Read On *(Chapter 36, pages 178–181)*

ASSESS

Lesson Assessment: Mother Jones (*Online*)

You will complete an online assessment covering the main objectives of this lesson. Your assessment will be scored by the computer.

LEARN

Activity 2: Mother Jones *(Online)*

Name Date

Child Labor Picture Analysis

Step 1. Observation

Look at the pictures of child laborers on page 173. Choose one photograph to analyze. Study it for two minutes. After you've taken a good, hard look, examine individual items in the photograph. Use the chart to list people, objects, and activities in the photograph.

People	Objects	Activities

Step 2. Inference

Photographs often tell you more than you can actually see in the picture. When you look at objects in the photograph you associate them with what you already know about life in general or about life during that time period. For example, when you look at a picture of a parent reading to kids tucked into bed, you imagine it is nighttime even if you don't see a clock or a dark window. The process of concluding something by reasoning it from what you see is called inference. Look at the photograph and your list again and then list three things you might infer from the picture.

____

____

____

____

____

____

Step 3. Questions

What questions does this photograph raise in your mind?

____

____

____

____

____

____

____

____

Student Guide
Lesson 4: Raking Muck

As a U.S. citizen you have the right to express your opinions in public. You can express them by talking about them, or by publishing them in newspapers, magazines, and books. The First Amendment to the Constitution, also known as Article I of the Bill of Rights, guarantees you these freedoms. But why do you think it is important for people to feel free to express their opinions in public? What do you think would happen if this freedom were restricted?

Lesson Objectives

- Demonstrate mastery of the content in this lesson.
- Explain the role of a free press in a democratic society.
- Define *muckraker*.
- Identify S.S. McClure as a supporter of good writers.
- Describe the effect of Ida Tarbell's writing about the Standard Oil Company.
- Identify at least two muckrakers near the turn of the twentieth century.
- Describe the subjects the muckrakers wrote about and the results of their writing.

PREPARE

Approximate lesson time is 60 minutes.

Materials

For the Student

- Consumer Safety
- Free Press in a Democratic Society
- Jefferson on the Value of a Free Press

A History of US (Concise Edition), Volume C (1865-1932) by Joy Hakim

History Journal

LEARN

Activity 1: The Free Press *(Offline)*

Instructions

A. Check Your Reading *(Chapter 36, pages 178–181)*

Review your reading by completing the Free Press in a Democratic Society sheet. Compare your answers with those in the Lesson Answer Key.

B. Use What You Know

People like Mother Jones and the muckrakers focused public attention on dangerous work conditions and dangerous consumer products. Public attention often forces government action that results in consumer safety laws and standards. That is democracy in action, and one result is that most of the things we buy, wear, and eat are safe to use.

- Complete the Consumer Safety sheet as you identify items in your home that have warnings, government inspection seals, or useful information. You may want an adult to help you with this activity. Add this sheet to your History Journal. Compare your answers with those in the Lesson Answer Key.
- Complete the Jefferson on the Value of a Free Press document analysis sheet. Compare your answers with those in the Lesson Answer Key.

C. Assessment

Take the assessment online.

D. Read On *(Chapters 37, pages 182–183)*

As you read, write a brief definition for the following terms in your History Journal. Compare your definitions with the definitions in the Keywords section of the Tackling Trusts lesson.

- exposé
- investigative journalism

ASSESS

Lesson Assessment: Raking Muck (*Online*)

You will complete an online assessment covering the main objectives of this lesson. Your assessment will be scored by the computer.

Name Date

Free Press in a Democratic Society

1. What does Article I of the Bill of Rights say about the press?

2. What do some people refer to as the fourth branch of our government?

3. What do most Americans believe that we need to solve our problems?

4. Why was the press so important to the American people at the turn of the century?

5. What are muckrakers?

6. How did Sam McClure support good writers?

Name Date

Consumer Safety

Look around your home—check the refrigerator, the medicine cabinets, the cleaning products under the sink or in the laundry room, the mattress tags and clothing labels, the toys and board games, and the electric appliances. Write down any consumer warning labels, government seals, or statements of quality that you find on the items listed below. For food items, be sure to look at lists of ingredients and nutritional information.

Consumer Item	Warning label, government seal, or statement of quality
Meat products	
Eggs	
Dairy products	
Other packaged foods	
Cleaning products	
Medications	
Clothes (small children's pajamas)	
Mattress or pillow tags	
Toys or board games	
Electrical appliances	

Name Date

Jefferson on the Value of a Free Press

Thomas Jefferson wrote and spoke about the role of the free press in a democratic society on numerous occasions.

> *"The way to prevent… [errors] of the people is to give them full information of their affairs through the channel of the public papers."*

1. Jefferson thought that the public would not make mistakes if they had all the facts. What kinds of mistakes could citizens make if they were not informed?

2. How can information prevent the public from making those mistakes?

> *"… were it left to me to decide whether we should have government without newspapers, or newspapers without government, I should not hesitate a moment to prefer the latter."*

3. If he had to choose between the two, why would Jefferson choose newspapers without government rather than government without newspapers?

4. Do you think a democracy (government by the people) can exist without a free press? How about free speech? Does the size of the population matter? Discuss this question with an adult.

Student Guide
Lesson 5: Tackling Trusts

In the late nineteenth century, many people—big business leaders, union leaders, political leaders, and many ordinary citizens—didn't seem to care about laws, or even about right and wrong. Muckrakers began looking around and picked up their pens to expose wrongdoings. Ida Tarbell led the way.

Lesson Objectives

- Identify S.S. McClure as a supporter of good writers.
- Describe the effect of Ida Tarbell's writing about the Standard Oil Company.
- Identify at least two muckrakers near the turn of the twentieth century.
- Describe the subjects the muckrakers wrote about and the results of their writing.

PREPARE

Approximate lesson time is 60 minutes.

Materials

For the Student

- Muckrakers, Exposés, and Reforms
- The News Boom

A History of US (Concise Edition), Volume C (1865-1932) by Joy Hakim

History Journal

Keywords and Pronunciation

exposé (ek-spoh-ZAY) : a publication that exposes wrongdoing to the public

investigative journalism : reporting by a journalist investigating wrongdoing that affects the public

---

LEARN

Activity 1: The Muckrakers *(Offline)*

Instructions

A. Check Your Reading: *(Chapter 37, pages 182–183)*

Compare the definitions you wrote in your History Journal for *exposé* (ek-spoh-ZAY) and for *investigative journalism* with those in the Keywords section online. Then complete the Muckrakers, Exposés, and Reforms sheet. Compare your answers with those in the Lesson Answer Key.

B. Use What You Know

In the late nineteenth century, new technologies and publishing techniques made it possible to produce inexpensive newspapers and distribute them to a wide audience. The population of the United States was growing quickly, and the literacy rate of that population was rising. The demand for newspapers grew, and publishers were happy to supply newspapers and magazines to meet that demand.

Complete the News Boom sheet, and compare your answers with those in the Lesson Answer Key.

C. Beyond the Lesson *(Optional)*

Muckrakers are interesting people. Select one to include in the Profiles in American History section of your History Journal. You can research online or offline. The online *New Book of Knowledge* encyclopedia is a good resource. Be sure to write a paragraph on why the muckraker you have chosen belongs in the Profiles in American History. Consider what lasting contribution that person made.

ASSESS

Lesson Assessment: Tackling Trusts (*Online*)

You will complete an online assessment covering the main objectives of this lesson. Your assessment will be scored by the computer.

Name Date

Muckrakers, Exposés, and Reforms

Muckrakers investigated their subjects carefully, and then wrote about them. The exposés they published often brought about reforms. Use your knowledge and what you've read to complete this chart.

Muckraker	Exposed	Reforms
Upton Sinclair	Meat-packing factories' filthy ways of butchering and preparing meat	Food-inspection laws were passed.
	The business practices of John D. Rockefeller and his Standard Oil Company trust.	
Lincoln Steffens		

Who made it possible for good writers to earn a living writing investigative articles and exposés? What was the name of his magazine?

____

____

____

Name Date

The News Boom

Use the information in the chart to answer the questions.

Year	Number of Daily Newspapers	Circulation
1860	387	1,478,000
1870	574	2,602,000
1880	971	3,566,000
1890	1,610	8,387,000
1900	2,226	15,102,000

1. Which twenty-year period showed the greatest growth in newspapers?

2. How much did readership increase between 1880 and 1900?

3. What can you conclude about the power of the press?

Student Guide
Lesson 6: (Optional) Your Choice

Lesson Objectives

- Explore knowledge and skills taught in this course.

PREPARE

Approximate lesson time is 60 minutes.

Materials

For the Student

Map of the United States

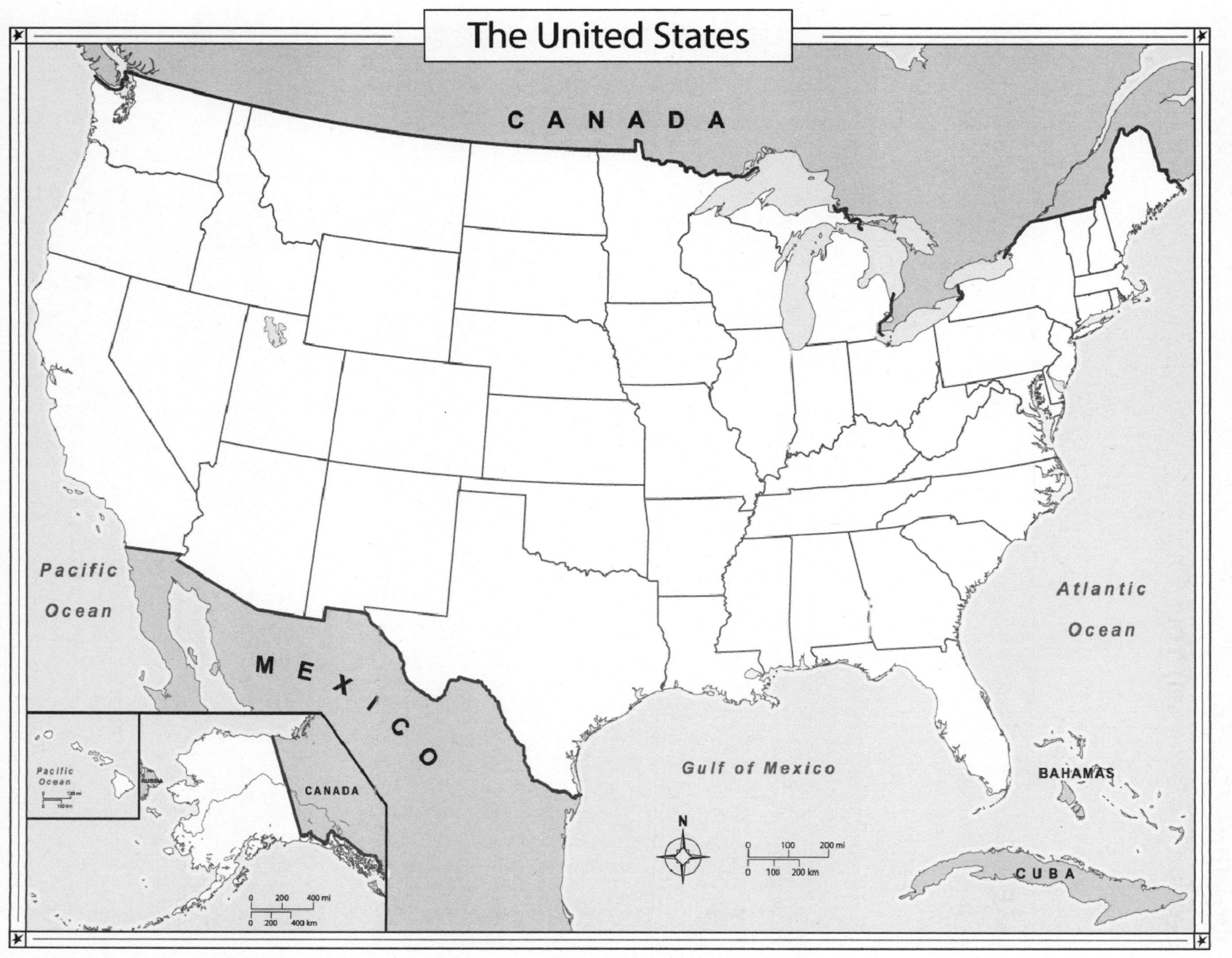
The United States
CANADA
Pacific Ocean
Atlantic Ocean
MEXICO
Gulf of Mexico
BAHAMAS
CUBA
N
0 100 200 mi
0 100 200 km
CANADA
RUSSIA
0 200 400 mi
0 200 400 km
Pacific Ocean

Student Guide
Lesson 7: Citizen of the Earth

"I might have been a millionaire," said naturalist John Muir. "I chose to become a tramp." Muir called himself a tramp because he loved hiking in the wilderness. He walked through Alaska, the Grand Canyon, and California's Yosemite Valley. He once hiked from Indiana to the Gulf of Mexico—about 1,000 miles! In his travels he noticed that civilization was taking over the wilderness and destroying the country's most beautiful places. What could he do to stop it?

Lesson Objectives

- Demonstrate mastery of the content in this lesson.
- Explain that Americans held differing views on land use and resources in the late 1800s.
- Identify John Muir as a preservationist.
- Recognize the purpose of the National Park System today.

PREPARE

Approximate lesson time is 60 minutes.

Materials

For the Student

The National Park System

This Land Is Our Land

A History of US (Concise Edition), Volume C (1865-1932) by Joy Hakim

History Journal

Keywords and Pronunciation

conservationist : a person who believes in using natural resources wisely while protecting their value by avoiding wasteful or destructive practices

John Muir (myur)

preservationist : a person who believes that natural resources should be kept in their natural state--untouched by man

---

LEARN

Activity 1: Preserving Nature *(Offline)*

Instructions

A. Read *(Chapter 38, pages 184–189)*

While you read, complete the This Land Is Our Land sheet. Compare your answers with those in the Lesson Answer Key.

B. Explore

Congress created the National Park Service in 1916 to "conserve the scenery and the natural and historic objects and the wild life therein…by such means as will leave them unimpaired for the enjoyment of future generations." John Muir's work helped people recognize the need to conserve and preserve nature.

Go to *The New Book of Knowledge* at Grolier's Encyclopedia. In the search field, type the words *National Park System*. Select the article entitled National Park System from the search results. Using the information in this article, complete the National Park System sheet.

ASSESS

Lesson Assessment: Citizen of the Earth *(Online)*

You will complete an online assessment covering the main points of this lesson. Your assessment will be scored by the computer.

LEARN

Activity 2. Optional: Citizen of the Earth *(Online)*

Name _______________ Date _______________

This Land Is Our Land

Answer the following questions based on the information in Chapter 38 in *A History of US, (Concise Edition), Volume C*.

1. By the end of the nineteenth century, the United States was growing fast. Population, industry, and agriculture were growing. Settlement of the land was expanding. The nation was rich with opportunity. How did the vastness of the American frontier affect the way in which Americans viewed their natural resources?

2. In 1890, the U.S. Census Bureau said there was no more frontier. How did that realization affect the way in which Americans viewed their natural resources?

3. Who was John Muir?

In 1890, three kinds of people were deciding the future of our national natural resources. Describe each group.

4. Preservationists: _______________

5. Conservationists: _______________

6. Others: ____

____

7. What is the purpose of the National Park System today?

____

____

Name ______________________ Date ______________________

The National Park System

Go to the National Park System article in the *New Book of Knowledge* at Grolier Online.

Read the first three paragraphs.

1. The places in the National Park System have been set aside for what purposes and for how long?

   ____

2. How many different places (units) are there in the National Park System?

   __________________ That's about one for every day in the year.

3. Approximately how many visitors from all over the world visit places in the National Park System every year? __________________

4. The system contains more than __________________ acres of land which is less than __________________ of the total land area of the United States.

5. This remarkable collection is made up of __________________, __________________, __________________, and other areas.

Read the section on the First National Parks.

6. What was the first national park, and when was it dedicated?

   ____

7. To whom does the park belong?

   ____

8. Identify three other early national parks. ______________________________

   ____

9. In 1906, Congress passed the Act for the Preservation of American Antiquities. It authorized the president to set aside what kinds of lands owned or controlled by the United States?

   ____

10. What are these lands called? ______________________________

11. During the early years, who managed the national parks and monuments?

____

12. What did Congress create in 1916 to manage the various parks and monuments already in existence? ______________________________

The people of the United States had a good idea in starting the National Park System. Many countries around the world have created national parks to conserve and preserve their natural treasures. Read about some of these in the National Park Systems Around the World section of the article.

13. Go back to the top of the page. Click Facts at a Glance. Look at all the links at the top of that page. They tell about all of the different kinds of places that are a part of the National Park System. Click a few of these links. Identify one or more places that are near you.

____

Click your browser's Back button until you get back to the main article. Click the small map near the top of the page to see the distribution of National Park Service sites in the country. When you have finished, close the browser window.

14. Click More Art to see regional maps. Click the map for your region of the country. Identify one or more National Parks or National Monuments near you. If you are not in the United States, click the World National Parks map. Is there a national park in the country where you live? When you have finished, close the browser window.

____

Finally, click the More Pictures link to see a small gallery of beautiful photos taken in some of the places in our National Park System.

Student Guide
Lesson 8: Woman of Peace

Jane Addams believed in helping poor immigrants. She moved into the slums of Chicago and set to work. She was good at solving problems and very determined—she wouldn't let anyone stand in her way. Jane Addams became the most admired woman in America and was awarded one of the most honored prizes in the world—the Nobel Peace Prize.

Lesson Objectives

- Demonstrate mastery of the content in this lesson.
- Describe the problems of immigrants in the cities of the late 1800s.
- Identify Jane Addams.
- Explore the history of the Nobel Prizes and those who have won Nobel Peace Prizes.

PREPARE

Approximate lesson time is 60 minutes.

Materials

For the Student

Better Cities for Immigrants

A History of US (Concise Edition), Volume C (1865-1932) by Joy Hakim

History Journal

LEARN

Activity 1: Getting Settled at Hull House *(Offline)*

Instructions

A. Read *(Chapter 39, pages 190–198)*

Complete the Better Cities for Immigrants sheet while you read. When you have finished, compare your answers with those in the Lesson Answer Key.

B. Discuss

How have the lives of immigrants in American cities changed during the last century?
There are thousands of immigrants from different lands, speaking different languages. Many of the immigrants are poor, have come to America to escape oppressive governments, and don't understand our system of government. Many of them also need help.

In your History Journal, write a list of problems that immigrants and the poor in the cities faced at the beginning of the twentieth century. Discuss the list with an adult. Do the same problems exist in U.S. cities today? How does our society try to address the problems? Do city governments provide services? Does the federal government provide services? Do private organizations provide services? Do churches provide services? Do settlement houses exist today?

C. Explore

Jane Addams won the Nobel Peace Prize in 1931. What is the Nobel prize? What kinds of Nobel prizes are there? What, or who was Nobel? Who awards the prize? How often is it awarded? Who has won it and what did they do to deserve it? You can find out in the online Grolier's encyclopedia.

Enter Nobel in the search field. Read the article on Alfred Bernhard Nobel. Then look at the list of winners in the Nobel Prizes link. Can you find Jane Addams?

ASSESS

Lesson Assessment: Woman of Peace *(Online)*

You will complete an online assessment covering the main points of this lesson. Your assessment will be scored by the computer.

Name ______________________________ Date ______________________________

Better Cities for Immigrants

1. Why did Joy Hakim use the term polyglot to describe U. S. cities in the late nineteenth century?

2. Describe the problems of immigrants in the cities in the late 1800s.

3. How were city bosses able to serve immigrants?

4. How did the city bosses pay themselves for helping immigrants? Give an example.

5. Why were immigrants willing to let city bosses control their lives?

6. Who was the founder of Hull House? ______________________________

7. Why did Jane Addams decide to live in the slums of Chicago?

8. Hull House was a neighborhood place known as a settlement house. Who did settlement houses serve, and what did settlement houses do?

9. Both settlement houses and city bosses offered services to the immigrants and the poor. How were their motives different?

10. Jane Addams is famous for establishing settlement houses, but she did many other things to improve the life of Chicago's poor. Name two other ways she helped them.

11. How and when was Jane Addams honored for her work?

Student Guide
Lesson 9: How Close Are We?

The urban America we know today began taking shape in the late 1800s. Changes in society and an increase in population led to the rapid growth of cities. During that period, millions of immigrants arrived in the United States, and many moved into urban areas. By 1914, as many Americans lived in cities as in rural areas. You can see how urban America changed over the years by looking at a population-density map.

Lesson Objectives

- Interpret population-density maps.
- Compare population-density maps from different time periods.
- Analyze immigrant population data.

PREPARE

Approximate lesson time is 60 minutes.

Materials

For the Student

Population Density Map

LEARN

Activity 1: The Growth of Cities *(Offline)*

Instructions

A. Focus on Geography

Population Density

What's the difference between New Jersey and Montana? You could probably list several differences.One item on your list should be people, or rather, the number of people who live in each state.

- Click Population Density at the bottom of the interactive map to display a population-density map for the United States. The map shows, in ranges, the number of people per square mile. Data for this map comes from the U.S. Census.
- Look at the may key. What is the lowest range of population density? The key shows that the color yellow represents a population density of 6 or fewer people per square mile. This is the lowest range of population density shown on the map.
- Find New Jersey on the map. If you're not sure where New Jersey is, check your U.S. wall map. What is the population density for the entire state of New Jersey?

New Jersey is colored the darkest orange. By looking at the key you can see that areas with this color have a population density of 90 or more people per square mile. New Jersey, therefore, has a population density of 90 or more people per square mile.

- Now find Montana. What is the population density for most of Montana?

Most of Montana is yellow. The key shows that yellow represents areas with a population density of 6 or fewer, so almost all of Montana has a population density of 6 or fewer people per square mile.

- Look at the coastal areas of the map. Compare these areas to the interior of the country. What patterns do you see? What do you think are the reasons for the patterns?

The coastal areas have denser populations. They were settled first and that's where cities first formed. Coastal cities grew quickly because they had easy access to shipping. Port cities also served as points of entry for immigrants arriving by boat.

Look at the year 1990 at the top of the map. It's pointing to a spot in central Missouri. This point represents the mean center of population of the United States in 1990.

What is the mean center of population? Imagine you have a flat, weightless, and rigid map of the United States. Now imagine you have millions of tiny weights—one for each person in the country—and that you place each weight on the map to represent the location of each person in the United States.

Now imagine carefully balancing that map on the point of a pencil. The point on the map that is resting on the pencil tip is the location of the mean center of population.

- Click Start. You'll see how the mean center of population moves eastward as you go back in time. Finally, you'll see a population density map of the United States for 1890. Population-density maps from different years can help you see how a population changes over time. These maps show how patterns of population density have changed over time.

On both maps you can see that the eastern half of the country is more densely populated than the western half. But what difference do you notice between 1890 and 1990?

- Although the eastern half of the United States is more densely populated than the western half in both maps, the difference is not as great in 1990.

In 1890, the population of the United States was 62 million. In 1990, it was almost 249 million. It makes sense that the 1990 map shows greater population density overall.

- Find where Los Angeles and the surrounding area would be on both maps. What do you notice?

In 1890, the area around Los Angeles had a population density of 6-18 people per square mile. In 1990, the population density was 90 or more people per square mile. The population density has increased dramatically in the last 100 years.

Immigration

The population of the United States has changed in many ways in the last 100 years. One change was an increase in population because more people were born in the United States. Population increases also came about because people immigrated to the States from many different countries and continents.

Click Immigration at the bottom of the interactive map. Click Immigration to the United States to display the graph. The graph shows the number of immigrants who arrived in the United States between 1890 and 1920. Each line on the graph represents immigrants from a different geographic region. For example, the green line represents immigrants from Southern and Eastern Europe.

Use the graph to answer the following questions:

1. Which geographic region had the most immigrants to the United States in 1910?
2. About how many immigrants came to the United States in 1900 from all regions?
3. In 1890, where did most immigrants to the United States come from?
4. Beginning in 1890, what was the trend in immigration? In other words, how would you describe immigration patterns beginning in that year?

Now click Countries of Origin. This graph shows the number of people living in the United States in 1910 who came from one of five different countries. These are the top five countries of origin. In other words, in 1910, more people came from these five countries than from anywhere else. Use this graph to answer the following questions:

5. How many people living in the U.S. in 1910 were born in Sweden?
6. The most foreign-born people living in the U.S. in 1910 came from what country?
7. Compare this graph with the Immigration to the U.S. graph. Notice that Ireland and Great Britain are two of the top five countries of origin for 1910. On the other graph, notice that immigration from Northern and Western Europe was a lot lower in 1910 than immigration from Southern and Eastern Europe. Why do you think Ireland and Great Britain are in the top five countries of origin.

Answers

1. Most immigrants to the U.S. in 1910 came from Southern and Eastern Europe.
2. About 480,000 immigrants came to the United States in 1900. (40,000 from Asia, Africa, and South America; 120,000 from Northern and Western Europe; and 320,000 from Southern and Eastern Europe)
3. In 1890, most immigrants to the U.S. came from Northern and Western Europe.

4. Beginning in 1890, the number of immigrants from Northern and Western Europe began to decrease. At the same time, the number of immigrants from Southern and Eastern Europe began to increase. Immigration from Asia, Africa, and South America also began to increase, but more gradually.
5. In 1910, 582,000 people living in the U.S. were born in Sweden.
6. In 1910, the largest number of foreign-born people living in the U.S. came from Germany
7. Before 1890, most immigrants came from countries in Northern and Western Europe, like Ireland and Great Britain. Many of these people were still alive in 1910. Even more immigrants came to the U.S. in 1910 from Southern and Eastern Europe, but not as many had come from these countries before 1890.

ASSESS

Lesson Assessment: How Close Are We? (*Online*)

You will complete an online assessment covering the main goals of this lesson. Your assessment will be scored by the computer.

Student Guide
Lesson 10: Progressing

Life was changing rapidly in the United States. A new middle class had emerged. Americans had more leisure time. But some groups were left out and change created new problems. The Populists had made Americans aware of the problems. Review the late 1800s and the changes that came about during that time.

Lesson Objectives

- Define *primary, initiative, referendum,* and *direct election of senators* as they relate to the Progressive movement.
- Review the history of the United States in the late 1800s.
- Describe the ways the nation was changing in the late 1800s.
- Identify groups left out of the prosperity of the late 1800s.
- Describe the Progressive movement.

PREPARE

Approximate lesson time is 60 minutes.

Materials

For the Student

Mixed-Up Time

A History of US (Concise Edition), Volume C (1865-1932) by Joy Hakim

History Journal

Keywords and Pronunciation

17th Amendment : a change to the Constitution that allowed the people (rather than the legislature) to choose their Senators

direct primary : a process by which the people choose candidates in party elections prior to the general election

initiative : a procedure by which a measure is placed on the ballot because a specific number of voters petitioned for it

referendum : a popular vote for or against a specific measure

---

LEARN

Activity 1: Haves and Have Nots *(Online)*

Instructions

Warm-Up

Begin the lesson by playing the Haves and Have Nots game to check your understanding.

A. Use What You Know

Print the Mixed-Up Time sheet and write about the many changes occurring in the United States during this period. Check your answers against the Lesson Answer Key.

B. Discuss *(Chapter 39, page 198)*

In 1902, Theodore Roosevelt said "When I say that I am for the square deal, I mean not merely to stand for fair play under the present rules of the game, but that I stand for having those rules changed so as to work for [greater] . . .equality of opportunity . . . ." Carefully reread the "Politically Speaking" section on page 198. Discuss with an adult how direct primaries, initiatives, referendums, and the 17th Amendment made the country more democratic.

ASSESS

Lesson Assessment: Progressing (*Online*)

You will complete an online assessment covering the main goals of this lesson. Your assessment will be scored by the computer.

Name Date

Mixed-Up Time

Each row across contains related questions. Write short but complete answers to each question.

1a. List some of the technological innovations.	**1b.** What effect did they have on the people?	**1c.** Who benefited?
2a. Why did cities grow?	**2b.** What problems did the growth cause?	**2c.** Who attempted to solve these problems?
3a. What was the impact of having fewer farmers?	**3b.** How were farmers doing in the late 1800s?	

4a. Describe the middle class.	**4b.** What benefit do they have in the Gilded Age that used to be reserved only for the rich?	**4c.** What innovations did they have in their homes?
5a. List the groups of people who were left out of the good times.	**5b.** What did the Progressives do to try to help them?	**5c.** What problem did the Progressives put aside?
6a. How was the Progressive movement linked to the Populist movement?	**6b.** How did the Progressive and Populist movements differ?	

Student Guide
Lesson 11: (Optional) Your Choice

Lesson Objectives

- Explore knowledge and skills taught in this course.

PREPARE

Approximate lesson time is 60 minutes.

Materials

For the Student

Map of the United States

The United States
CANADA
Pacific Ocean
MEXICO
Atlantic Ocean
Gulf of Mexico
BAHAMAS
CUBA
N
0 100 200 mi
0 100 200 km
Pacific Ocean
RUSSIA
CANADA
0 200 400 mi
0 200 400 km

Student Guide
Lesson 12: Unit Review

You have finished the unit! It's time to review what you've learned. You will take the Unit Assessment in the next lesson.

Lesson Objectives

- Demonstrate mastery of important knowledge and skills in this unit.

PREPARE

Approximate lesson time is 60 minutes.

Materials

For the Student

A History of US (Concise Edition), Volume C (1865-1932) by Joy Hakim

History Journal

LEARN

Activity 1: A Look Back *(Online)*

Refresh your memory by reviewing your History Journal and the online activities.

A. History Journal Review

When you look over your History Journal, be sure to:

- Look at activity sheets you've completed for this unit.
- Review unit Keywords and definitions.
- Read through any writing assignments you did during the unit.
- Review the assessments you took.

Don't rush through. Take your time.

B. Online Review

To be sure you're ready for the Making Things Better unit assessment review these activities on the following pages.

- Flash Cards
- Photo Analysis - Triangle Shirtwaist Factory Fire
- Radical or Reasonable?
- Get a Clue: Organizing Unions
- Get a Clue: Child Labor
- Haves & Have Nots game

Student Guide
Lesson 13: Unit Assessment

You've finished the unit! Now it's time to take the Unit Assessment.

Lesson Objectives

- Explain the purpose of unions.
- Describe the public reaction to unions.
- Compare and contrast the goals of socialists and anarchists with those of Gompers.
- Identify Mother Jones as a champion of child labor laws.
- Explain the role of a free press in a democratic society.
- Describe the effect of Ida Tarbell's writing about the Standard Oil Company.
- Describe the subjects the muckrakers wrote about and the results of their writing.
- Analyze immigrant population data.
- Recognize differing views on government regulation and the use of land and natural resources in the late 1800s.
- Distinguish between the goals of socialists and those who support regulation of capitalism.
- Identify John Muir as a preservationist.
- Identify the Haymarket Square incident.
- Define *muckraker*.
- Describe the problems of immigrants in the cities of the late 1800s.
- Identify Jane Addams.
- Explore the history of the Nobel Prizes and those who have won Nobel Peace Prizes.
- Identify individuals and groups who worked toward reform in conservation, city life, factories, and child labor and the resistance they faced.
- Explain the role of a free press in a democracy and give examples of its power through the muckrakers of the late nineteenth and early twentieth centuries.
- Differentiate between population density and population distribution.
- Recognize the purpose of the National Park System today.

PREPARE

Approximate lesson time is 60 minutes.

Materials

For the Student

- Word Bank

ASSESS

Unit Assessment: Making Things Better, Part 1 *(Online)*

Complete the computer-scored portion of the Unit Assessment. When you have finished, complete the teacher-scored portion of the assessment and submit it to your teacher.

Unit Assessment: Making Things Better, Part 2 *(Offline)*

Complete the teacher-scored portion of the Unit Assessment and submit it to your teacher.

Student Guide

Unit 5: Taking a Position
Lesson 1: Choosing a Topic

American society changed rapidly between 1877 and 1900. As businesses and cities grew, new opportunities emerged. Some people reaped great profits and benefits, but many social problems resulted. Many of the problems still exist today. In this unit, you will take a position on one of those issues and write an essay to support your position.

Before you can start writing an essay to support your position, you need to have one. A position, that is. To help you begin to focus on a topic, we've limited it to issues that emerged in the United States between 1877 and 1900. Your first step is to do some research and narrow that broad topic down to something more specific.

Lesson Objectives

- Review the history of the United States between 1877 and 1900.
- Identify major individuals or groups who influenced the period and the roles they played.

PREPARE

Approximate lesson time is 60 minutes.

Materials

For the Student

Then and Now

A History of US (Concise Edition), Volume C (1865-1932) by Joy Hakim

History Journal

LEARN

Activity 1: Choosing a Topic *(Offline)*

Instructions

To get started, print the Then and Now sheet and get Volume C of *A History of US (Concise Edition).* With these tools, you'll be ready to do a little research and narrow down that broad topic.

Before you work on the Then and Now sheet, look at the Time Line: 1865-1890 and the Time Line: 1891-1918. Quickly refresh your memory about the major people and events between 1877 and 1900. As you review the time lines, try to mentally place each important person and event into one of the following three historical themes:

- Corporate Responsibility
- Social Reform
- Conservation

Name Date

Then and Now

Background: At the end of the nineteenth century and the beginning of the twentieth, cities and businesses were expanding rapidly. Some business leaders gathered enormous profits and didn't seem to care how their actions affected the people or places around them.

Some courageous reformers decided to do something about the abuses they saw. First they had to expose the situation and convince people that it needed to be changed. To do that, they picked up their pens and wrote persuasive stories in newspapers and magazines.

In this unit, you'll have a chance to write about an important issue. The topic you will consider is: Did one person make a difference in an area of society that we can still see the effects of their efforts today?

Part 1: Then

1. You will need to cite historical events from the late 1800s to support your opinion. To refresh your memory about the people and events of the late 1800s, scan the time lines. You'll note that many changes took place as businesses expanded and journalists took on a more critical role. Reformers focused on social problems and conservationists starting worrying about the environment.

   As you review the time lines, mentally place the people and events into the following three themes:

   - Corporate Responsibility: (Chapters 22–24, 33, 34, 37)
   - Social Reform: (Chapters 18–20, 34, 35, 39)
   - Conservation: (Chapter 38)

   Which theme interests you the most? Which issues are still important today? For your essay, pick the theme that interests you most, and write it down at the top of the chart on the next page.

2. When you've chosen a theme, scan the chapters (given above) that relate to that theme. As you read, jot down facts, details, and ideas in the appropriate row of the chart. As you review and organize the information, consider the roles that individuals played in changing society. Keep in mind that the focus is on the idea of one person making a difference in an area of society that is still affected by that person's efforts today.

3. In the Choosing a Position lesson you'll develop your position and write the thesis statement for your essay.

Then

Historical Theme: ______________________

People/Groups	**What They Did and Why**	**Result(s)**

Part 2: Now

As you begin developing your essay, keep your goal in mind: supporting the idea of one person making a difference that we can still see today.

Now that you have chosen and researched a theme that was important a century ago, you'll need to find out about issues related to that theme today. Write the name of the theme at the top of the chart on the next page. With an adult, explore websites that are related to your theme and support your position.

- Corporate Responsibility
- Conservation
- Social Reform

Now you should have enough information to answer the following question:

> Has any one person made a difference in an area of society that is still affected by that person's efforts today?

Look at the charts you completed. In the past, were there individuals who made a difference? Can we still see the effects today?

It's time to write your thesis statement, expressing your position on the issue. Several sample thesis statements are included to help you.

Sample Thesis Statements:

- One person improved the environment.
- One person couldn't affect corruption in corporate America.
- One person did reduce corruption in corporate America.

Your Thesis Statement:

____

____

____

Now

Historical Theme ______________ Issue: ______________

People/Groups	What They Did and Why	Result(s)

Student Guide

Lesson 2: (Optional) Your Choice

Lesson Objectives

- Explore knowledge and skills taught in this course.

PREPARE

Approximate lesson time is 60 minutes.

Materials

For the Student

Map of the United States

The United States
CANADA
Pacific Ocean
Atlantic Ocean
MEXICO
Gulf of Mexico
BAHAMAS
CUBA
N
0 100 200 mi
0 100 200 km
Pacific Ocean
0 100 mi
0 100 km
RUSSIA
CANADA
0 200 400 mi
0 200 400 km

Student Guide
Lesson 3: Choosing a Position

You've gathered some information about a theme related to American history between 1877 and 1900. Now it's time to find out about the issues today. Once you've finished the research, you'll be able to make the connections between the issues today and during the late 1800s and decide on your own position.

Lesson Objectives

- Connect issues important in the United States between 1877 and 1900 to the present.

PREPARE

Approximate lesson time is 60 minutes.

LEARN

Activity 1: Choosing a Position *(Online)*

Before you can write your essay, you need to take a position on an issue. Completing Part 2 of the Then and Now sheet will help you do that.

Student Guide
Lesson 4: (Optional) Your Choice

Lesson Objectives

- Explore knowledge and skills taught in this course.

PREPARE

Approximate lesson time is 60 minutes.

Materials

For the Student

Map of the United States

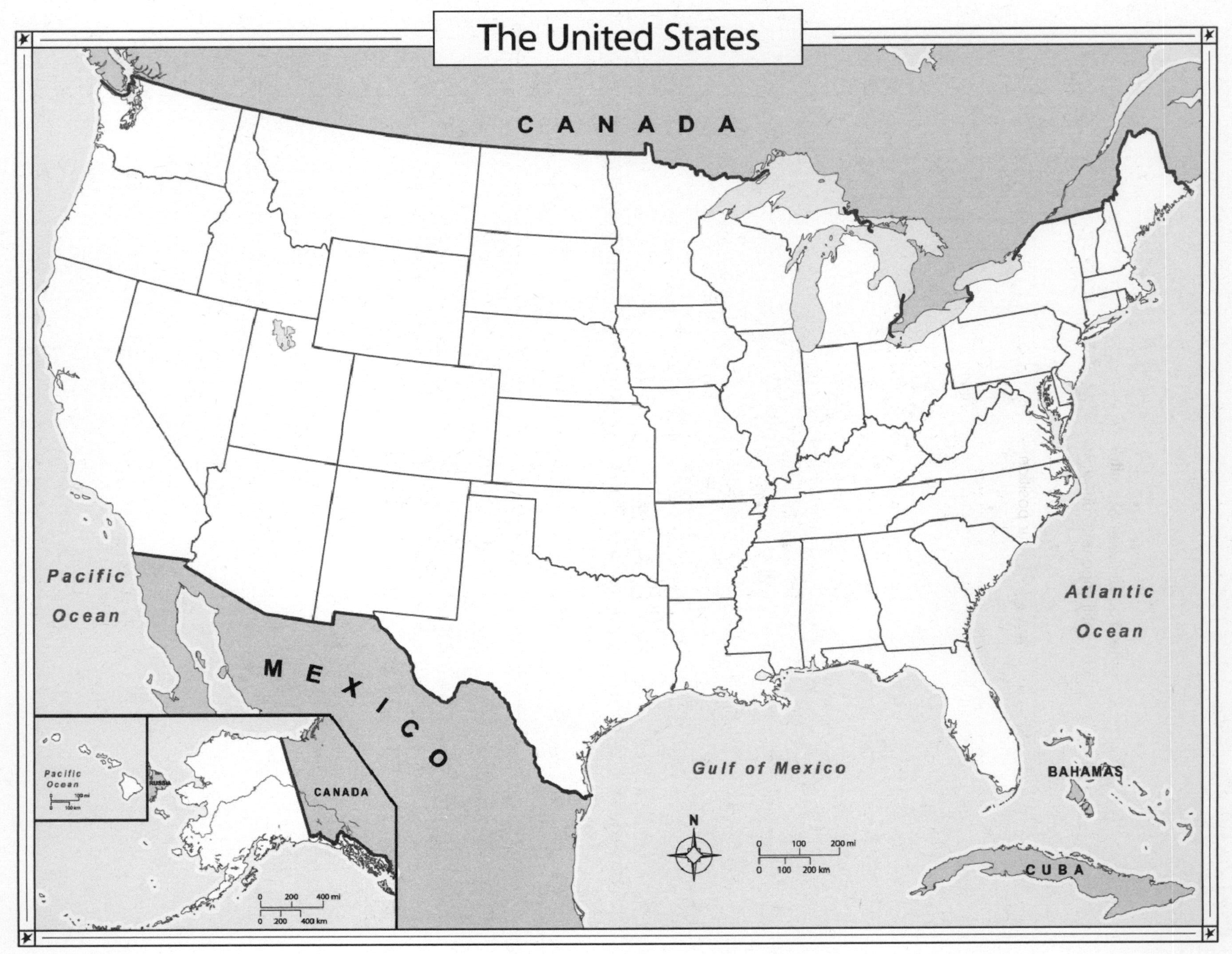
The United States
CANADA
MEXICO
Pacific Ocean
Atlantic Ocean
Gulf of Mexico
BAHAMAS
CUBA
N
0 100 200 mi
0 100 200 km
CANADA
RUSSIA
0 200 400 mi
0 200 400 km
Pacific Ocean

Student Guide
Lesson 5: Writing the Essay

You've researched a historical theme. You've taken a position on an important issue. You've seen how this issue was important in the past and is still important today. Now it's time to write your essay.

Lesson Objectives

- Write a five-paragraph essay to support your position.

PREPARE

Approximate lesson time is 60 minutes.

Materials

For the Student

Essay Plan and Outline

LEARN

Activity 1: Writing the Essay *(Online)*

Instructions

To get started on writing your essay, print the Essay Plan and Outline sheet. You can take this sheet, some loose-leaf paper and a pencil, and finish the lesson away from the computer.

An adult will assess your essay.

ASSESS

Lesson Assessment: Writing the Essay (*Offline*)

You will complete an offline assessment covering some of the main points of this lesson. Your assessment will be scored by the teacher.

Name Date

Essay Plan and Outline

An essay may be organized in the following way:

Introduction: The essay begins with a paragraph that includes the thesis statement.

Body: The body presents evidence that supports your thesis statement.

Conclusion: The essay ends with a paragraph that summarizes your position.

Directions:

Step 1: Prepare an Outline

On the Then and Now sheets, you organized the facts you will use to your position. Now you will organize them in the way you will use them in your essay, in outline form. Use the blank outline on pages 2-5.

- **Introduction:** Your thesis statement will be the introduction to your essay. Write your thesis statement below Roman numeral I on the outline. If you chose the Corporate Leadership theme, your thesis statement might be something like "One person couldn't affect corruption in corporate America."
- **Main Topics:** Your outline will contain three main topics—three reasons supporting your position. Main topics in an outline are listed next to Roman numerals. The first main topic in your outline is the first reason that supports your position. Write a topic sentence stating this reason below Roman numeral II on your outline. For example, "One person couldn't affect corruption in corporate America because corporations had so much more money and power than individuals."
- **Subtopics:** Now decide what pieces of information you will use to support your first reason, and what order that information should be in. In an outline, these pieces of information are called subtopics, and they are listed next to capital letters (A., B., C.) You may not need all the capital letters on the outline, or you may add more if you need them.

  Using the information from the Then and Now sheets, add subtopics to your outline under the first main topic. You must list at least two subtopics under each main topic. One subtopic might be "In the 1880s, Rockefeller's Standard Oil Trust owned 90 percent of the oil industry."

- **Specific Facts:** Now add some specific facts about the subtopics. In an outline, specific facts are listed next to Arabic numerals (1., 2., 3.). List at least two facts under each subtopic.
- Finally, check the information on the Then and Now sheets. You will probably not use all the information you recorded, but be sure you have not left out anything you think is important to support your position. Remember, your essay will follow the outline exactly. When you have completed the section for the first main topic, follow the same procedure for the other main topics.
- **Conclusion:** Your essay will contain a concluding paragraph that summarizes your position and restates the thesis. You may want to include a strong, thought-provoking statement or an emotional appeal that supports your position. Jot down a few ideas for the conclusion below Roman numeral V on the outline.

OUTLINE

I. Introduction: Thesis Statement

____

____

____

____

II. First Main Topic: First reason that supports your position

Topic Sentence:

____

____

____

____

A. ____________________________________

1. __________________________________

2. __________________________________

B. ____________________________________

1. __________________________________

2. __________________________________

C. ______

1. ______

2. ______

D. ______

1. ______

2. ______

III. Second Main Topic: Second reason that supports your position

Topic Sentence:

______

______

______

______

A. ______

1. ______

2. ______

B. ______

1. ______

2. ______

C. ______

1. ______

2. ______

D. ______

1. ______

2. ______

IV. Third Main Topic: Third reason that supports your position

Topic Sentence:

____

____

____

____

A. ______________________________

1. ______________________________
2. ______________________________

B. ______________________________

1. ______________________________
2. ______________________________

C. ______________________________

1. ______________________________
2. ______________________________

D. ______________________________

1. ______________________________
2. ______________________________

V. Conclusion:

____

____

____

____

Step 2: Write Your Essay

Now it's time to write your essay. Keep your Then and Now sheets where you can refer to them.

- Write the introduction. This paragraph presents your thesis statement and captures the reader's attention. You may add some general information if you wish.

  Do not use specific examples in the introduction. Write in a general way. Write three to five sentences.

- Write the body:

  1. Use the main topic sentences to state the main idea of each paragraph.
  2. Explain each topic sentence using the information listed in the subtopics and specifics in that section of the outline.
  3. Write a concluding sentence that connects back to the topic sentence.

- Write a concluding paragraph that summarizes the major ideas of your essay and restates your thesis in some way. Consider making an emotional or thought-provoking appeal to the reader to support your position. Write three or four sentences.

Step 3: Revise and Refine

- Read back through the whole essay. Do you think your essay supports your position? Are all your ideas clearly written? If not, reword or rewrite any sections you think need to be revised.

- Make sure your essay follows this format:

  Introduction: The essay begins with a paragraph that includes the thesis statement.
  Body: The body presents evidence that supports your thesis statement.
  Conclusion: The essay ends with a paragraph that summarizes your position.

- Correct any spelling, grammar, or punctuation mistakes you see. Reading the essay aloud will help you spot errors.

- Share your essay with an adult.

Student Guide
Lesson 6: (Optional) Your Choice

Lesson Objectives

- Explore knowledge and skills taught in this course.

PREPARE

Approximate lesson time is 60 minutes.

Materials

For the Student

Map of the United States

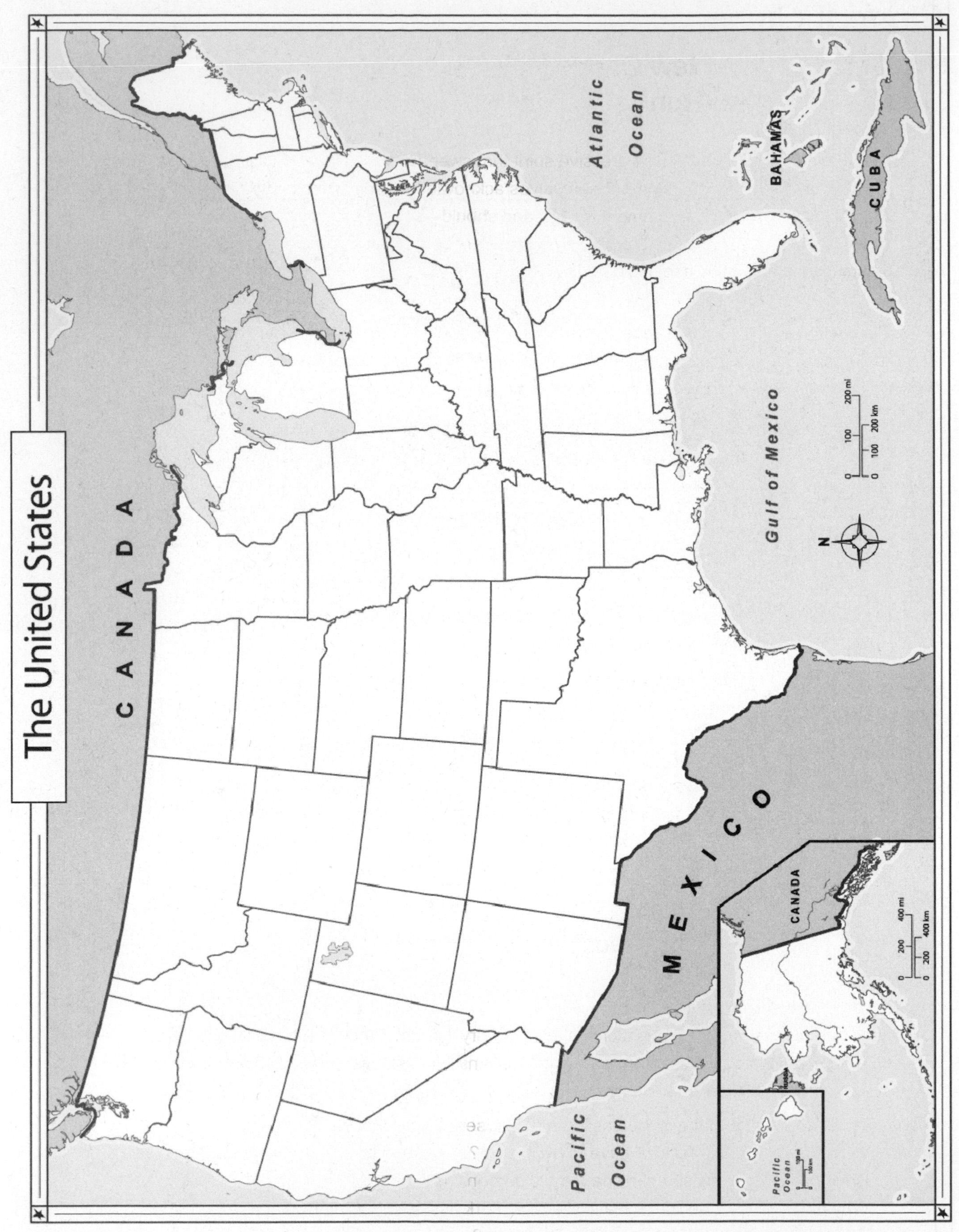
The United States
CANADA
Atlantic Ocean
BAHAMAS
CUBA
Gulf of Mexico
N
0 100 200 mi
0 100 200 km
MEXICO
CANADA
0 200 400 mi
0 200 400 km
Pacific Ocean
Pacific Ocean

Student Guide

Unit 6: Entering a New Century
Lesson 1: Born to Run

Theodore Roosevelt embodied the progressive spirit that swept the country at the beginning of the twentieth century. Energetic, educated, confident Progressives acknowledged the problems the Populists had publicized. They believed the government could—and should—solve those problems and bring equity to the working classes. When Woodrow Wilson became president he was ready to fight to end injustice. But conflict in Europe pulled the United States into a terrible war.

Even as a youngster "Teedie" Roosevelt showed great curiosity and drive. He threw himself into everything. He said, "There were all kinds of things which I was afraid of at first, . . . but by acting as if I was not afraid I gradually ceased to be afraid." He grew up to become a very bold, energetic president.

Lesson Objectives

- Describe the early life of Theodore Roosevelt and the obstacles he had to overcome.

PREPARE

Approximate lesson time is 60 minutes.

Materials

For the Student

A Portrait of Teddy

A History of US (Concise Edition), Volume C (1865-1932) by Joy Hakim

History Journal

Keywords and Pronunciation

anti-imperialist : a person who does not believe in expanding a nation by taking other lands
expansionism : imperialism, the policy or practice of taking lands to increase the size of the country
philanthropist : a person who works to help others, often by giving money to charitable causes

---

LEARN

Activity 1: Getting to Know Teddy *(Online)*

Instructions

A. Read *(Chapter 40, pages 200–204)*

As you read, answer the following questions in your History Journal. When you have finished, compare your answers with the ones in the Lesson Answer Key. Your answers to Questions 1, 2, 3 and 7 will be used to assess how well you understood the lesson.

1. What were some of the unique aspects of Roosevelt's childhood?
2. What hardships did "Teedie" have to overcome?
3. How do you think his struggle shaped his personality?
4. Why did Roosevelt decide to leave the New York Assembly for the Badlands?
5. What are some of the features of the Badlands?

6. What adventures did Teddy Roosevelt experience in the Badlands?
7. How did Roosevelt show his love and respect for the wilderness when he returned to the East?

Define the following terms and write them in your History Journal. When you have finished, compare your definitions with the ones in the Keywords section of this lesson.

- anti-imperialist
- expansionism
- philanthropist

B. Use What You Know

Print and complete the A Portrait of Teddy sheet. Compare your answers to those in the Lesson Answer Key.

ASSESS

Lesson Assessment: Born to Run *(Online)*

You will complete an online assessment covering the main points of this lesson. Your assessment will be scored by the computer.

Name Date

A Portrait of Teddy

In Chapter 40 the author paints a sympathetic picture of Theodore Roosevelt to help you understand the young man before he became president.

1. Identify struggles or events in Teddy's life that shaped him.

2. Identify some key terms or adjectives to describe Teddy.

3. On the next page, draw a sketch of Teddy based on the description of him.

4. Choose phrases from the events and terms in the first two questions of this worksheet and add them to the borders.

Student Guide
Lesson 2: Wanting War

Newspaper headlines in the late 1800s fueled American anger against Spain. In 1898 when the U.S. battleship *Maine* exploded in Havana harbor—killing 260 American sailors—Americans demanded war.

Lesson Objectives

- Describe the results of the Spanish-American War.
- Describe Theodore Roosevelt's role in the Spanish-American War and how it affected his political life.
- Explain the causes of the Spanish-American War.
- Summarize the arguments over the justification for the Spanish-American War.

PREPARE

Approximate lesson time is 60 minutes.

Materials

For the Student

A History of US (Concise Edition), Volume C (1865-1932) by Joy Hakim

History Journal

Keywords and Pronunciation

yellow journalism : news reporting that exploits, distorts, or exaggerates the news to create sensation and attract readers

---

LEARN

Activity 1: Growing Pains *(Offline)*

Instructions

A. Read *(Chapter 41, pages 205–211)*

As you read, take notes in your History Journal about:

- The causes of the war with Spain
- The results of the Spanish-American War
- Different American views on American imperialism
- How Theodore Roosevelt's war experience ultimately affected the entire country

You will use the information to complete the Use What You Know assignment.

Write a definition for *yellow journalism* in your History Journal. Read page 205 carefully, then explain why this was an issue in the Spanish-American War.

B. Use What You Know

Yellow journalism played an important role in stirring American desire for war against Spain. If you had been a journalist then, how would you have written the news? If you were writing newspaper articles now, looking back to that time, how would you write about the events?

Using your reading notes, create a newspaper front page about the Spanish-American War. Decide if you want your paper to reflect the yellow journalism of Theodore Roosevelt's era, or the perspective of a journalist today looking back at the war. Create headlines and articles covering the following topics from that perspective:

- Causes of the Spanish-American War
- Results of the Spanish-American War
- Americans' views on American imperialism
- Theodore Roosevelt's war experience and his path to the presidency

You may wish to create your front page on poster board, using markers to create bold headlines and using paste or a glue stick to mount your articles. If time permits, you may even wish to add a political cartoon or an advertisement.

After you have finished, compare your newspaper articles with the Lesson Answer Key to see if you included the main ideas for each topic.

ASSESS

Lesson Assessment: Wanting War *(Online)*

You will complete an online assessment covering the main points of this lesson. Your assessment will be scored by the computer.

LEARN

Activity 2. Optional: Wanting War *(Online)*

Visit this website if you would like to see film footage of the The Spanish-American War.
Film used back then tends to be grainy and it may be difficult to see the picture clearly at times. In order to understand what the film portrays, be sure to read the website text describing the film clip before viewing it.

Student Guide
Lesson 3: Wanting More

When you think of Hawaii do you think of hula dancers? Did you know the ancient hula dance was a religious ritual, not just tourist entertainment? After the Polynesians settled the Hawaiian Islands, the people lived undisturbed for more than 1,000 years. They developed a rich oral tradition, irrigated plantations, and had a religion centered on a system of taboos. Then, in the nineteenth century, European and American businessmen, missionaries, and governments brought enormous change to the beautiful islands.

Lesson Objectives

- Summarize the history of the Hawaiian Islands, including their annexation and U.S. statehood.
- Use maps to gain familiarity with U.S. territories.
- Describe the citizenship of people in U.S. territories.

PREPARE

Approximate lesson time is 60 minutes.

Materials

For the Student
- All About Hawaii
- Outlying Areas of the United States
- A History of US (Concise Edition), Volume C (1865-1932) by Joy Hakim
- History Journal

LEARN

Activity 1: Aloha Oe *(Offline)*

Instructions

A. Read *(Chapter 42, pages 212–217)*
As you read, write brief notes and phrases in your History Journal that will help you remember:

- The early history of the Hawaiian islands
- How Hawaii was annexed by the United States
- How Hawaii became the 50th state

You will use the information to complete the Use What You Know assignment.

B. Use What You Know
Print the All About Hawaii sheet. Using your notes and textbook, complete the spider map. Compare your answers with the ones in the Lesson Answer Key. Discuss with an adult any topics you found hard to understand.

C. Explore

Print the Outlying Areas of the United States sheet. After you have read about them, locate each territory on your world wall map. This activity will be part of your Lesson Assessment.

ASSESS

Lesson Assessment: Wanting More (*Online*)

You will complete an online assessment covering the main goals of this lesson. Your assessment will be scored by the computer.

LEARN

Activity 2. Optional: Wanting More *(Online)*

Go to the following website to learn more about Hawaiian history, the people, language, geography and nature: The Hawaiian Historical Society.

Name Date

Outlying Areas of the United States

Using the chart, draw conclusions about how each cause helped bring about World War I. Support your conclusions with details from your reading.

You know that the United States has 50 states. But did you know that the United States also has several island territories in the Pacific Ocean and Caribbean Sea? These "outlying areas" are part of the United States. The islands are considered U.S. soil, but since they're not states, they're not full members of the Union.

The people who live on most of these islands are U.S. citizens. They can travel throughout the United States without immigration restrictions. They enjoy the fundamental rights guaranteed by the U.S. Constitution, such as the right to free speech and the right to a fair trial. And they share many of the same government services as people in the states. For example, people in the territories use the American dollar as their currency and American stamps to send mail. (Outlying areas have zip codes for mail delivery, just like other parts of the United States.)

In many ways, people in the outlying areas govern themselves. They have their own governments and make their own local laws, just as the 50 states do. And, like the 50 states, they are also subject to federal laws. The U.S. government in Washington often has a great deal to say about how things are run in the territories. The islands are considered "partially self-governing" areas since they are possessions of the United States but haven't been granted statehood.

One important difference between living in a territory and a state is that people in the territories don't have full representation in Congress. In the main outlying areas, people elect a delegate to the U.S. House of Representatives. The delegates may vote in House committees. But they don't get a vote when the full House of Representatives decides whether or not to pass a law. Citizens living in outlying areas don't get to vote in U.S. presidential elections either.

According to the U.S. Constitution, Congress has the power to admit a territory to the Union as a state. It has happened many times. In fact, 31 of the 50 states were territories before they became states. Alaska and Hawaii were the last territories to become states, both in 1959.

The following are the main outlying areas of the United States:

- Puerto Rico
- The Virgin Islands of the United States
- Guam
- The Northern Mariana Islands
- American Samoa

Puerto Rico lies about 1,000 miles southeast of Florida in the Caribbean Sea. About four million people live there. Spain surrendered the island to the United States in 1898 at the end of the Spanish-American War. Puerto Ricans elect a governor and a legislature, which consists of a senate and house of representatives.

The Virgin Islands of the United States are also in the Caribbean Sea. This territory consists of three islands: St. Croix, St. Thomas, and St. John. About 125,000 people live there. The U.S. Virgin Islands were purchased from Denmark in 1917 for $25 million. The people there elect their own governor and one-house legislature, which consists of 15 members. The U.S. Congress can void any acts passed in the Virgin Islands if it chooses to.

Guam was acquired from Spain in 1898, after the Spanish-American War. This Pacific island lies in the southern Mariana Islands, about 1,300 miles east of the Philippines. About 165,000 people live there. The people of Guam elect a governor and one-house legislature. The U.S. Department of the Interior supervises Guam for the federal government. The United States maintains an important air and naval base there.

The Northern Mariana Islands is a chain of 16 small islands in the Pacific Ocean, about 1,000 miles south of Japan. Some 77,000 people live there. The United States gained control of the islands in 1944 during World War II, and in 1986 the islands became self-governing. The people there elect a governor and two-house legislature to handle internal affairs. The United States is responsible for defense and foreign affairs.

American Samoa consists of a group of seven islands about 2,300 miles southwest of Hawaii. The United States acquired them between 1920 and 1925.About 69,000 people live there. The U.S. Department of the Interior supervises the territory. Samoans elect their own governor and two-house legislature. American Samoa's people are not U.S. citizens but are considered U.S. nationals, which means that they owe their loyalty to the United States.

The United States possesses several other small outlying islands. For example, Wake Island lies in the west-central Pacific. It's used mainly for emergency stopovers for airplanes and ships, as well as a weather research station. About 100 people live there. And tiny Navassa Island, in the Caribbean, is uninhabited. It's reserved for a lighthouse and administered by the U.S. Coast Guard.

Name Date

All About Hawaii

Describe the history of Hawaii by completing the spider map.

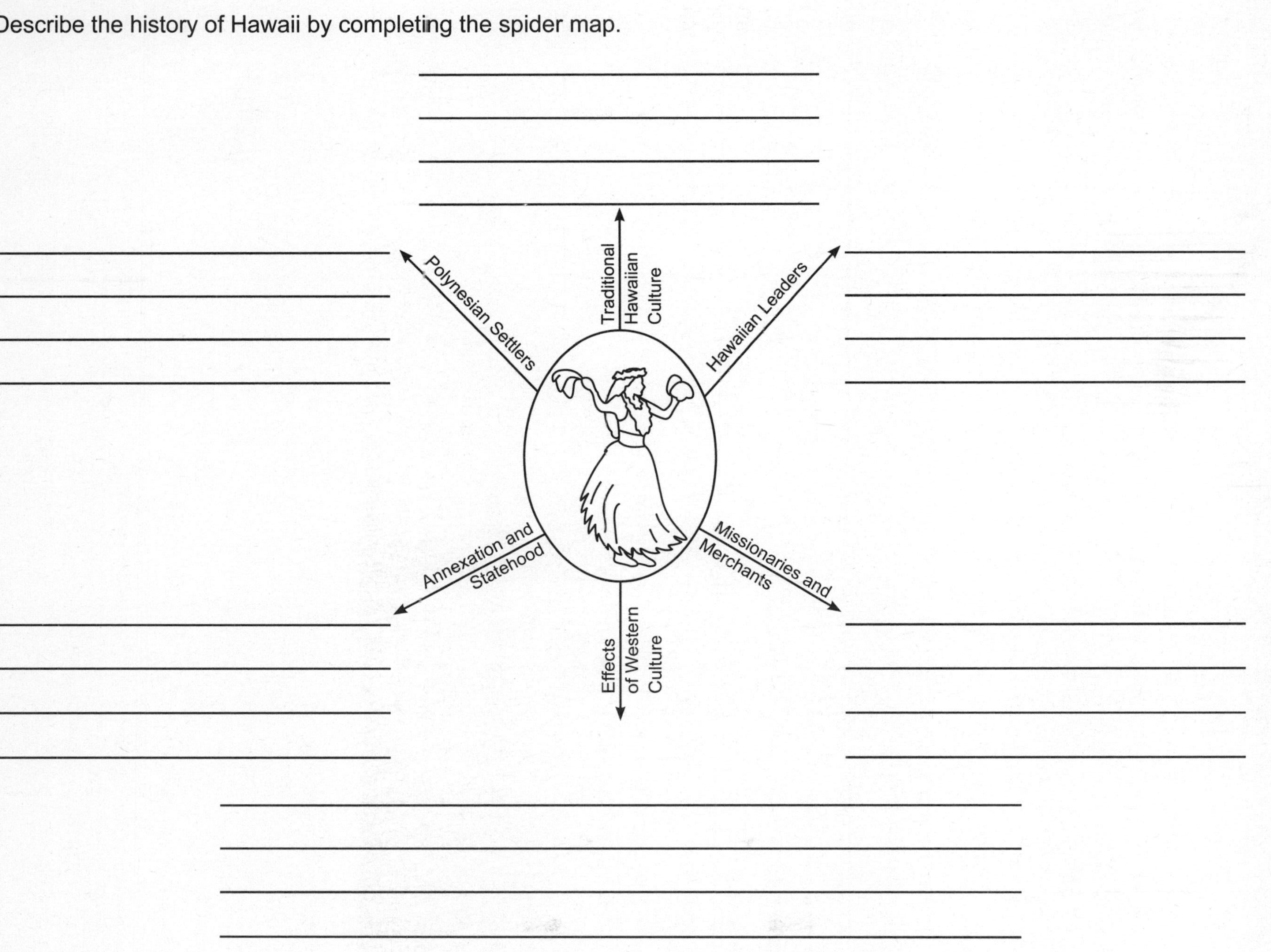

Student Guide
Lesson 4: Our Youngest President

Theodore Roosevelt was "dee-lighted to be president" and the people loved him! One day in 1907, he invited anyone (who was clean and not drunk) to the White House to shake the president's hand. He set a record shaking 8,150 hands that day. His enthusiasm and energy reshaped America's domestic and foreign policies.

Lesson Objectives

- Demonstrate knowledge gained in previous lessons.
- Recognize the changes Theodore Roosevelt initiated as president.
- Describe Theodore Roosevelt's foreign policy.
- Recognize major immigrant groups of the late 1800s and their challenges, opportunities, and contributions.
- Identify individuals, groups, or movements that helped or hindered the growth of civil rights and opportunity in the late 1800s.

PREPARE

Approximate lesson time is 60 minutes.

Materials

For the Student

About Theodore Roosevelt

A History of US (Concise Edition), Volume C (1865-1932) by Joy Hakim

History Journal

LEARN

Activity 1: Teddy Bear President *(Offline)*

Instructions

A. Read *(Chapter 43, pages 218–221)*

As you read, take notes in your History Journal about Theodore Roosevelt's policies. Be sure to include key ideas and phrases to help you recall the following later:

Domestic initiatives

- Pure food and drug laws
- Enforcement of antitrust laws
- Opposition to racial prejudice
- Conservation

Foreign policy

- Construction of the Panama Canal
- "Big Stick" policy

You will use this information to complete the Explore assignment.

B. Explore

Print the About Theodore Roosevelt sheet. Use your notes from today's reading and previous lessons to write about his life. You can also review the Time Line to help you remember key events. You will write about Theodore Roosevelt's domestic and foreign policies and two other aspects of his life. (You'll find suggestions on the About Theodore Roosevelt sheet.) Illustrate each section you write with pictures you copy from books, find and print from the Internet, or draw by hand.

When you have finished, compare your answers with those in the Lesson Answer Key. The first two questions of this writing activity will be used as the assessment for this lesson.

ASSESS

Lesson Assessment: Our Youngest President *(Online)*

You will complete an online assessment covering the main points of this lesson. Your assessment will be scored by the computer.

LEARN

Activity 2. Optional: Our Youngest President *(Online)*

Theodore Roosevelt was responsible for the construction of the Panama Canal, which connected the Atlantic Ocean and the Pacific Ocean. To understand what a phenomenal accomplishment that was, view the Smithsonian's website Make the Dirt Fly!

Name Date

About Theodore Roosevelt

Describe Theodore Roosevelt's domestic and foreign policies on the first page. Select two other areas of Theodore Roosevelt's life or character that interest you (e.g., TR as a boy, Rough Rider during the Spanish-American War, outdoorsman, conservationist, governor of New York, family man, etc.) and complete the second page. Illustrate each section with a picture you copy, print, or draw. This writing activity will be used as the assessment for this lesson.

Insert TR domestic policy picture here

1. TR's Domestic Policies

2. TR's Foreign Policies

Insert TR foreign policy picture here

3.

Insert picture here

4.

Insert picture here

Student Guide
Lesson 5: (Optional) Your Choice

You may use today's lesson time to do one or more of the following:

- Complete work in progress.
- Visit two websites to learn more: About Theodore Roosevelt (www.Theodoreroosevelt.org) and Theodore Roosevelt: His Life and Times on Film (www.memory.loc.gov/ammem/trfhtml/trfhome.html). Then finish the visual essay.
- Locate and identify the 50 states (www.yourchildlearns.com/dirmpusa.htm).
- Go on to the next lesson.

Please mark this lesson complete in order to proceed to the next lesson in the course.

Lesson Objectives

- Explore knowledge and skills taught in this course.

PREPARE

Approximate lesson time is 60 minutes.

Materials

For the Student

Map of the United States

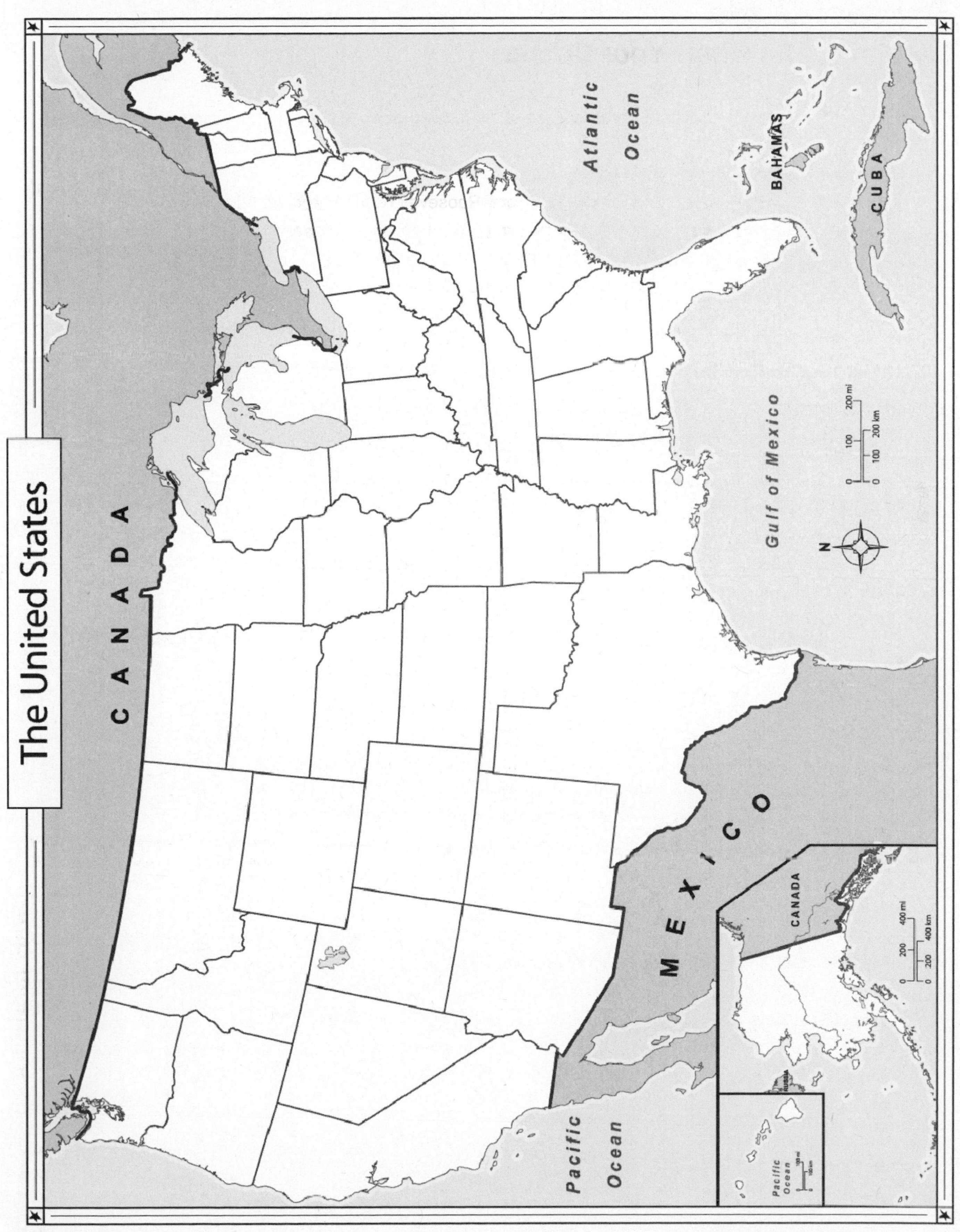
The United States
CANADA
Atlantic Ocean
BAHAMAS
CUBA
Gulf of Mexico
N
0 100 200 mi
0 100 200 km
MEXICO
Pacific Ocean
CANADA
0 200 400 mi
0 200 400 km
Pacific Ocean

Student Guide
Lesson 6: Our Biggest President

Teddy Roosevelt helped put William Howard Taft into the White House. But when they disagreed, Roosevelt challenged Taft by starting his own political party. The split among Republicans thrust a new breed of progressive into the presidency—scholarly, serious Woodrow Wilson.

Lesson Objectives

- Explain the disagreement between President Taft and former President Roosevelt that led to the formation of a third party and Democratic victory in 1912.
- Explain the reasons for, and the effect of, the growth of government regulation since the late 1800s.

PREPARE

Approximate lesson time is 60 minutes.

Materials

For the Student

Election of 1912

A History of US (Concise Edition), Volume C (1865-1932) by Joy Hakim

History Journal

LEARN

Activity 1: Divide and Conquer *(Offline)*

Instructions

A. Read *(Chapter 46, pages 229–232)*

As you read, answer the following questions in your History Journal:

1. Why did Theodore Roosevelt oppose William Howard Taft in 1912?
2. How did Theodore Roosevelt's candidacy help the Democrat, Woodrow Wilson, win the election?

When you have finished, compare the answers in your History Journal with the ones in the Lesson Answer Key. Ask an adult for help with any questions you found difficult.

B. Use What You Know

Print and complete the Election of 1912 sheet. When you have finished, compare your answers with the ones in the Lesson Answer Key. Ask an adult for help if you have trouble with any of the answers.

C. Discuss

Review "Some Political Theory: A Discussion" on pages 231–232. Then discuss the following questions with an adult.

1. The text reads "When people get together and form a government, they make rules—laws—that limit freedom." But what is freedom? Abraham Lincoln said that "The world has never had a good definition of the word liberty." What does freedom mean to you?
2. The people in the Gilded Age were worried about losing their freedom. Why?
3. Why do you think we have more laws today than Americans had in 1900?
4. We have found that some people abuse freedom. Give at least two examples.
5. During the Gilded Age, the government began actively to help people, which was a new role for government. In your History Journal, list some of the groups the government helped. (Your list will be used as part of the assessment for this lesson.) Compare your list to the list in the Lesson Answer Key.

D. Read On (*Chapter 47, pages 233–236*)

As you read, answer the following questions in your History Journal.

1. What were some of the obstacles Woodrow Wilson overcame to become a professor and later a president?
2. What were some of Wilson's progressive goals when he was president? Did he accomplish those goals?
3. What areas of reform did he neglect?
4. What role did Wilson think the United States should play in world affairs? How did his opinion differ from that of the presidents just before him?

ASSESS

Lesson Assessment: Our Biggest President (*Online*)

You will complete an online assessment covering the main points of this lesson. Your assessment will be scored by the computer.

Name Date

The Election of 1912

Using the information on the table, place the 1912 election results on the map below. First write the abbreviations for all the states on their correct spots on the map. Then color-code the map, choosing one color for each of the three political parties. When you are finished, answer the Questions 1–5.

Candidate	Party	States Won	% of Popular Vote
Teddy Roosevelt	Progressive	WA, CA, SD, MN, MI, PA	27.4
William Taft	Republican	UT, VT	23.2
Woodrow Wilson	Democratic	Remaining States	41.9

1. What new party showed up in the 1912 election? ____________________

2. Who ran as its candidate? ____________________

3. Why was this new party established? ____________________

____

____

4. Which party won the election? ____________________

5. Historians say that the divided Republicans had no chance against the united Democrats. What do they mean by this? (Hint: look at the column listing the percentage of the popular vote.)

Student Guide
Lesson 7: Professor President

Nine-year-old Woodrow Wilson had a problem. He just couldn't seem to master his ABCs. Even when he was older he struggled with his reading. But sometimes problems can become strengths. Wilson overcame his childhood handicaps and became a distinguished writer, a brilliant professor, and eventually, president of the United States. Though he revealed a different handicap—a blind spot when it came to racism and women's rights—he was one of the most competent presidents the country had ever seen.

Lesson Objectives

- Describe the obstacles Woodrow Wilson overcame to become a professor and later president.
- Identify areas in which Wilson was not a reformer.
- Identify areas in which Wilson promoted reform.
- Recognize Wilson's view on foreign policy and explain how this view was different from those of the presidents just before him.
- Recognize and define *monopoly, trust, command economy, market economy, hybrid economy, corporation,* and *tariff.*

PREPARE

Approximate lesson time is 60 minutes.

Materials

For the Student

All About Woodrow Wilson

A History of US (Concise Edition), Volume C (1865-1932) by Joy Hakim

History Journal

LEARN

Activity 1: Woodrow Wilson, Professor and President *(Offline)*

Instructions

A. Check Your Reading *(Chapter 47, pages 233–236)*

Compare your answers to these questions with the ones in the Lesson Answer Key. Ask an adult for help with any questions you found difficult.

1. What were some of the obstacles Woodrow Wilson overcame to become a professor and later a president?
2. What were some of Wilson's progressive goals as president? Did he accomplish those goals?
3. What areas of reform did he neglect?
4. What role did Wilson think the United States should play in world affairs? How did his opinion differ from that of the presidents just before him?

B. Use What You Know

Summarize what you've learned about Woodrow Wilson by completing the All About Woodrow Wilson sheet. Then check your answers with those in the Lesson Answer Key.

C. Read On *(Chapter 48, pages 237–243)*

- As you read, identify the Central and Allied (A-liyd) Powers and locate them on the world wall map.
- Answer the following questions in your History Journal:
    1. In what ways was World War I different from other wars?
    2. What policy did Wilson try to follow?
    3. Why was this policy impossible to follow?

ASSESS

Lesson Assessment: Professor President (*Online*)

You will complete an online assessment covering the main goals of this lesson. Your assessment will be scored by the computer.

LEARN

Activity 2. Optional: Professor President *(Online)*

Name Date

All About Woodrow Wilson

Describe the different stages of Woodrow Wilson's life by completing the spider map.

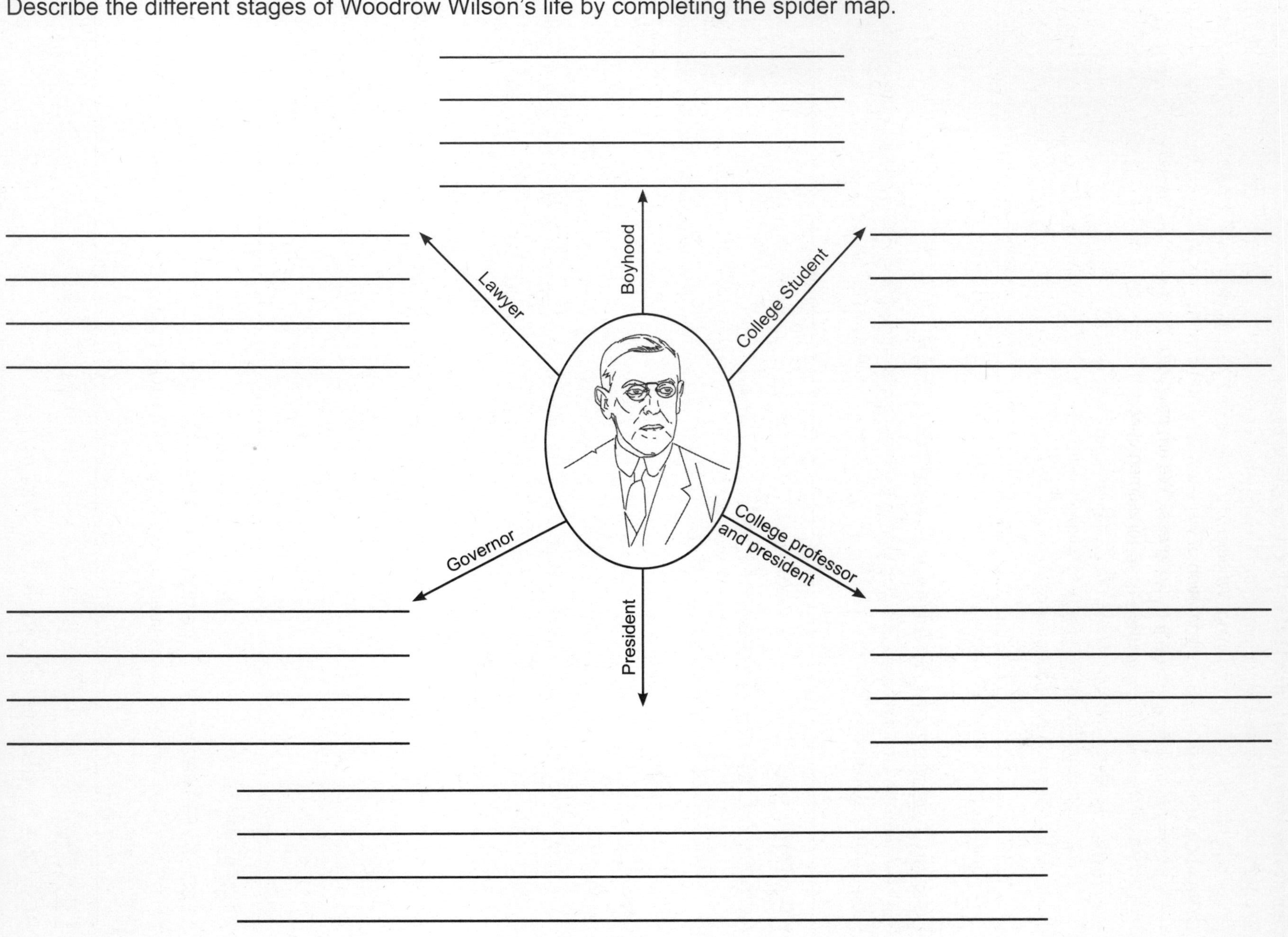

Student Guide
Lesson 8: Entangled in War

In the quiet of an early April morning, Woodrow Wilson sat on the south veranda of the White House and typed out a message. It was a declaration of war—a war he had tried very hard to keep his country out of. The next day he delivered his message to Congress. "We are accepting the challenge," he said. "The world must be made safe for democracy." While the congressmen cheered, Wilson went back to his office and wept.

Lesson Objectives

- Summarize the major causes of World War I.
- Describe the ways in which World War I was more destructive than people thought it would be.
- Identify Wilson's policy of neutrality and peacemaking and the reasons for abandoning the policy.
- Identify the Central Powers and the Allied Powers and locate them on a map.

PREPARE

Approximate lesson time is 60 minutes.

Materials

For the Student

Causes of World War I

A History of US (Concise Edition), Volume C (1865-1932) by Joy Hakim

History Journal

Keywords and Pronunciation

alliance (uh-LIY-uhnts)

allied (A-liyd)

LEARN

Activity 1: The Great War *(Online)*

In 1917, the United States entered the Great War—now known as World War I. As young men went confidently off to Europe, some Americans were singing. Before you begin today's lesson, turn to page 243 in your book to find the lyrics of "Over There."

Then continue to the next screen and read more about World War I and how it started.

ASSESS

Lesson Assessment: Entangled in War (*Online*)

You will complete an online assessment covering the main points of this lesson. Your assessment will be scored by the computer.

LEARN

Activity 2. Optional: Entangled in War *(Online)*

Name Date

Causes of World War I

Using the chart, draw conclusions about how each cause helped bring about World War I. Support your conclusions with details from your reading.

Cause	How It Helped Bring About World War
Nationalism	
Imperialism	
Militarism	
Alliances	

Student Guide
Lesson 9: Ending War

By November 1918, the Great War was over, thanks to the help of the United States under Woodrow Wilson's leadership. Now the Allied leaders gathered in France to decide the fate of the Central Powers. Wilson didn't believe in revenge, he believed in kindness. He came up with fourteen ideas about how to bring about a lasting peace. Not everyone liked Wilson's ideas. "God gave us his Ten Commandments and we broke them," said France's prime minister. "Wilson gave us his Fourteen Points—we shall see."

Lesson Objectives

- Analyze Wilson's goal for U.S. involvement in the Great War.
- Describe the reasons for U.S. entry into the war on the Allied side and the result of U.S. mobilization.
- Identify the Fourteen Points as Wilson's plan for peace and the League of Nations.
- Recognize that the U.S. did not join the League of Nations and explain why.

PREPARE

Approximate lesson time is 60 minutes.

Materials

For the Student

A History of US (Concise Edition), Volume C (1865-1932) by Joy Hakim

History Journal

LEARN

Activity 1: Armistice Day *(Offline)*

Instructions

A. Read *(Chapter 49, pages 244–246; Chapter 50, pages 247–252)*

As you read, answer the following questions in your History Journal. Compare your answers to those in the Lesson Answer Key.

1. What did President Woodrow Wilson see as one of the chief goals of the United States in the war?
2. What and when was Armistice Day?
3. What was the document known as the Fourteen Points?
4. What were the major goals of the Fourteen Points?
5. Why did Wilson consider the League of Nations the most important of his Fourteen Points?
6. Why didn't the United States join the League of Nations?
7. In 1918, why was the influenza considered a pandemic?
8. How did the disease compare in the number of deaths to the Great War?

B. Use What You Know

Imagine that you are riding the train with Woodrow Wilson as he travels around the United States. He is trying to convince people that America should join the League of Nations, but so far the response hasn't been encouraging.

You are on the president's staff but you don't know him very well. You want to explain to him why Americans might not want to join the league, and you decide to do so in a short letter. In the chapters you read today, look for evidence (maps, photographs, and letters) to support your reasons, and include this evidence in your letter. Write the letter in your History Journal.

ASSESS

Lesson Assessment: Ending War (*Online*)

You will complete an online assessment covering the main points of this lesson. Your assessment will be scored by the computer.

Student Guide
Lesson 10: Unit Review

You have finished the unit! It's time to review what you've learned. You will take the Unit Assessment in the next lesson.

Lesson Objectives

- Demonstrate mastery of important knowledge and skills in this unit.

PREPARE

Approximate lesson time is 60 minutes.

Materials

For the Student

A History of US (Concise Edition), Volume C (1865-1932) by Joy Hakim

History Journal

LEARN
Activity 1: A Look Back *(Online)*

Instructions

A. History Journal Review

Review what you learned in this unit by going through your History Journal.

- Look at activity sheets you completed for this unit. Be sure to review the Outlying Areas sheet.
- Review unit Keywords and definitions.
- Read through any writing assignments you did during the unit.
- Review the assessments you took.

Don't rush through. Take your time. Your History Journal is a great resource for a unit review.

B. Online Review

Review the following online activities:

- Time Line:1891–1918
- Online Unit Review

Student Guide
Lesson 11: Unit Assessment

You've finished the unit! Now it's time to take the Unit Assessment.

Lesson Objectives

- Describe the growth of a consumer middle class in the late 1800s and the groups left out of prosperity.
- Analyze the Progressive movement in terms of its goals, methods, and achievements.
- Summarize the causes and results of the Spanish-American War and the imperialism it reflected.
- Recognize the reasons for and results of the United States' entry into World War I on the Allied side.
- Summarize the ways in which the United States acquired or controlled new territory near the turn of the century.
- Recognize current U.S. territories on a map.
- Describe the civil rights and responsibilities of people living in U.S. territories today.
- Recognize the Populist and Progressive proposals that are part of our democratic tradition today.
- Demonstrate knowledge and skills gained in this unit.
- Summarize the qualifications, philosophies, policies, achievements, and failures of the three Progressives who served as president between 1900 and 1920.
- Describe Woodrow Wilson's plan for world peace and the reasons for the plan's failure.

PREPARE

Approximate lesson time is 60 minutes.

ASSESS

Unit Assessment: Entering a New Century, Part 1 *(Online)*

Complete the computer-scored portion of the Unit Assessment. When you have finished, complete the teacher-scored portion of the assessment and submit it to your teacher.

Unit Assessment: Entering a New Century, Part 2 *(Offline)*

Complete the teacher-scored portion of the Unit Assessment and submit it to your teacher.

Student Guide

Unit 7: A Fascinating Era
Lesson 1: Amending Behavior

The Great War brought enormous changes to the United States. When it was over, people wanted a return to what Warren Harding called "normalcy." Some people promoted traditional ideas and resisted change, but others embraced innovations, inventions, fashions, sports, and music. Although class conflict and economic instability lay just beneath the surface and threatened to bring hard times, the decade known as the Roaring Twenties was a colorful and fascinating era.

Many people think that drinking alcohol is bad. In the early part of the 1900s, so many Americans thought it was bad that they decided that no one in the country should have access to alcohol. It took about 20 years, but the government finally passed a Constitutional amendment that made it illegal to make or sell liquor anywhere in the United States. Thirteen years later that amendment was repealed. Find out why.

Lesson Objectives

- Explain the arguments in favor of Prohibition.
- Describe the intended and unintended consequences of Prohibition.
- Explore the amendment process under the Constitution, including the need for a new amendment to cancel an existing amendment.

PREPARE

Approximate lesson time is 60 minutes.

Materials

For the Student

- Amending the Constitution
- Know, Want to Know, and Learn

A History of US (Concise Edition), Volume C (1865-1932) by Joy Hakim

History Journal

Keywords and Pronunciation

bootlegger : a person who makes, sells, or transports liquor illegally

Prohibition : the 18th Amendment to the Constitution, in force from 1920-1933, which outlawed making, selling, or transporting alcoholic beverages except for medicinal and religious purposes

speakeasy : a place where alcoholic beverages were sold illegally during Prohibition

temperance movement : an effort to promote moderation and, more often, complete abstinence in alcohol consumption

LEARN

Activity 1: A Lost Generation? *(Offline)*

Instructions

A. Read (*Chapter 51, pages 253–255)*

- As you read, complete the Know, Want to Know, and Learn sheet.
- Define these terms. When you have finished, compare your definitions to those in the Keywords section of this lesson.

bootlegger
prohibition
speakeasy
temperance movement

B. Use What You Know

Complete the Prohibition activity online.

C. Focus on Civics

It is important to understand the difference between a law and an amendment. An amendment becomes part of the Constitution itself. That is, it becomes part of the basic plan for the structure of the United States government. A law, on the other hand, regulates people's actions and can be passed or changed fairly easily as needs change. The Founders made it very difficult to amend, or change, the Constitution.

Look again at the feature on Article V of the Constitution. Then answer the questions on the Amending the Constitution sheet and compare your answers to those in the Lesson Answer Key.

ASSESS

Lesson Assessment: Amending Behavior *(Online)*

You will complete an online assessment covering the main points of this lesson. Your assessment will be scored by the computer.

Name Date

Know, Want to Know, and Learn

When you think of *history*, what comes to mind? Do you think of dates and wars and people's names? Do you think of cause and effect, of events happening because of other events? History is all of these things, but how can you keep track?

To help order your thoughts, start by making a chart like the one below. Divide the chart into three columns. List all the things you already know about the subject in the first column ("Know"). Write down all the questions you have and the things you want to find out in the second column ("Want to Know"). As you learn the answers to your questions, write them in the third column ("Learned").

Try using the chart as you study life after World War I. Begin with Chapter 51. Do you know what Prohibition is? If so, write it down along with anything else you know about Prohibition in the first column of the chart. Next, write down anything you would like to know about the movement.

PROHIBITION		
Know	**Want to Know**	**Learned**

As you read the chapter, write down any answers to your questions in the "Learned" column. Also, continue recording further questions. When you have finished, compare what you first knew about Prohibition with what you have now learned. Did this approach help you keep track of things as you were reading?

You may find you want to make some changes in the chart. For example, not all the answers to your questions will be found in *A History of US*. You might want to add another column ("How") to keep track of how and where you found your information. Then, when you are looking for answers to other questions, you will have some ideas about where to do research.

Name ____________________________ Date ____________________________

Amending the Constitution

1. What are the requirements for passing an amendment as stated in Article V of the Constitution?

2. Why did the writers of the Constitution make it so hard to pass an amendment?

3. How many amendments have been made to the Constitution so far?

4. How many have been proposed?

Student Guide
Lesson 2: Doubling Voters

While American soldiers fought the Central Powers in Europe, a different kind of conflict was taking place back at home. Women were fighting for their rights. All over the country, suffragists protested, picketed, and spoke out in the name of equality for women. They even marched back and forth in front of the White House to get the president's attention. President Wilson, however, was focused on winning the war. He didn't think giving women the vote was all that important. Could it be that ordinary citizens sometimes understand democracy better than their president does?

Lesson Objectives

- Explain the methods used to gain support for the 19th Amendment.
- Identify the 19th Amendment.
- Describe the amendment process under the Constitution.

PREPARE

Approximate lesson time is 60 minutes.

Materials

For the Student

Tracing the History of the 19th Amendment

A History of US (Concise Edition), Volume C (1865-1932) by Joy Hakim

History Journal

Keywords and Pronunciation

suffrage (SUH-frihj) : the right to vote

suffragist : a person who supports extension of the right to vote, especially to women

---

LEARN

Activity 1: Bring On the Vote *(Offline)*

Instructions

A. Read *(Chapter 52, pages 256–259)*

- Answer the following questions and write the answers in your History Journal. When you have finished, compare your answers to those in the Lesson Answer Key.
  1. What methods did suffragists use to bring attention to their cause?
  2. Why were women picketing in front of the White House in 1917?
  3. Why were they arrested? What happened to them after they were arrested?
  4. How did American women finally get the right to vote, and in what year did it happen?
- Define the following terms. When you have finished, check your definitions against those in the Keywords section.

  suffrage
  suffragist

B. Looking Back

Complete the Tracing the History of the 19th Amendment sheet. When you have finished, check your answers against those in the Lesson Answer Key.

C. Use What You Know

Design a political cartoon showing reasons to support or oppose either the 18th or 19th Amendment. You may look back at the last lesson, Amending Behavior, and this lesson for ideas and supporting information.

ASSESS

Lesson Assessment: Doubling Voters *(Online)*

You will complete an online assessment covering the main points of this lesson. Your assessment will be scored by the computer.

Name Date

Tracing the History of the 19th Amendment

Study the flowchart and answer the questions.

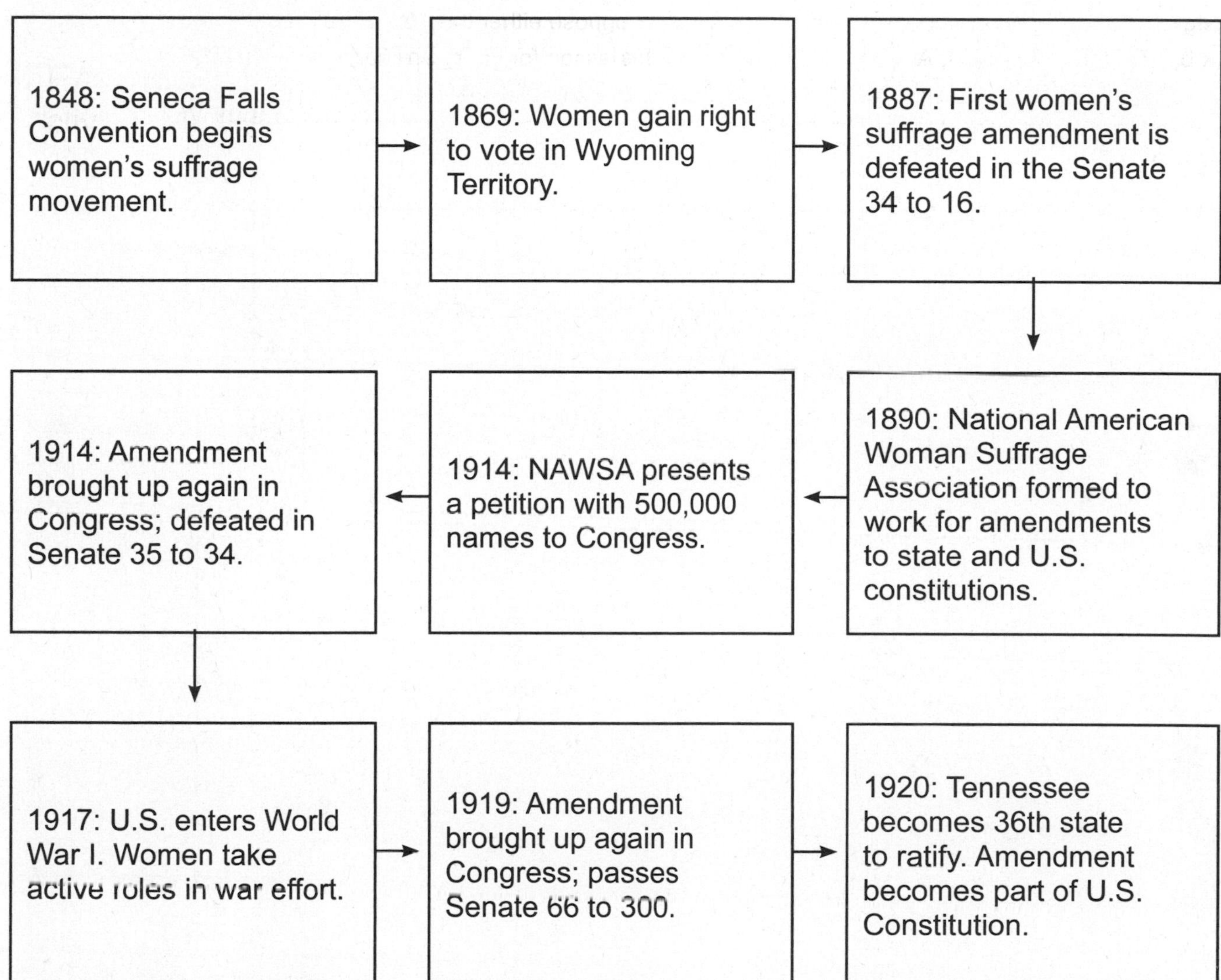

1. How many years passed after the Seneca Falls Convention before women won the right to vote in Wyoming? In the country as a whole? ______________________

2. Describe how Senate support for the 19th Amendment changed over time.

____

____

____

3. Why did the Senate change the way it voted? What methods did suffragists use to influence this change?

4. Which event in the flowchart do you think had the greatest impact on getting the 19th Amendment passed? Why?

Student Guide
Lesson 3: Seeing Red

During a two-day period in 1920, the U.S. government rounded up nearly 5,000 people from cities around the country and threw them in jail. Those who were not U.S. citizens were sent to Russia. Most of these people had not broken any laws. So why did the government arrest them?

Lesson Objectives

- Summarize the major events that led Russia to adopt communism and made people in the United States fear communism.
- Recognize that constitutional abuses took place during the Red Scare.
- Distinguish between legislation against actions and legislation against the expression of ideas.

PREPARE

Approximate lesson time is 60 minutes.

Materials

For the Student

A History of US (Concise Edition), Volume C (1865-1932) by Joy Hakim

History Journal

Keywords and Pronunciation

alien law : a law that prevented certain people from immigrating to the United States
anarchist (A-nuhr-kihst) : a person who does not believe in any form of government
communism : a political and economic system in which the state owns most of the land and property and shares them with the citizens
Reds : a nickname for communists or people thought to be communists
sedition law : a law that made it a crime for anyone to speak against the government

---

LEARN

Activity 1: The Red Scare *(Offline)*

Instructions

A. Read *(Chapter 53, pages 260–262)*

- As you read, answer the following questions in your History Journal. Compare your answers to those in the Lesson Answer Key.

1. Describe the events in Russia that led the country to adopt communism.
2. Why were people in the United States worried about the communist revolution in Russia?
3. Why were people in the United States worried about communism?
4. How did Attorney General Palmer try to deal with communists and anarchists?
5. What constitutional rights did the government violate during the Red Scare?
6. Give an example in your reading of a law against an action and an example of a law against an expression of an idea.

- Write a brief definition for each of the following terms in your History Journal. When you have finished, compare your definitions with those in the Keywords section of this lesson.
  alien law
  anarchist (A-nuhr-kihst)
  communism
  Reds
  sedition law

B. Use What You Know

- Access the Grolier's online encyclopedia, *The New Book of Knowledge*. Review information on the Bill of Rights. Focus your attention on the First, Fourth, Fifth, Sixth, and Eighth Amendments. To quickly access this information, follow these steps:

  1. Use the Search Grolier Online feature to search for the Bill of Rights.
  2. Click the first Bill of Rights link.
  3. Scroll to the "What the Bill of Rights Says" section.

- In your History Journal, write a letter to the editor protesting the actions of Attorney General Palmer. Base your objections on your understanding of the Bill of Rights.

ASSESS

Lesson Assessment: Seeing Red (*Online*)

You will complete an online assessment covering the main objectives of this lesson. Your assessment will be scored by the computer.

Student Guide
Lesson 4: The Twenties

If a movie director were casting a president's part, he might have picked Warren G. Harding. With silver hair and tanned skin, Harding *looked* like a president. Indeed, he was one of the most popular presidents ever. But was Harding a *good* president?

Calvin Coolidge, who took office after Harding, was also very popular. During his administration the stock market went up, land values boomed, and people were able to buy things they couldn't buy before. Was Coolidge a good president?

Lesson Objectives

- Summarize the varied duties of a U.S. president and the consequences of Harding's failure to meet his responsibilities.
- Describe the black migration of the 1920s.
- Identify the cultural changes that characterized the 1920s.
- Recognize key events and characteristics of Harding and Coolidge administrations.

PREPARE

Approximate lesson time is 60 minutes.

Materials

For the Student

Presidential Time Line

A History of US (Concise Edition), Volume C (1865-1932) by Joy Hakim

History Journal

Keywords and Pronunciation

black migration : the movement of more than one million black people from the rural South to the cities of the North

evolution : the theory that life on Earth started from simple one-celled creatures and developed into complex plants, animals, and humans

flappers : young women of the 1920s who dressed in a bold, new style

---

LEARN

Activity 1: A Decade of Change *(Offline)*

Instructions

A. Read *(Chapter 54, pages 263–265)*

- As you read, answer the following questions in your History Journal. When you have finished, compare your answers to those in the Lesson Answer Key.

1. What are some of the qualities a good president must have?
2. How did scandal mar President Harding's administration?
3. In his first message to Congress, what were some of Calvin Coolidge's goals?
4. Why did most Americans at the time think that Coolidge was a splendid president?

- Write a brief definition for each of the following terms in your History Journal. When you have finished, compare your definitions with those in the Keywords section of this lesson.
  black migration
  evolution
  flappers

B. Use What You Know
Complete a Presidential Time Line sheet for Warren G. Harding and Calvin Coolidge. Be sure to include some of the following:

- Personal characteristics that influenced the presidency
- Presidential accomplishments

Compare the information on your Presidential Time Line with the information in the Lesson Answer Key. Display your Time Line sheets with other Presidential Time Line sheets or put them in the Presidents section of your History Journal.

ASSESS

Lesson Assessment: The Twenties (*Online*)

You will complete an online assessment covering the main goals of this lesson. Your assessment will be scored by the computer.

Name Date

Presidential Time Line

If you can find a picture of this president, attach it here.

Name: ____________________

Years in Office: _____ – ________

Number of Terms: _____

Vice president: ____________________

First Lady: ____________________

_________ President

Name ______________________ Date ______________________

Presidential Time Line

If you can find a picture of this president, attach it here.

Name: ______________________

Years in Office: ______ – ______

Number of Terms: ______

Vice president: ______________________

First Lady: ______________________

______ President

Student Guide
Lesson 5: The Jazz Age

The 1920s was a giddy decade of change. Blacks were packing up and leaving the farms of the South and heading to the new factories and growing cities of the North. The streets were filling up with shiny new automobiles. Many people had a few extra bucks in their pockets and they were frantically spending them on having a good time and trying something new. Women spent their money on short skirts, makeup, and daring new short haircuts. People bought radios and flocked to movies, baseball games, and dance contests. Creative new books, art, and music filled the air and helped the decade earn the nickname the Roaring Twenties.

Lesson Objectives

- Recognize cultural trends and achievements of the 1920s including film, literature, music, art, and the Harlem Renaissance.
- Describe the black migration of the 1920s.

PREPARE

Approximate lesson time is 60 minutes.

Materials

For the Student

The Jazz Age

A History of US (Concise Edition), Volume C (1865-1932) by Joy Hakim

History Journal

Keywords and Pronunciation

Creole (KREE-ohl) : a person of Spanish or French and African-American descent

---

LEARN

Activity 1: A Slide Show *(Online)*

Activity 2: A New Way of Living *(Offline)*

Instructions

A. Browse *(Chapter 55, pages 266–273; Chapter 56, pages 274–277)*

During the next several lessons you will learn about the Jazz Age and how life in the United States changed in the 1920s. You will complete the Jazz Age sheets during the first three lessons. In the Tell Us What It Means lesson, you will create a newspaper using the information on your Jazz Age sheets. As you browse through the chapters, complete the Society section of the Jazz Age sheets. The assessment will be based on the information you fill in on the Jazz Age sheets.

Write a brief definition for the term *Creole* in your History Journal. When you have finished, compare your definition with the one in the Keywords section of this lesson.

ASSESS

Lesson Assessment: The Jazz Age *(Online)*

You will complete an online assessment covering the main points of this lesson. Your assessment will be scored by the computer.

LEARN

Activity 3. Optional: The Jazz Age *(Online)*

Name Date

The Jazz Age

Describe the changes in each area of society during the 1920s.

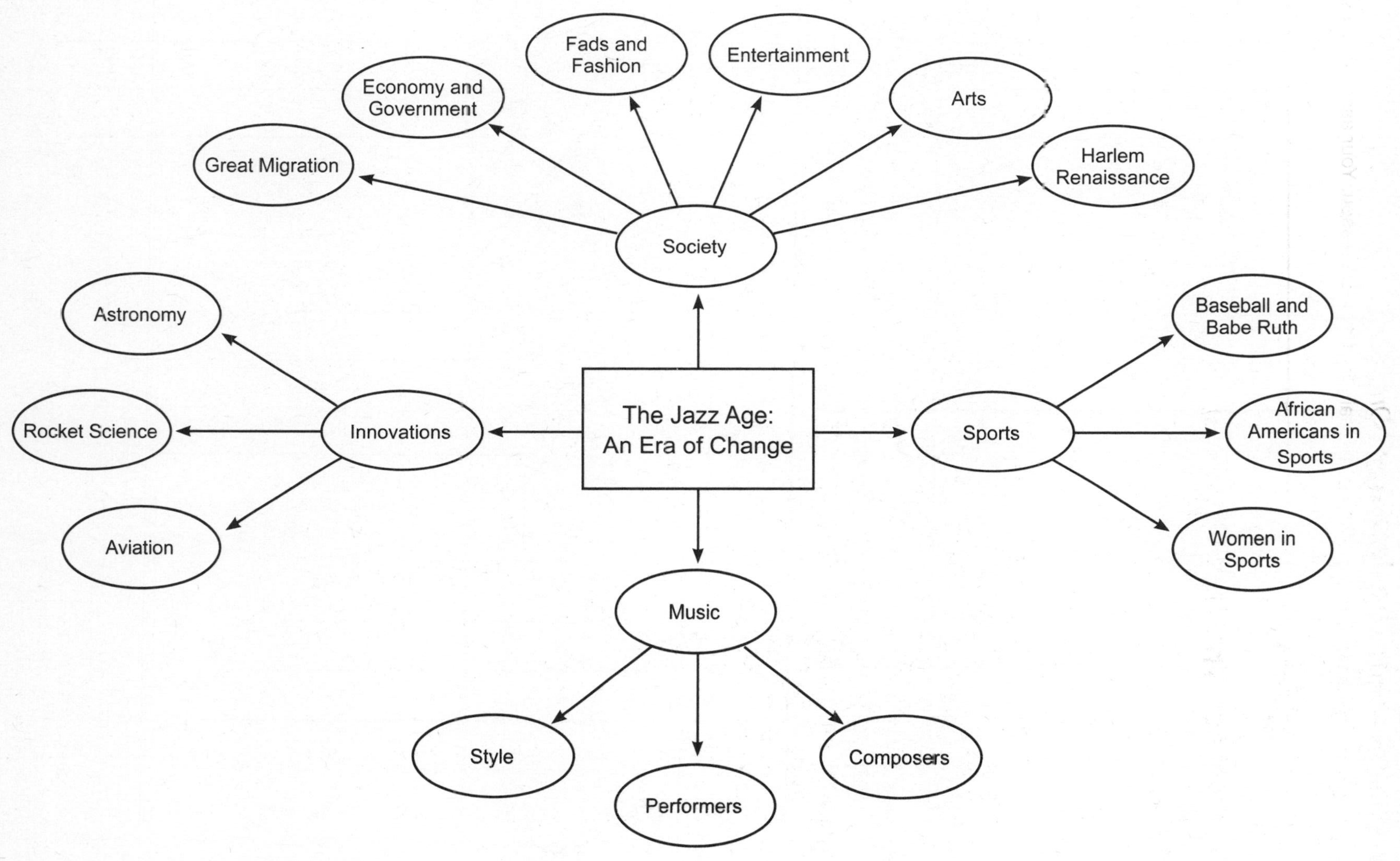

The Jazz Age

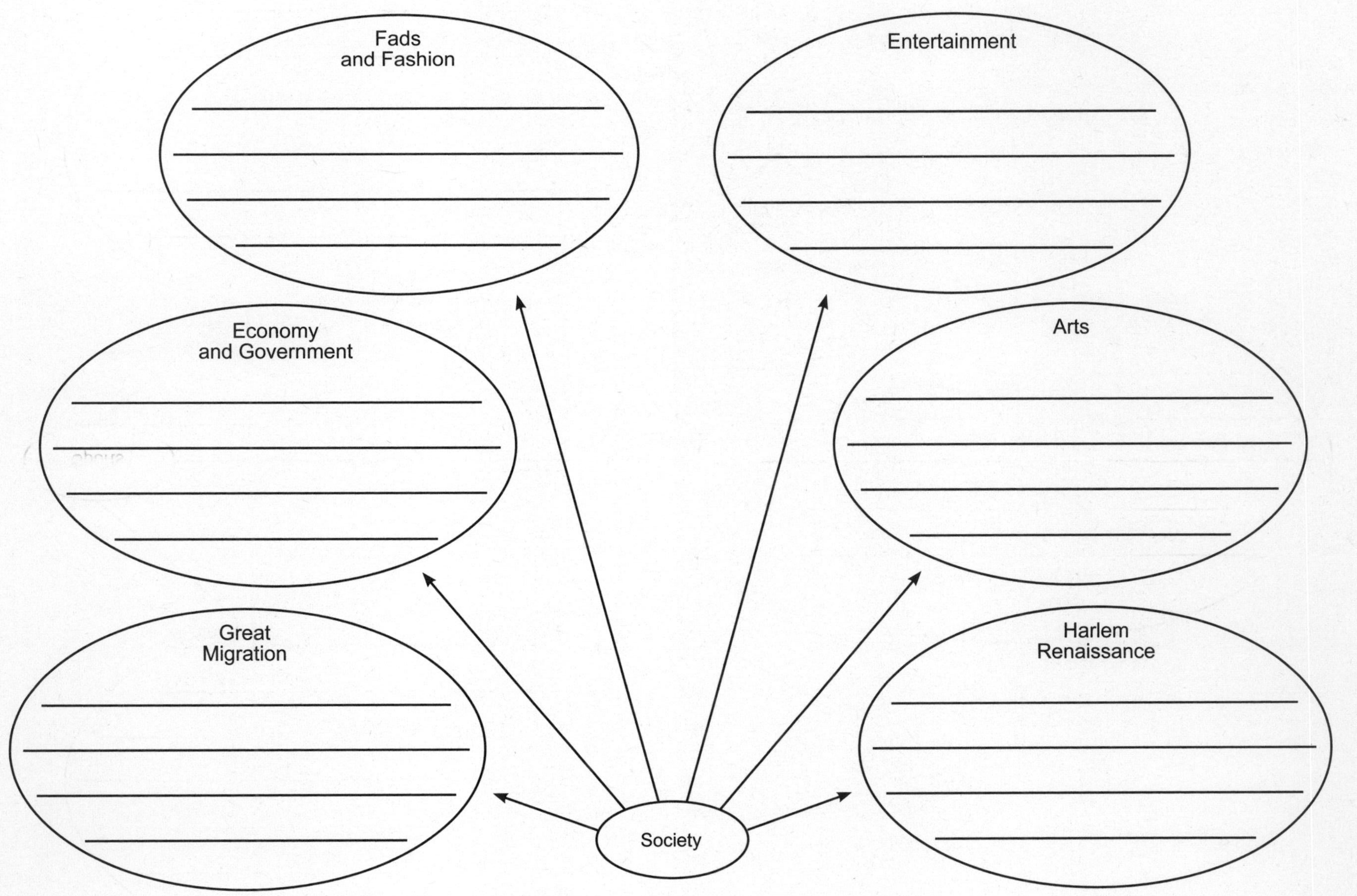
Fads
and Fashion
Entertainment
Economy
and Government
Arts
Great
Migration
Harlem
Renaissance
Society

The Jazz Age

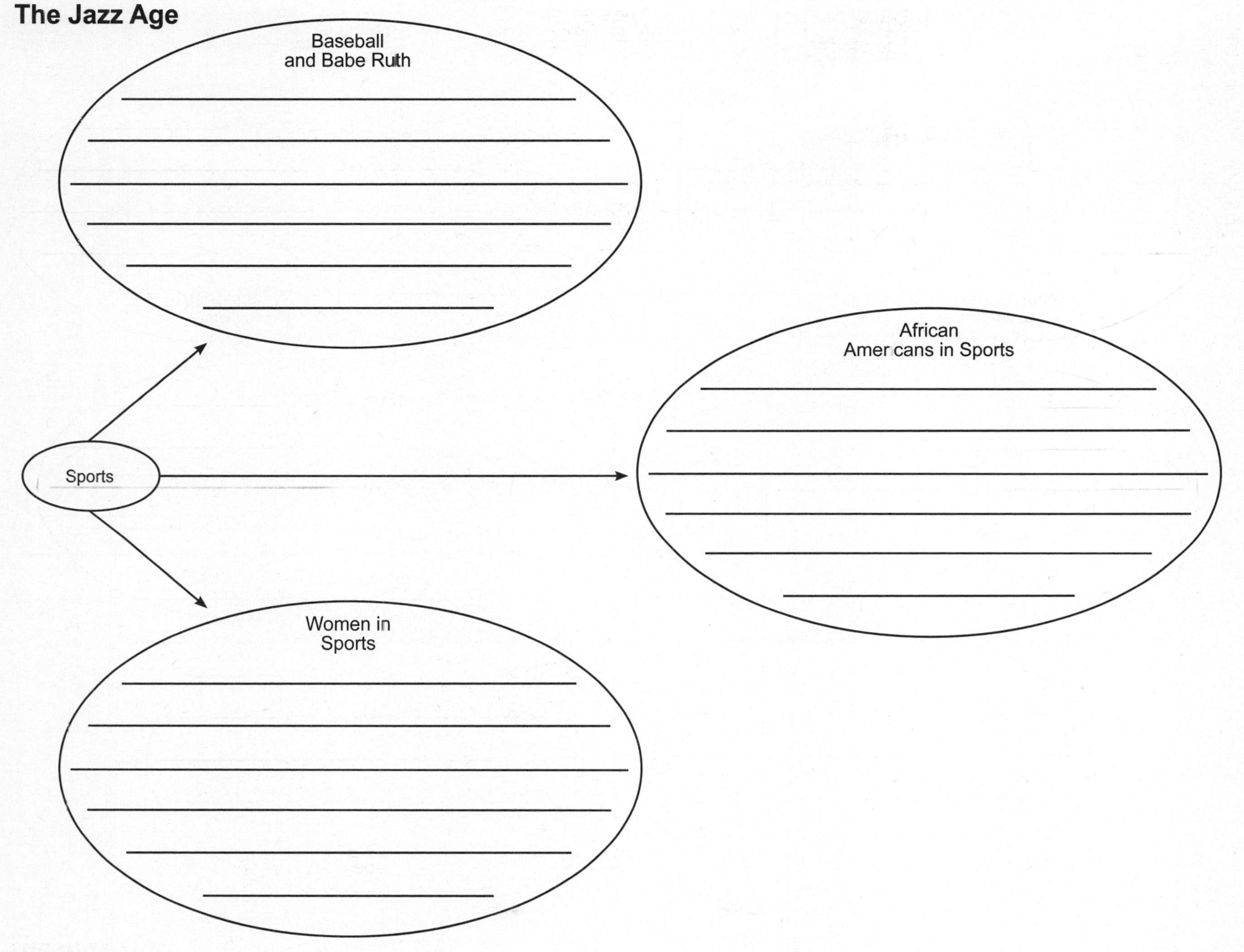
Baseball
and Babe Ruth
Sports
African
Americans in Sports
Women in
Sports

The Jazz Age

Music

Style

Compoers

Performers

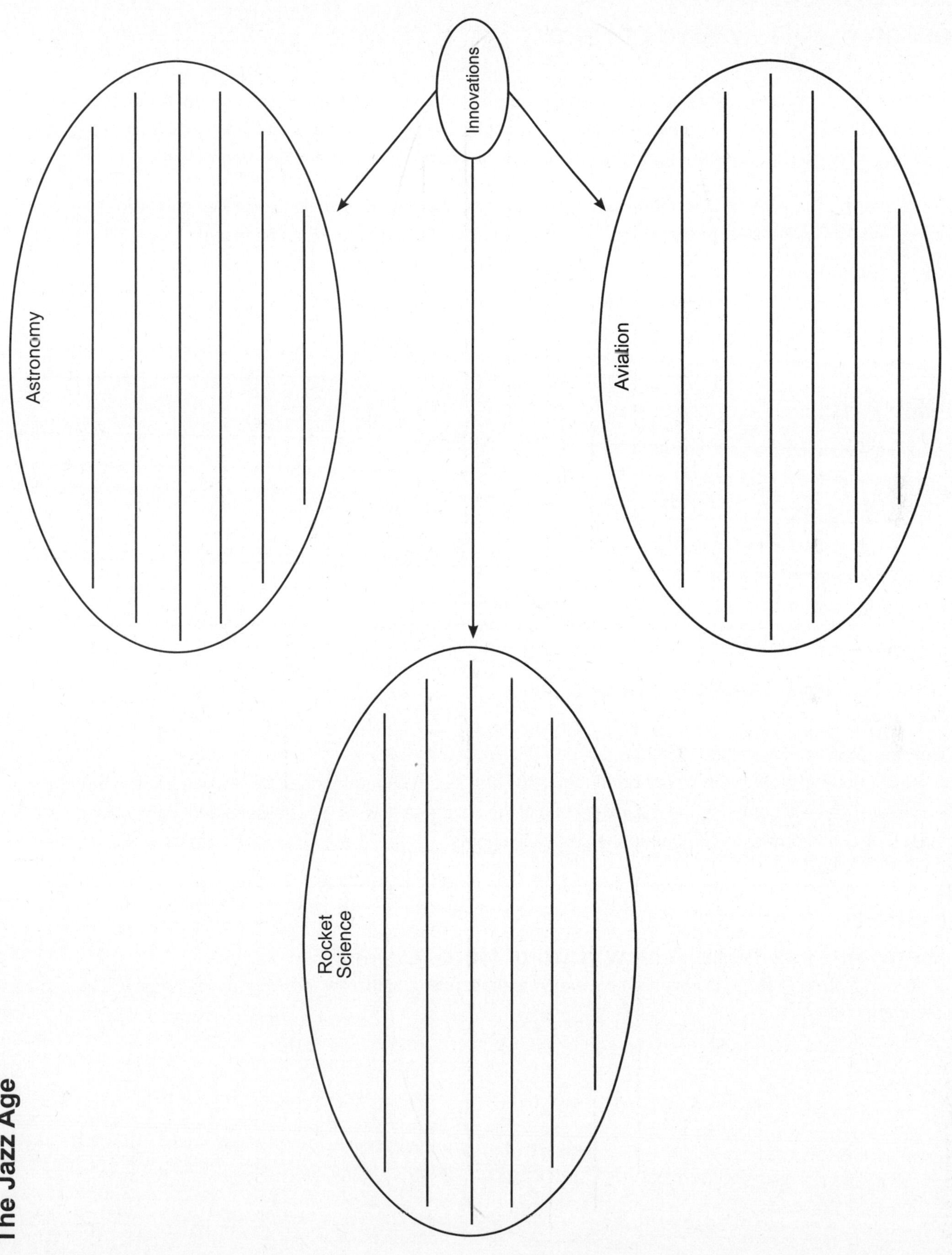
Innovations
Astronomy
Aviation
Rocket Science

Student Guide
Lesson 6: A New Kind of Hero

Organized sports became very popular during the Roaring Twenties. With more leisure time, Americans could go to the ballparks or listen to games on radio. They could also play sports themselves. By the end of the '20s, Americans were hard at play, and golf courses and tennis courts were popping up everywhere.

Sports stars, such as George Herman Ruth, who was known as "the Babe," became American heroes. Women and African Americans were also contributors to the sports arena. Read on to learn more.

Lesson Objectives

- Recognize cultural trends and achievements of the 1920s including film, literature, music, art, and the Harlem Renaissance.

PREPARE

Approximate lesson time is 60 minutes.

Materials

For the Student

A History of US (Concise Edition), Volume C (1865-1932) by Joy Hakim

History Journal

LEARN

Activity 1: New American Heroes *(Offline)*

Instructions

A. Browse *(Chapter 57, pages 278–281; Chapter 58, pages 282–284)*

You will continue exploring the Jazz Age of the 1920s and its effect on American life. As you browse through the chapters, you will complete the Sports section of the Jazz Age sheets. Your assessment in this lesson will be based on the information you add to the Jazz Age sheets.

ASSESS

Lesson Assessment: A New Kind of Hero *(Online)*

You will complete an online assessment covering the main points of this lesson. Your assessment will be scored by the computer.

Student Guide
Lesson 7: More Jazz

A spirited new sound swept the nation. Born in New Orleans, jazz blended African rhythms with European forms to create a uniquely American sound. As jazz traveled north to Chicago and New York, musicians were constantly improvising and changing it. Great performers like Louis Armstrong and Duke Ellington, and great composers like Charles Ives and Aaron Copland emerged to create distinctive American music. But bold experimentation and innovation were not limited to music. The Roaring Twenties saw other remarkable advances. Charles Lindbergh, Jr., flew across the Atlantic Ocean, Robert Goddard launched rockets, and Edwin Hubble expanded our knowledge of the universe.

Lesson Objectives

- Recognize cultural trends and achievements of the 1920s including film, literature, music, art, and the Harlem Renaissance.
- Analyze inventions and innovations of the 1920s and their effect on the American way of life.

PREPARE

Approximate lesson time is 60 minutes.

Materials

For the Student

A History of US (Concise Edition), Volume C (1865-1932) by Joy Hakim

History Journal

Keywords and Pronunciation

Aaron Copland (AIR-uhn KOHP-luhnd)

LEARN

Activity 1: Catchy Terms of the 1920s *(Online)*

Activity 2: All That Jazz and More *(Offline)*

Instructions

A. Browse *(Jazz: An American Original, pages 272–273; Chapter 59, pages 285–289; Chapter 60, pages 290–294)*

You will continue exploring the Jazz Age of the 1920s and its effect on American life. As you browse through the chapters, you will complete the Music and Innovations sections of the Jazz Age sheets. Your assessment in this lesson will be based on the information you add to the Jazz Age sheets. In the Tell Us What It Means lesson, you will create a newspaper using the information from your Jazz Age sheets.

ASSESS

Lesson Assessment: More Jazz *(Online)*

You will complete an online assessment covering the main points of this lesson. Your assessment will be scored by the computer.

LEARN

Activity 3. Optional: More Jazz *(Online)*

Student Guide
Lesson 8: Tell Us What It Means

When the traumatic First World War ended Americans breathed a sigh of relief and plunged into experimenting. During the Roaring '20s they turned to new pastimes–sports, radio, movies, dancing, and music. African Americans introduced dynamic rhythms to music and spread the popularity of jazz across the nation. Talented African Americans gathered in Harlem, daring aviators flew across the ocean, and scientists expanded our knowledge of the universe. Chronicle the tumultuous years and amazing achievements in your newspaper.

Lesson Objectives

- Demonstrate knowledge gained in previous lessons.
- Recognize that there was class conflict and tension in the United States during the 1920s.
- Describe the black migration of the 1920s.
- Recognize cultural trends and achievements of the 1920s including film, literature, music, art, and the Harlem Renaissance.
- Analyze inventions and innovations of the 1920s and their effect on the American way of life.

PREPARE

Approximate lesson time is 60 minutes.

Materials

For the Student

K12 Herald

paper, construction, 12" x 12"

LEARN

Activity 1: In the News *(Offline)*

Instructions

A. Use What You Know

Today you will be the reporter, editor, and publisher for the *K[12] Herald*. You will use the information from the Jazz Age sheets to create a multiple-page newspaper. The newspaper will explain how the various innovations and cultural achievements affected American life during the 1920s. As an editor, you will also write an editorial.

An editorial is an article that expresses the editor's opinion. You will write about the changes and conflicts that occurred in the United States during the 1920s. Think of a new name for the Roaring Twenties or Jazz Age and explain your choice to the readers of your paper. Consider the following questions before you write:

- In what ways did the culture of the twenties bring Americans together?
- In what ways did changes in technology bring Americans closer together?
- Where did most change take place? Where did life stay much like it had been?
- Who seemed to be most enthusiastic about the changes of the 1920s?

- Who seemed to resist or fear change?
- The Roaring Twenties were packed with fun. Was it also a time of tension in the country?

Today's assessment will be based on the information you write in your newspaper.
You may use any of the following to help you create the newspaper.

- The K[12] Herald sheet: You will use this sheet as a layout guide. You should cut out the headings and strategically place them on a large sheet of plain paper or white construction paper. You will need more than one sheet.
- A word processing program: You may use a word processor or computer to create the entire newspaper (make sure you use the headings from the K[12] Herald sheet) or to just type your text, and then place the text under the proper headings on the large piece of plain paper.
- Images: You may use images from other sources or print the images from the slideshow in the Jazz Age lesson or the Gallery in this lesson.
- Websites: For additional information or images, you may want to visit the websites listed in the Beyond the Lesson sections of this lesson and the two previous lessons.

ASSESS

Lesson Assessment: Tell Us What It Means *(Offline)*

You will complete an offline assessment covering some of the main points of this lesson. Your assessment will be scored by the teacher.

LEARN

Activity 2. Optional: Tell Us What It Means *(Online)*

Name Date

K[12] Herald

Cut out the various headings to use as part of the newspaper layout.

Specal Edition Date: Anywhere USA

The Roaring Twenties Changed American Life

The Great Migration: Blacks on the Move

Fads and Fashions: The Cat's Meow

Entertainment: In the morning, in the evening, ain't we got fun!

The Harlem Renaissance: An Explosion of Creativity

U.S. Economy: Is Everybody Happy?

Music and All That Jazz

Innovations: What a Nifty Idea!

Sports: Record-breaking . . . !

Editorial

Student Guide
Lesson 9: (Optional) Your Choice

You may use today's lesson time to do one or more of the following:

- Complete work in progress.
- Visit a website to learn more about the1920s.
- Locate the 50 states in the game or print the outline map and see how many of the 50 states you can identify.
- Go on to the next lesson.

Please mark this lesson complete in order to proceed to the next lesson in the course.

Lesson Objectives

- Explore knowledge and skills taught in this course.

PREPARE

Approximate lesson time is 60 minutes.

Materials

For the Student

Map of the United States

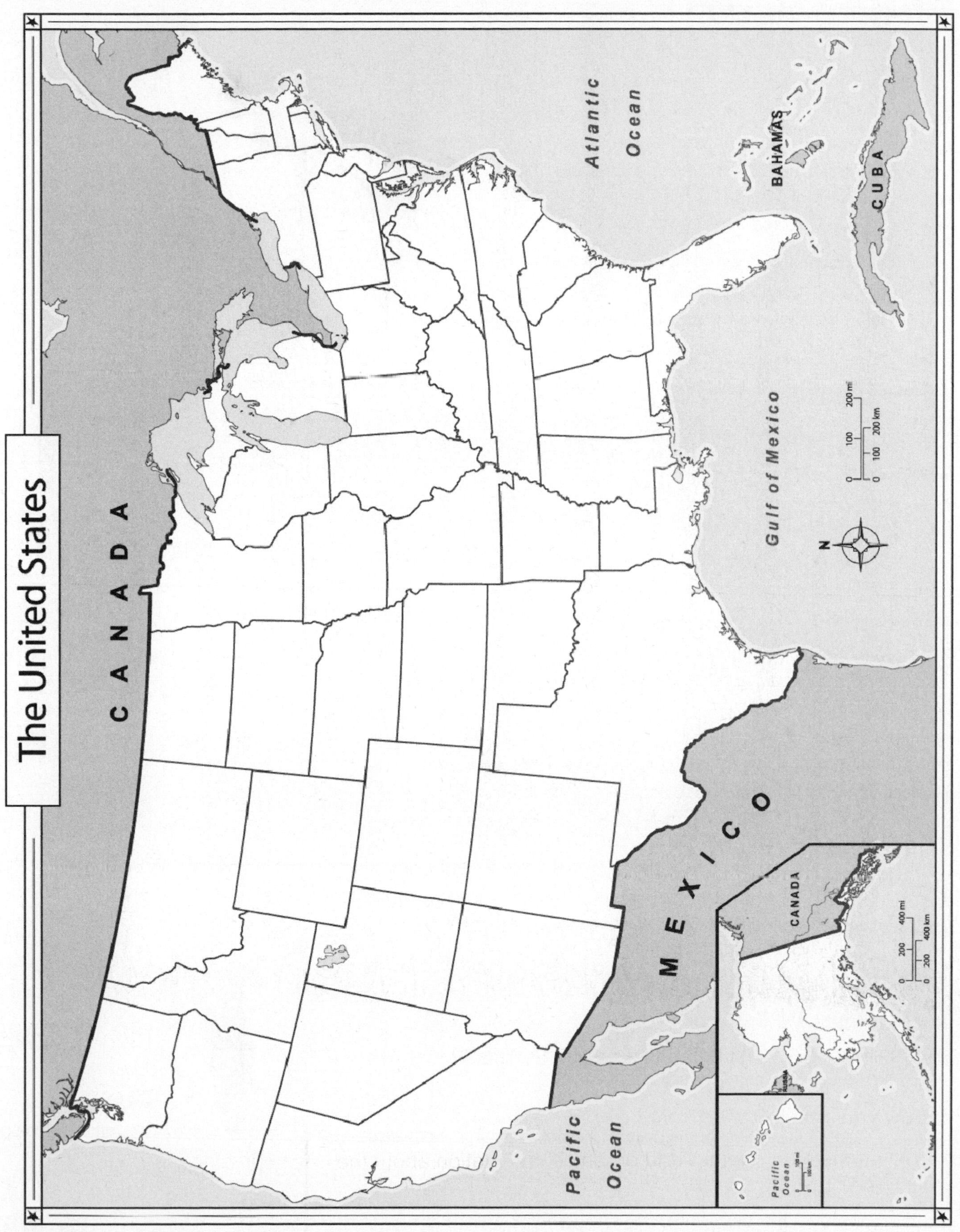
The United States
CANADA
Atlantic Ocean
BAHAMAS
CUBA
Gulf of Mexico
MEXICO
Pacific Ocean
CANADA
RUSSIA
Pacific Ocean
N
0 100 200 mi
0 100 200 km
0 200 400 mi
0 200 400 km

Student Guide
Lesson 10: Boom and Bust

During the 1928 presidential campaign Herbert Hoover's supporters appealed to the American voters' worst traits. Hoover won. Many Americans were happy that year because the stock market was booming. People were borrowing money freely to invest in stocks. They were hoping to make a quick fortune, but then the market crashed.

Lesson Objectives

- Describe Herbert Hoover's background.
- Describe the campaign against Al Smith.
- Recognize the basic structure of the stock system for financing corporations.

PREPARE

Approximate lesson time is 60 minutes.

Materials

For the Student

Money Matters

A History of US (Concise Edition), Volume C (1865-1932) by Joy Hakim

History Journal

Keywords and Pronunciation

bear market : a nickname brokers use when the stock market is down
bull market : a nickname brokers use when the stock market is up
share : a piece of ownership of a corporation
stock : shares in a company
stock exchange : the place where stocks are bought and sold
stock market : the business of buying and selling stocks
stockbroker : the person who buys and sells stock for another person

---

LEARN

Activity 1: Hoover's Promise *(Online)*

Activity 2: Prosperity *(Offline)*

Instructions

A. Read *(Chapter 61, pages 295–299)*

As you read, answer the following questions.

1. What job qualifications did Herbert Hoover bring to the presidency?
2. On what grounds did many of Hoover's supporters attack candidate Al Smith during the election campaign?
3. How do many large companies raise the money needed for growth and expansion?

4. Why do stock prices go up and down?
5. How does buying stocks on margin cause problems for many people?
6. How did the sharp drop in the stock market affect people's property, the banks, and jobs?

Write a brief definition for each of the following terms in your History Journal. When you have finished, compare your definitions with those in the Keywords section of this lesson.

- bear market
- bull market
- share
- stock
- stock market

B. Use What You Know

Complete the Money Matters sheet. When you have finished, compare your answers with those in the Lesson Answer Key.

ASSESS

Lesson Assessment: Boom and Bust (*Online*)

You will complete an online assessment covering the main goals of this lesson. Your assessment will be scored by the computer.

Name ______________________ Date ______________________

Money Matters

Case 1: Mr. Jones

You are Mr. Jones. You had $1,000 in savings and everyone told you to buy stock.

So you borrowed money from a stockbroker and bought as many shares of ABC stock as you could. You bought them on margin for $10 a share when they were selling for $100 a share.

- How many shares did you buy? ____________________
- If you bought the stocks for $10 a share when they were worth $100 a share, you must have borrowed $90 per share from the stockbroker. How much do you owe the stockbroker? ____________________

What a lucky day for you, Mr. Jones! You just learned that your stock is now worth $200 per share!

- How much are all our shares worth now? ____________________
- How much money have you made? Don't forget to pay back the stockbroker first.

  ____

But wait, you haven't actually made the money yet. You only make the money if you sell your stock when it is worth $200 a share. You didn't sell your stock and neither did your stockbroker because you thought it would keep going up and up in value. You just got a call from your stockbroker. The price on your stock fell. Then it fell some more. Your stockbroker sold it—for $10 a share.

- How much did the stock sell for if the stockbroker sold all your shares for $10 a share?

  ____

- The stockbroker keeps this money. Mr. Jones, how much do you owe him?

  ____

Case 2: Mr. Thomas

It's November 1929. Everyone you know is trying to make money the easy way, but not you.

You watched your pennies and put your savings in the bank. You didn't buy a fancy car or go to speakeasies. You didn't buy stock. You saved.

It's a good thing you did save Mr. Thomas, because you just lost your job at U.S. Steel. Now you'll really need those savings in the bank. What? You can't get your money? It's gone? How can that be?

- Why can't you get your money from the bank?

____

____

____

____

____

- What does a bank do with your money when you put it in an account there?

____

____

____

____

____

Student Guide
Lesson 11: Suffering

Everyone suffered during the Great Depression--rich people, poor people, city people, and farmers. Many lost their money, their jobs, and their homes. Some families moved in together; others lived in houses made of cardboard boxes. On the Great Plains—the Dust Bowl during the Great Depression—drought ravaged the land and the farmers' lives. These were hard times for all.

Lesson Objectives

- Summarize the financial problems farmers faced during the 1920s and '30s.
- Explain the causes of the Dust Bowl.
- Describe the shantytowns and the reasons for them.

PREPARE

Approximate lesson time is 60 minutes.

Materials

For the Student

- Picture Power
- The Dust Bowl

A History of US (Concise Edition), Volume C (1865-1932) by Joy Hakim

History Journal

Keywords and Pronunciation

depression : a time of decline in business activity, accompanied by high unemployment and falling prices

Dust Bowl : the name given to the region that was devastated by drought during the Depression years

---

LEARN

Activity 1: Hard Times for All *(Offline)*

Instructions

A. Read *(Chapter 62, pages 300–303)*

While you are reading, take notes in your History Journal about:

- The financial problems farmers faced during the 1920s and 1930s.
- The reasons shantytowns sprang up and what they were like.

B. Focus on Geography

Print The Dust Bowl sheet. Referring to your wall map, label the names of the states that had severe damage from the dust storms. Then label the remaining states that had damage. Describe the natural and man-made causes of the Dust Bowl in your History Journal. Compare your answers with those in the Lesson Answer Key.

C. Use What You Know

"A picture is worth a thousand words," or so the saying goes. Print the Picture Power sheet and analyze the painting *Migration* by William Gropper on page 303.

ASSESS

Lesson Assessment: Suffering (*Online*)

You will complete an online assessment covering the main goals of this lesson. Your assessment will be scored by the computer.

LEARN

Activity 2. Optional: Suffering *(Online)*

Name Date

The Dust Bowl

Referring to your wall map, label the states that had severe damage from the dust storms. Then label the remaining states that had damage.

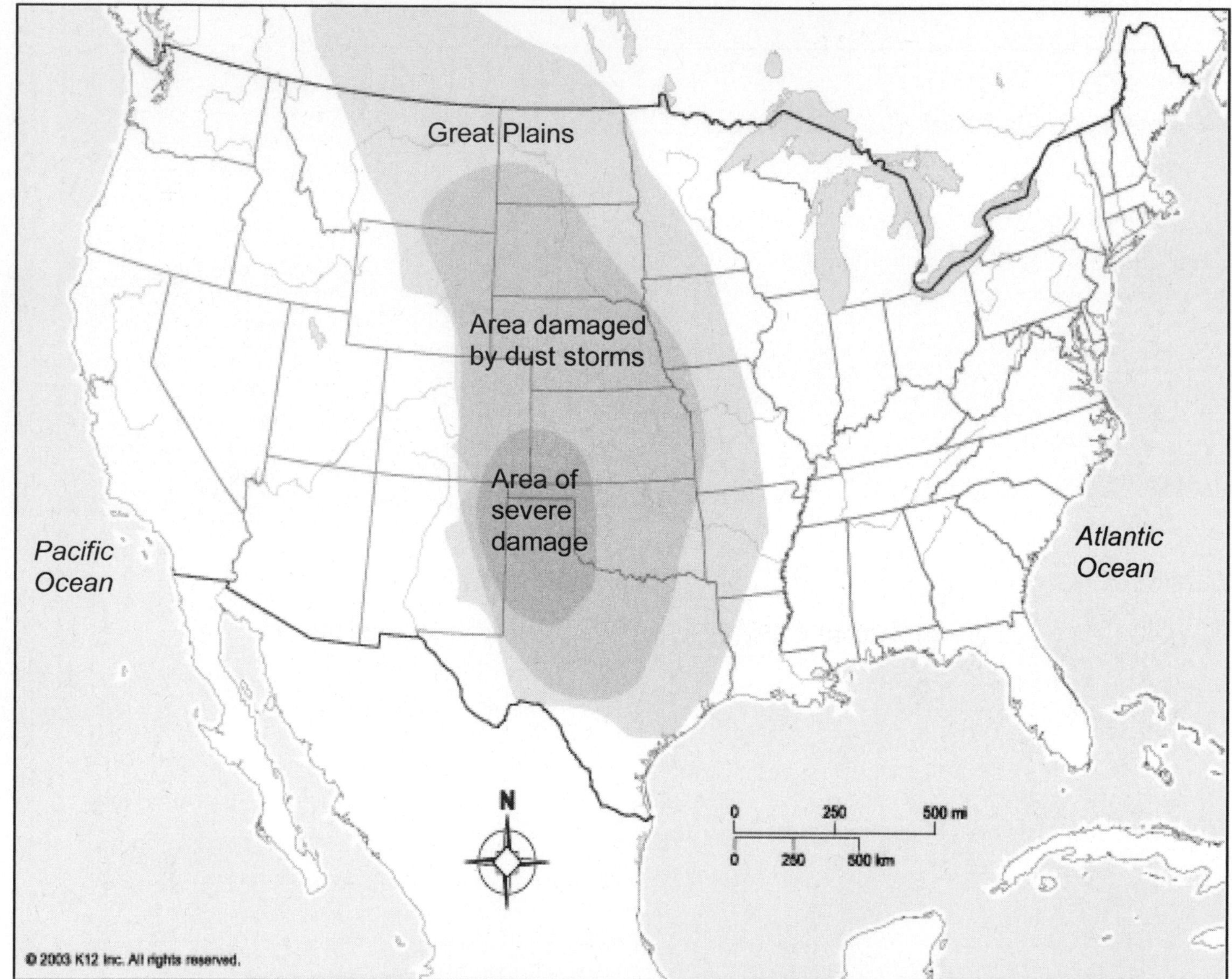

Name Date

Picture Power

Analyze William Gropper's painting Migration on page 303. Answer the following questions about the painting.

Observation

1. Describe the people in the painting.

2. Describe the setting in the painting.

3. Describe the activities in the painting.

Interpretation

1. Based on your observations, write three things you might infer from this painting.

2. Why was this painting created?

3. Who might have made this painting?

Evaluation

1. What questions does this painting raise in your mind?

2. What new ideas about history have you learned from this painting?

Student Guide
Lesson 12: Democracy in Danger

The crisis of the Great Depression was threatening American ideals. People were starving in the land of plenty. The Bonus Army marched on Washington. Some Americans thought foreign dictators had good ideas. What would President Hoover do?

Lesson Objectives

- Describe the Bonus March.
- Explain Hoover's philosophy of government responsibility.
- Give examples of Americans who admired other government systems and the leaders they admired.

PREPARE

Approximate lesson time is 60 minutes.

Materials

For the Student

A History of US (Concise Edition), Volume C (1865-1932) by Joy Hakim

History Journal

Depression Song

Keywords and Pronunciation

Bonus Army : the name given to 20,000 World War I veterans who marched to Washington to see President Hoover in an effort to get the bonus Congress had promised them for their war service
capitalism : the economic system in which individuals or companies, rather than the government, own most factories and businesses, and in which laborers produce products for a wage
communism : a political and economic system in which the people own goods and businesses in common, but the government manages and controls them
pacifist (PA-suh-fist) : a person who is opposed to the use of force under any circumstance

---

LEARN

Activity 1: Democracy at Risk *(Offline)*

Instructions

A. Read *(Chapter 63, pages 304–306)*
Answer the following questions as you read. Check your answers with the Lesson Answer Key.
Use the terms in the Word Bank to fill in the blanks below.
Word Bank: Italy, Russia, Germany, Adolf Hitler, Benito Mussolini

1. Match each leader with the country he ruled.
- Adolf Hitler :___________________
- Benito Mussolini: ________________
- Joseph Stalin: __________________

2. Match each American with the foreign leader he thought had good ideas.
- Charles Lindbergh: ________________
- Philip LaFollette: ________________

3. Why did some people in the 1930s say positive things about some dictators in Europe?

Reread Herbert Hoover's statements at the beginning of the chapter.

1. Why do you think the author placed these quotes at the beginning of the chapter?
2. Explain President Hoover's view of the role of government in difficult economic times.
3. Do you think President Hoover was in a position to understand what was happening to millions of people?

Define the following terms in your History Journal, and then compare your definitions with the ones in the Keywords section of this lesson.
Bonus Army
capitalism
communism
pacifist

B. Discuss
When the Bonus Army marched to Washington to see President Hoover and ask that their promised bonuses be paid then instead of in 1945, Hoover would not see them. When the police asked the Bonus Army to leave, they refused. President Hoover then sent the army to deal with them.

Why do you think the army attacked the Bonus Army? Should President Hoover have spoken to representatives of the Bonus Army? Discuss the issue with an adult. Remember to use facts from the book to support your position.

ASSESS

Lesson Assessment: Democracy in Danger (*Online*)

You will complete an online assessment covering the main goals of this lesson. Your assessment will be scored by the computer.

LEARN

Activity 2. Optional: Democracy in Danger *(Online)*

Print the Depression Song sheet and listen to "Brother, Can You Spare a Dime?" Pay close attention to the words of the song. What story do they tell?

Imagine you and your family are living through the Great Depression. You have no income, no home, and now you are losing hope.

Write your own lyrics to tell your Depression story. You may want to come up with a catchy title for your song that helps convey your message.

Name Date

Depression Song

Listen to "Brother Can You Spare a Dime?" Pay close attention to the words of the song. What do they tell? Imagine you are living through the Great Depression with your family—no income, no home, and now you are losing hope. Write your lyrics to your own Depression story.

Brother, Can You Spare a Dime?

They used to tell me I was building a dream
And so I followed the mob.
When there was earth to plow or guns to bear,
I was always there, right on the job.
They used to tell me I was building a dream
With peace and glory ahead—
Why should I be standing in line,
just waiting for bread?

Once I built a railroad, I made it run,
Made it race against time.
Once I built a railroad, now it's done—
Brother, can you spare a dime?

Once I built a tower, up to the sun,
brick and rivet and lime.
Once I built a tower, now it's done—
Brother, can you spare a dime?

Once in khaki suits, gee, we looked swell
Full of that Yankee Doodle-de-dum.
Half a million boots went slogging through hell,
And I was the kid with the drum.

Say, don't you remember they called me Al,
It was Al all the time.
Why don't you remember, I'm your pal—
Say, buddy, can you spare a dime?

Student Guide
Lesson 13: Unit Review

You have finished the unit! It's time to review what you've learned. You will take the Unit Assessment in the next lesson.

Lesson Objectives

- Demonstrate mastery of important knowledge and skills in this unit.

PREPARE

Approximate lesson time is 60 minutes.

Materials

For the Student

A History of US (Concise Edition), Volume C (1865-1932) by Joy Hakim

History Journal

LEARN

Activity 1: A Look Back *(Online)*

A. History Journal Review

Review what you've learned in this unit by going through your History Journal. You should:

- Look at activity sheets you completed for this unit.
- Review unit Keywords and definitions.
- Read through any writing assignments you did during the unit.
- Review the assessments you took.

Don't rush through. Take your time. Your History Journal is a great resource for a unit review.

B. Online Review

Review the following online activities:

- Flash Cards
- Time Line
- The Roaring Twenties

Student Guide
Lesson 14: Unit Assessment

You've finished the unit! Now it's time to take the Unit Assessment.

Lesson Objectives

- Describe the intended and unintended consequences of Prohibition.
- Explain the methods used to gain support for the 19th Amendment.
- Identify the 19th Amendment.
- Summarize the major events that led Russia to adopt communism and made people in the United States fear communism.
- Describe the black migration of the 1920s.
- Identify the cultural changes that characterized the 1920s.
- Recognize that there was class conflict and tension in the United States during the 1920s.
- Describe the campaign against Al Smith.
- Recognize the basic structure of the stock system for financing corporations.
- Identify individuals, groups or actions that promoted or diminished the ideals of democracy under the Constitution during the 1920s.
- Summarize the philosophies and policies of the three Republican presidents who served between 1921 and 1933.
- Give examples of cultural and social change over time during the 1920s.
- Trace the causes and results of the migration of blacks from the rural South to the cities of the North during the 1920s.
- Compare and contrast the changes in government during the Great Depression in the U.S. and those countries that turned to totalitarianism.
- Explore the amendment process under the Constitution, including the need for a new amendment to cancel an existing amendment.
- Summarize the varied duties of a U.S. president and the consequences of Harding's failure to meet his responsibilities.
- Recognize cultural trends and achievements of the 1920s including film, literature, music, art, and the Harlem Renaissance.
- Analyze inventions and innovations of the 1920s and their effect on the American way of life.
- Review the basic principles of the U.S. economy.

PREPARE

Approximate lesson time is 60 minutes.

ASSESS

Unit Assessment: A Fascinating Era, Part 1 *(Online)*

Complete the computer-scored portion of the Unit Assessment. When you have finished, complete the teacher-scored portion of the assessment and submit it to your teacher.

Unit Assessment: A Fascinating Era, Part 2 *(Offline)*

Complete the teacher-scored portion of the Unit Assessment and submit it to your teacher.

Student Guide
Lesson 15: Semester Review: Units 1–3

You've finished! Now it's time to pull together what you have learned this semester. You've learned a lot, so we'll review it unit by unit. Let's start by taking a look at Units 1–3.

Lesson Objectives

- Demonstrate mastery of important knowledge and skills taught in the Changing and Growing unit.
- Demonstrate mastery of important knowledge and skills taught in the Politics, Power, and the People unit.
- Demonstrate mastery of important knowledge and skills taught in the Reformers, Newcomers, and Innovators unit.

PREPARE

Approximate lesson time is 60 minutes.

Materials

For the Student

Unit Snapshot

A History of US (Concise Edition), Volume C (1865-1932) by Joy Hakim

History Journal

LEARN

Activity 1: Units 1–3 *(Online)*

Instructions

Let's review! Study your work from Units 1–3. As you review the units, complete the Unit Snapshot sheets. When you have finished your offline review, complete the online interactive review.

Name Date

Unit Snapshot: Unit _____

Categorize important information from this unit.

Significant People	Significant Events

Significant Places	Symbols of the Period
	(What do you associate with this time period? Example: 1840s—covered wagons)

What was your favorite lesson? Why?

Name Date

Unit Snapshot: Unit ____

Categorize important information from this unit.

Significant People	Significant Events

Significant Places	Symbols of the Period
	(What do you associate with this time period? Example: 1840s—covered wagons)

What was your favorite lesson? Why?

Name ______________________ Date ______________________

Unit Snapshot: Unit ____

Categorize important information from this unit.

Significant People	Significant Events

Significant Places	Symbols of the Period
	(What do you associate with this time period? Example: 1840s—covered wagons)

What was your favorite lesson? Why?

Name Date

Unit Snapshot: Unit ____

Categorize important information from this unit.

Significant People	Significant Events

Significant Places	Symbols of the Period
	(What do you associate with this time period? Example: 1840s—covered wagons)

What was your favorite lesson? Why?

Student Guide
Lesson 16: Semester Review: Units 4, 6, and 7

Let's continue pulling together what you have learned this semester. You've learned a lot, so we'll review it unit by unit. Let's take a look at Units 4, 6, and 7.

Lesson Objectives

- Demonstrate mastery of important knowledge and skills taught in the Making Things Better unit.
- Demonstrate mastery of important knowledge and skills taught in the Entering a New Century unit.
- Demonstrate mastery of important knowledge and skills taught in the A Fascinating Era unit.

PREPARE

Approximate lesson time is 60 minutes.

Materials

For the Student

Unit Snapshot

A History of US (Concise Edition), Volume C (1865-1932) by Joy Hakim

History Journal

LEARN

Activity 1: Units 4, 6, and 7 *(Online)*

Let's review! Study your work from Units 4, 6, and 7. As you review the units, complete the Unit Snapshot sheets. When you have finished your offline review, complete the online interactive review.

Name Date

Unit Snapshot: Unit ____

Categorize important information from this unit.

Significant People	Significant Events

Significant Places	Symbols of the Period
	(What do you associate with this time period? Example: 1840s—covered wagons)

What was your favorite lesson? Why?

Name Date

Unit Snapshot: Unit _____

Categorize important information from this unit.

Significant People	Significant Events

Significant Places	Symbols of the Period
	(What do you associate with this time period? Example: 1840s—covered wagons)

What was your favorite lesson? Why?

Name Date

Unit Snapshot: Unit ____

Categorize important information from this unit.

Significant People	Significant Events

Significant Places	Symbols of the Period
	(What do you associate with this time period? Example: 1840s—covered wagons)

What was your favorite lesson? Why?

Student Guide
Lesson 17: Fifty States Review and Assessment

Now it's time to review the locations of the 50 states. For your review you may use the U.S. Map Puzzle, or you may print the Map of the United States and use it to identify states. When you have finished the review, take the Fifty U.S. States Assessment.

Lesson Objectives

- Locate the 50 U.S. states on a map.

PREPARE

Approximate lesson time is 60 minutes.

Materials

For the Student

Map of the United States

ASSESS

Lesson Assessment: Fifty States Review and Assessment *(Online)*

You will complete an online assessment covering the main points of this lesson. Your assessment will be scored by the computer.

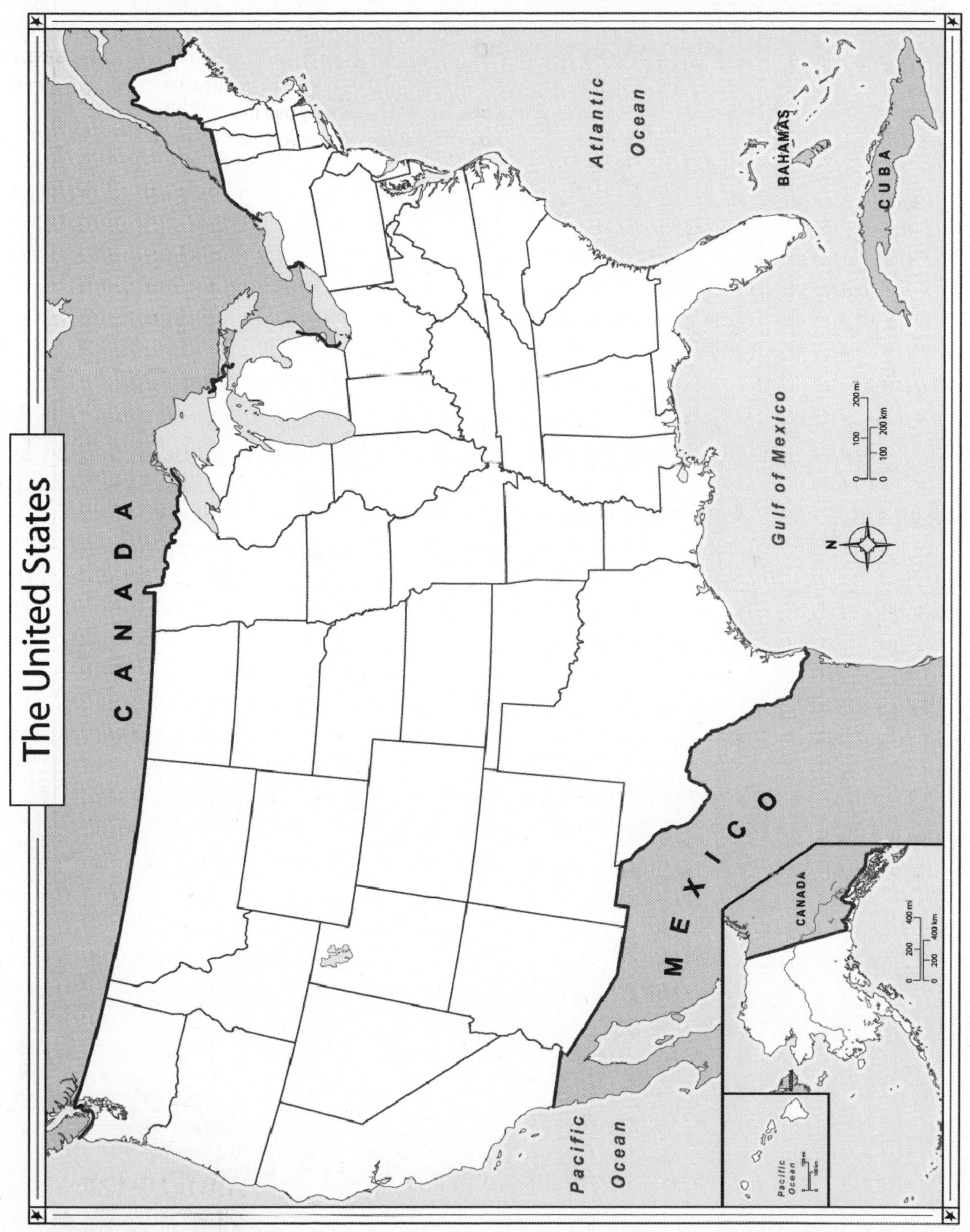
The United States
CANADA
Atlantic Ocean
BAHAMAS
CUBA
Gulf of Mexico
0 100 200 mi
0 100 200 km
N
MEXICO
Pacific Ocean
CANADA
0 200 400 mi
0 200 400 km

Student Guide
Lesson 18: Semester Assessment

You've finished the first semester! Now it's time to take the Semester Assessment.

Lesson Objectives

- Identify the major reasons for the move to restrict immigration.
- Identify groups left out of the prosperity of the late 1800s.
- Demonstrate mastery of important knowledge and skills taught in the Making Things Better unit.
- Demonstrate mastery of important knowledge and skills taught in the Entering a New Century unit.
- Demonstrate mastery of important knowledge and skills taught in the A Fascinating Era unit.
- Identify at least two of the following American writers of the early nineteenth century and their contributions to American literature: Emerson, Thoreau, Alcott, and Longfellow.
- Summarize Hakim's reasons for calling the late 1800s an age of extremes.
- Explain the causes of the Spanish-American War.
- Identify the Nez Perce Indians and their leader, Chief Joseph.
- Identify Boss Tweed as the leader of a political machine that ran New York by using bribery and intimidation.
- Identify Thomas Nast as the political cartoonist who helped bring down Tweed.
- Identify Mark Twain as the pen name of Samuel Clemens, the author of *The Adventures of Tom Sawyer, Adventures of Huckleberry Finn,* and other novels.
- Identify Jacob Riis as a Danish immigrant who photographed immigrant life to make people aware of the problems immigrants faced.
- Identify Booker T. Washington.
- Identify W.E.B. DuBois.
- Recognize and define *monopoly, trust, command economy, market economy, hybrid economy, corporation,* and *tariff.*
- Identify Samuel Gompers.
- Identify Mother Jones as a champion of child labor laws.
- Explain the arguments in favor of Prohibition.
- Identify the 19th Amendment.
- Describe how Andrew Carnegie rose from poverty to become one of the world's richest men.
- Compare and contrast Rockefeller and Morgan in terms of their rise to power, business practices, and use of wealth.
- Identify John Muir as a preservationist.

PREPARE

Approximate lesson time is 60 minutes.

ASSESS

Semester Assessment: MS American History Since 1865 Semester 1 (*Online*)

You will complete an online assessment covering the main points of this semester. Your assessment will be scored by the computer.

Student Guide

Unit 8: Hard Times
Lesson 1: Young Franklin

The Great Depression gripped the nation and the world, sending families into the streets and stripping people of their livelihoods and dignity. Some nations turned to totalitarian dictators who promised help. In the United States, a man who had grown up with everything, but had learned courage and humility in his battle with polio, rose to the challenge. His optimism and progressive spirit gave millions of Americans hope for the future.

Young Franklin grew up with all the benefits a privileged background could provide. But his family also taught him that it was his responsibility to make the world a better place.

Lesson Objectives

- Describe the early life of Franklin Roosevelt.

PREPARE

Approximate lesson time is 60 minutes.

Materials

For the Student

The Roosevelts

A History of US (Concise Edition), Volume D (1929 to Present) by Joy Hakim

History Journal

Keywords and Pronunciation

poliomyelitis (poh-lee-oh-miy-uh-LIY-tuhs) : a highly infectious disease of the nervous system caused by a virus that can cause paralysis; today it can be prevented by a series of vaccinations

---

LEARN

Activity 1: A Good Start *(Offline)*

Instructions

A. Read *(Chapter 1, pages 2–4; Chapter 2, pages 5–8)*

As you read, answer the following questions in your History Journal. Compare your answers with the ones in the Lesson Answer Key.

1. How did young Franklin learn about the history of his country?

2. What did young Franklin admire about Thomas Jefferson and Alexander Hamilton?

3. What were some of the advantages Franklin Roosevelt enjoyed during his childhood years?

4. What influences or experiences prevented Roosevelt from becoming arrogant or spoiled?

B. Use What You Know

Print The Roosevelts sheet. In this lesson, you will begin collecting information about the young Franklin Delano Roosevelt and will complete his section of the page. (You will add information about his wife, Eleanor Roosevelt, in another lesson.) Be sure to keep this sheet in a safe place so you will have it for later use.

ASSESS

Lesson Assessment: Young Franklin (*Online*)

You will complete an online assessment covering the main goals of this lesson. Your assessment will be scored by the computer.

LEARN

Activity 2. Optional: Young Franklin *(Online)*

Name Date

The Roosevelts

During today's lesson, answer the questions about Franklin Delano Roosevelt. You will answer these same questions about Eleanor Roosevelt in another lesson.

	Franklin Delano Roosevelt	**Eleanor Roosevelt**
1. Describe his/her family.		
2. Name the people who influenced him/her.		
3. What values did they teach him/her?		
4. How was he/she educated?		
5. What personal challenges did he/she overcome?		
6. What effect do you think this had on him/her?		

Student Guide
Lesson 2: A Woman of Courage

Do you remember the fairy tale about the ugly duckling that became a beautiful swan? Eleanor Roosevelt considered herself ugly (although FDR didn't). Although she had an awful, lonely childhood, she grew up to become one of the most beloved and influential Americans of the twentieth century.

Lesson Objectives

- Describe Eleanor Roosevelt's early life.
- Identify the ways in which Eleanor Roosevelt changed the traditional role of First Lady.
- Summarize Eleanor Roosevelt's work on behalf of the poor and minorities.

PREPARE

Approximate lesson time is 60 minutes.

Materials

For the Student

The First Lady

A History of US (Concise Edition), Volume D (1929 to Present) by Joy Hakim

History Journal

Keywords and Pronunciation

Civilian Conservation Corps : a New Deal program created to give unemployed workers jobs preserving the natural resources of the United States

---

LEARN

Activity 1: A Good Start *(Offline)*

Instructions

A. Read *(Chapter 3, pages 9–12)*

As you read, complete the questions about Eleanor Roosevelt on The Roosevelts sheet. Then compare your answers with the ones in the Lesson Answer Key.

B. Use What You Know

Eleanor Roosevelt changed and expanded the role of First Lady. Fill out a job description for the First Lady on the The First Lady sheet. Use Eleanor Roosevelt as an example. Start by using your book to identify the many activities, or tasks, she carried out while sharing the White House with FDR.

Note: When you write a job description, it is customary to start each task or function statement with a verb (for example: Write a letter). It doesn't have to be a complete sentence.

To fill out the columns underneath, do a little brainstorming about what Eleanor needed to know, and what she needed to be able to do, to perform the tasks. What values or beliefs contributed to her performance as First Lady? Write down everything that comes to mind, no matter how outrageous or silly it seems at first. Then go back and look closely at your answers and compare them to those in the Lesson Answer Key. Do they give you any clues about what made Eleanor Roosevelt tick? Why was she one of *Time* magazine's Top 100 Persons of the Century?

ASSESS

Lesson Assessment: A Woman of Courage (*Online*)

You will complete an online assessment covering the main goals of this lesson. Your assessment will be scored by the computer.

LEARN

Activity 2. Optional: A Woman of Courage *(Online)*

Name Date

The First Lady

Write a job description for the First Lady, using Eleanor Roosevelt as an example. First, using your book, list the many activities (called tasks) she performed. Then brainstorm ideas about what she needed to know, needed to be able to do, and the values she needed to be a good First Lady.

Job Tasks

☆☆☆☆☆☆☆

Knows	Able to Do	Believes In

Student Guide
Lesson 3: Polio and Politics

Franklin Delano Roosevelt's struggle to live a full life after he contracted polio made him stronger and more focused. Learn how those aspects affected his political career.

Lesson Objectives

- Describe Franklin Roosevelt's experience with polio.
- Identify the New Deal as Roosevelt's plan for ending the Great Depression.
- Describe the economic problems the nation faced in 1933 and FDR's ideas for dealing with the Depression.

PREPARE

Approximate lesson time is 60 minutes.

Materials

For the Student

FDR: The Man for the Times

A History of US (Concise Edition), Volume D (1929 to Present) by Joy Hakim

History Journal

Keywords and Pronunciation

New Deal : The programs and policies introduced during the 1930 by President Franklin D. Roosevelt, designed to promote economic recovery and social reform.

LEARN

Activity 1: A Blessing in Disguise? *(Offline)*

Instructions

A. Read *(Chapter 4, pages 13–15)*

As you read, define New Deal in your History Journal. When you have finished, compare your definition with the one in the Keywords section of this lesson.

B. Use What You Know

Print the FDR: The Man for the Times sheet and answer the questions. Compare your answers with the ones in the Lesson Answer Key.

C. Discuss

Why was it so important for FDR to break with tradition and appear personally at the 1932 Democratic National Convention to accept the party's nomination? Discuss your ideas with an adult.

ASSESS

Lesson Assessment: Polio and Politics (*Online*)

You will complete an online assessment covering the main goals of this lesson. Your assessment will be scored by the computer.

LEARN

Activity 2. Optional: Polio and Politics *(Online)*

Name Date

FDR: The Man for the Times

Using what you know, answer the following questions about FDR, the economic problems of the country, and how he planned to solve them.

1. How did Franklin Delano Roosevelt respond to a crippling attack of polio?

2. In what ways did polio make FDR a better candidate?

3. Describe the economic problems facing the country when FDR took office. How severe were they?

4. Many of FDR's ideas for addressing the country's problems were based on Progressive ideas. List them.

Student Guide
Lesson 4: A Powerful President

Franklin Delano Roosevelt swept into the presidency like a whirlwind, and his agenda was geared toward ending the Depression quickly. The centerpiece of the agenda was a program called the New Deal. The New Deal made government more involved in the lives of citizens, and vice versa—it gave power to people who had never had power before, including women and minorities. But FDR's ideas also sparked a debate that continues to this day—how big a role should government really play in the lives of the American people?

Lesson Objectives

- Compare and contrast FDR's philosophy of government with those of Coolidge and Hoover.
- Recognize the changes in the role of government during the 1930s.
- Give examples of the ways in which FDR increased citizen participation in government.

PREPARE

Approximate lesson time is 60 minutes.

Materials

For the Student

How to Lead

A History of US (Concise Edition), Volume D (1929 to Present) by Joy Hakim

History Journal

LEARN

Activity 1: FDR Changes Government *(Offline)*

Instructions

A. Read *(Chapter 5, pages 16–23)*

B. Making Connections

Complete the How to Lead sheet and compare Roosevelt's ideas on how to end the Depression with the ideas of Coolidge and Hoover.

C. Use What You Know

Prepare and deliver a "fireside chat" in which Franklin and Eleanor address the nation on a radio broadcast. Your completed chat should be about two minutes long.

- In Franklin's chat, summarize the president's actions during his first 100 days in office.
- In Eleanor's chat, describe her goal—the need for justice for all Americans.

ASSESS

Lesson Assessment: A Powerful President *(Online)*

You will complete an online assessment covering the main points of this lesson. Your assessment will be scored by the computer.

Name Date

How to Lead

1. FDR's leadership style and philosophy contrasted sharply with that of the two previous presidents – Coolidge and Hoover. Compare their leadership in the following areas:

	Coolidge	Hoover	F.D. Roosevelt
Purpose of government			To be an active participant in people's lives.
Relationship between business and government	Government should provide conditions to support business.		
Strategies to end the Depression			

How to Lead

2. How did the role of government change during the 1930s?

3. List two ways FDR increased citizen participation in government.

-
-

Student Guide
Lesson 5: The Government Grows

During the Great Depression, thousands of banks, stores, and factories closed and millions of people lost their jobs. Most U.S. leaders gave up trying to figure a way out of the crisis. But Franklin Delano Roosevelt had a plan. First he would help Americans get back to work. Then he would try to make sure a similar situation never happened again.

Lesson Objectives

- Recognize ways in which New Deal programs made the federal government an active participant in people's lives and in the U.S. economy.
- Describe programs of the New Deal that still exist today.

PREPARE

Approximate lesson time is 60 minutes.

Materials

For the Student

Still Working

A History of US (Concise Edition), Volume D (1929 to Present) by Joy Hakim

History Journal

LEARN

Activity 1: What a Deal! *(Offline)*

Instructions

A. Read *("New Ideas for a New Deal," Chapter 5, page 19)*

B. Use What You Know

Complete the online activity Relief, Recovery, Reform.

C. Explore

Roosevelt's New Deal

There were many parts to Franklin Roosevelt's New Deal. The Tennessee Valley Authority was a program to create jobs for unemployed Americans and bring prosperity to those living in the Tennessee Valley. The Civilian Conservation Corps put thousands of unemployed young men to work planting trees and fighting soil erosion.

Complete the following activity in your History Journal.

Complete the following activity in your History Journal.

1. Refer to the feature on the New Deal programs on page 19.
2. Then select one of the New Deal programs still in existence today to research.
3. Investigate its role today. Why do you think it has lasted?
4. Use the Still Working sheet to prepare a summary of the program's history and its present status.

- Securities and Exchange Commission (SEC) (SEC)
- Federal Deposit Insurance Corporation (FDIC) (FDIC)
- Social Security Act (SSA) (SSA)

  (SSA)—Use the link under Quick Intro on the left. The FAQ section in each is a good place to start.
- Tennessee Valley Authority (TVA) (TVA)

ASSESS

Lesson Assessment: The Government Grows *(Online)*

You will complete an online assessment covering the main points of this lesson. Your assessment will be scored by the computer.

LEARN

Activity 2. Optional: The Government Grows *(Online)*

Name Date

Still Working

1. Refer to the summary of New Deal programs in the feature on page 19. Select one of the programs still in existence to research.

Program: ______________________ Logo:

What is the history of the program?

What did this program hope to accomplish?

Was it successful?

What is its role today?

Why do you think it has lasted so long?

Think It Through

2. Many New Deal programs created jobs for people. The goal of these programs was relief because the money from the jobs enabled people to buy food and other necessities. The jobs were also intended to help get the economy going again (recovery). How would jobs for only some of the people in one town help the economy of the whole town? Before you answer, think about what people do with the money they earn.

3. Some New Deal programs gave people jobs building roads, bridges, and other infrastructure. How might these roads, bridges, and so forth help farmers and business owners make profits?

Student Guide
Lesson 6: (Optional) Your Choice

You may use today's lesson time to do one or more of the following:

- Complete work in progress.
- Prepare for your state standardized test.
- Visit two websites to learn more about FDR (Franklin Delano Roosevelt Memorial and Franklin D. Roosevelt Presidential Library and Museum).
- See if you can name and locate the state capitals in the U.S. State Capitals Quiz or on the outline map.
- Go on to the next lesson.

Please mark this lesson complete in order to proceed to the next lesson in the course.

Lesson Objectives

- Explore knowledge and skills taught in this course.

PREPARE

Approximate lesson time is 60 minutes.

Materials

For the Student

Map of the United States

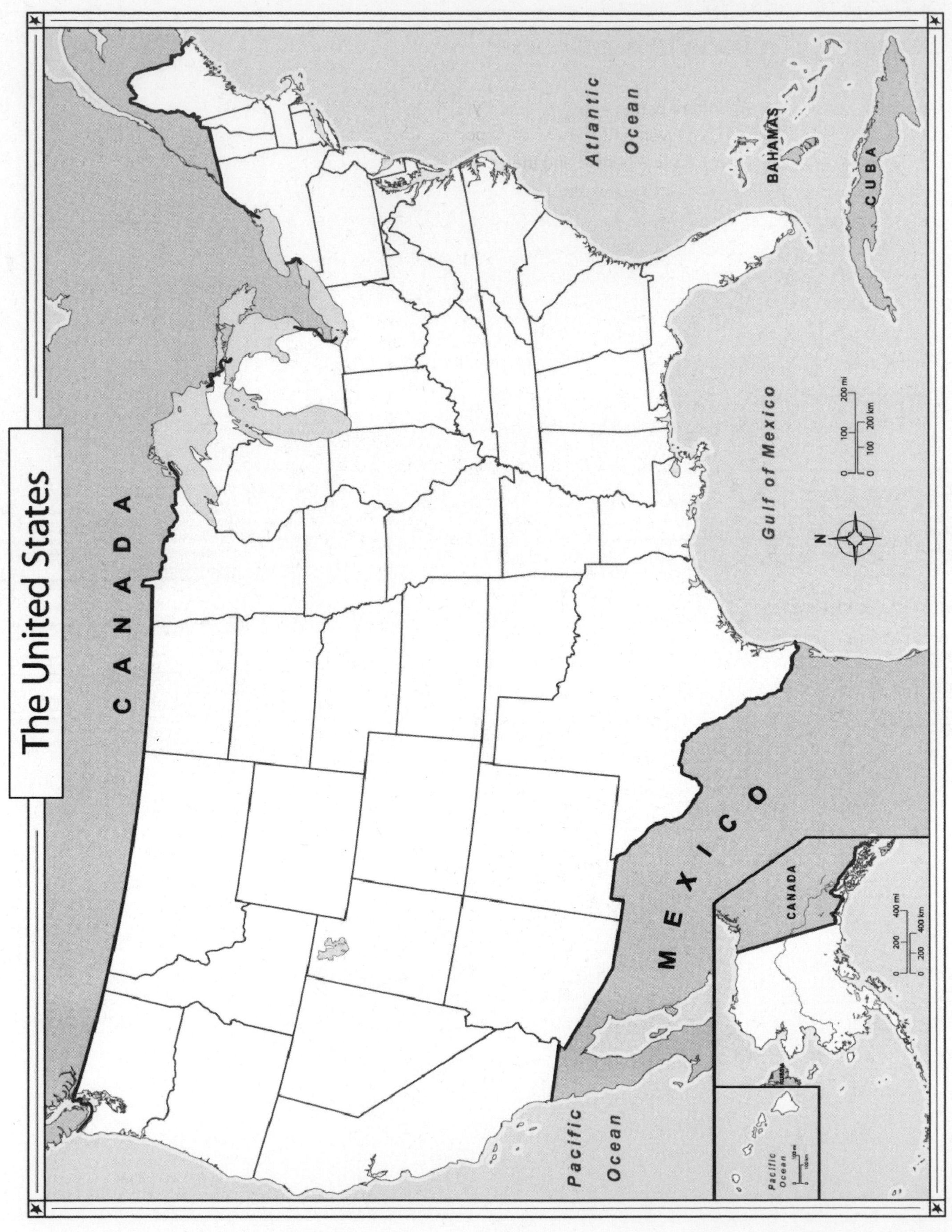
The United States
CANADA
Atlantic Ocean
BAHAMAS
CUBA
Gulf of Mexico
0 100 200 mi
0 100 200 km
N
MEXICO
Pacific Ocean
CANADA
0 200 400 mi
0 200 400 km
Pacific Ocean

Student Guide
Lesson 7: Choosing a Topic

Many people played an important part in American history between 1900 and 1940. Artists, scientists, politicians, businesspeople, and even entertainers and sports figures all had a big effect on the United States. You'll review some of those important people and then choose one to write about.

Lesson Objectives

- Review major individuals of the period 1900-1940 to assess their impact on the United States.

PREPARE

Approximate lesson time is 60 minutes.

Materials

For the Student

- The Person of the Era: 1900-1940
- History Journal

LEARN

Activity 1: Choosing a Topic *(Offline)*

Instructions

To get ready, you'll print The Person of the Era: 1900–1940 sheet and look through the Entering a New Century, A Fascinating Era, and Hard Times units in your History Journal to find activity sheets about people. Then start the lesson by reviewing some online resources.

Name Date

The Person of the Era: 1900–1940

Directions:

1. Use the following to review the important events, people, movements, and inventions that shaped the early twentieth century. As you review, think about the people who had the greatest effect on the United States in the years from 1900 to 1940.
   - Time Line: 1891–1918
   - Time Line: 1919–1945
   - People: 1891–1918
   - People: 1919–1945
   - Activity sheets in your History Journal with relevant content
2. Then choose five people, one for each of the following categories, who you think had the biggest effect.
   - Arts/Entertainment
     (writers, actors, musicians, artists, etc.)
   - Science/Technology/Medicine
     (scientists, inventors, physicians, medical researchers, etc.)
   - Public Service/Government
     (presidents, teachers, activists, politicians, reformers, etc.)
   - Sports
     (athletes, coaches, etc.)
   - Business
     (businessmen and women, financiers, industrialists, entrepreneurs, etc.)

As you make your choices, ask yourself:

- Did this person have an unusual and enduring influence on the nation?
- Did this person change the course of History?
- Was this person a pioneer in his/her field?
- Was this person fascinating?
- How did the United States change as a result of this person's actions?

Your answers will help you narrow your choices.

3. Use the chart on the next page to help you gather and organize information about the five people.

Area of Achievement	Person	Accomplishments/ Achievements	Effect of Achievements
Arts/Entertainment			
Science/Technology/Medicine			
Public Service/ Government			
Sports			
Business			

4. Now it's time to choose the person that you will write about in your essay. Use your chart to rank the people according to their importance and influence. Number the people you have listed on your chart from most important (1) to least important (5).

Ask yourself the same questions you asked when you narrowed your choices earlier. To make sure that you have chosen a significant person, also ask yourself "Will this person still be remembered one hundred years from now?" Then choose the person that you think has contributed the most to United States history in his/her field or to the nation as a whole.

The person I will write about is ______________________________.

Student Guide
Lesson 8: Forming a Thesis

It's easy to say "Theodore Roosevelt was an important person in American history." But it would take a little work to support that claim. Why is he considered important? What did he do? Did he have a significant effect on the United States?

Now that you've chosen a person to write about, it's time to do a little research. You need to be able to explain why this person was so important. To do that, you'll need to analyze some primary sources and read some secondary sources.

Lesson Objectives

- Explain the significance of one individual from the period 1900-1940.
- Analyze primary sources to gain information.
- Read secondary sources for information.

PREPARE

Approximate lesson time is 60 minutes.

Materials

For the Student

Notes and Thesis

LEARN

Activity 1: Forming a Thesis *(Online)*

Instructions

To get started, print the Notes and Thesis sheet. It will guide you through today's lesson.

On the next screen you'll find links to websites that will help you complete the activity.

Name Date

Notes and Thesis

Directions:

1. Begin your research on the person you selected in the Choosing a Topic lesson by reading general background information. An encyclopedia is a good place to begin. You can use Grolier's online encyclopedia, *The New Book of Knowledge*.

2. After you've gained some general background information about the person, read and take notes from other sources. The websites listed online will lead you to many primary and secondary sources with good information about the individual you have chosen. Use the chart on the next page to guide your research and help organize the information you find.

3. As you research, remember that you are looking for specific information that will support your position that the person you have chosen has had a significant effect on the history of the United States. You will probably end up with more information in some columns than others. It is even possible that one of the columns will be empty (it depends upon the individual you have chosen). Always keep the Guiding Question in mind.

Guiding Question: Who is the person whom you believe has contributed the most to U.S. history from 1900 to 1940 in his/her field or to the nation as a whole, and why?

Category	Notes
Character Traits and Evidence of the Traits	Example: bravery – risked his life in WWI to save another man; pulled him to safety with “bullets flying”
Obstacles Overcome and Details	
Specific Accomplishments	
Other Information, Details, and Facts to Support Your Claim	
Business	

Writing the Thesis

Now it's time to answer the Guiding Question:

> Who is the person that you believe has contributed the most to U.S. history from 1900-1940 in his/her field or to the nation as a whole, and why?

As you begin to compose the answer to this question in your mind, use the chart to help you think about three main points you want to make. The answers to the following questions may help in this task.

- Why do you think this person is more important than others?
- What did this person accomplish?
- What are the long-term and short-term results or impact of the accomplishments?
- What character traits did the person exhibit?
- What obstacles did the person have to overcome to achieve greatness?

Write your answer to the Guiding Question below in one or two clear sentences. Your brief answer will be the thesis of your essay. Use third person—don't use the words "I", "we", or "you". Do not use any specific details in the short answer. You will add specifics and details later.

Thesis:

____

____

____

____

Sample Thesis:

Franklin Delano Roosevelt was one of the most important people in History between 1900 and 1940 because he overcame obstacles to become a great leader, and his New Deal economic policies greatly affected the nation.

Student Guide
Lesson 9: (Optional) Your Choice

You may use today's lesson time to do one or more of the following:

- Complete work in progress.
- Prepare for your state standardized test.
- See if you can name and locate the state capitals in the U.S. State Capitals Quiz or on the outline map.
- Go on to the next lesson.

Please mark this lesson complete in order to proceed to the next lesson in the course.

Lesson Objectives

- Explore knowledge and skills taught in this course.

PREPARE

Approximate lesson time is 60 minutes.

Materials

For the Student

Map of the United States

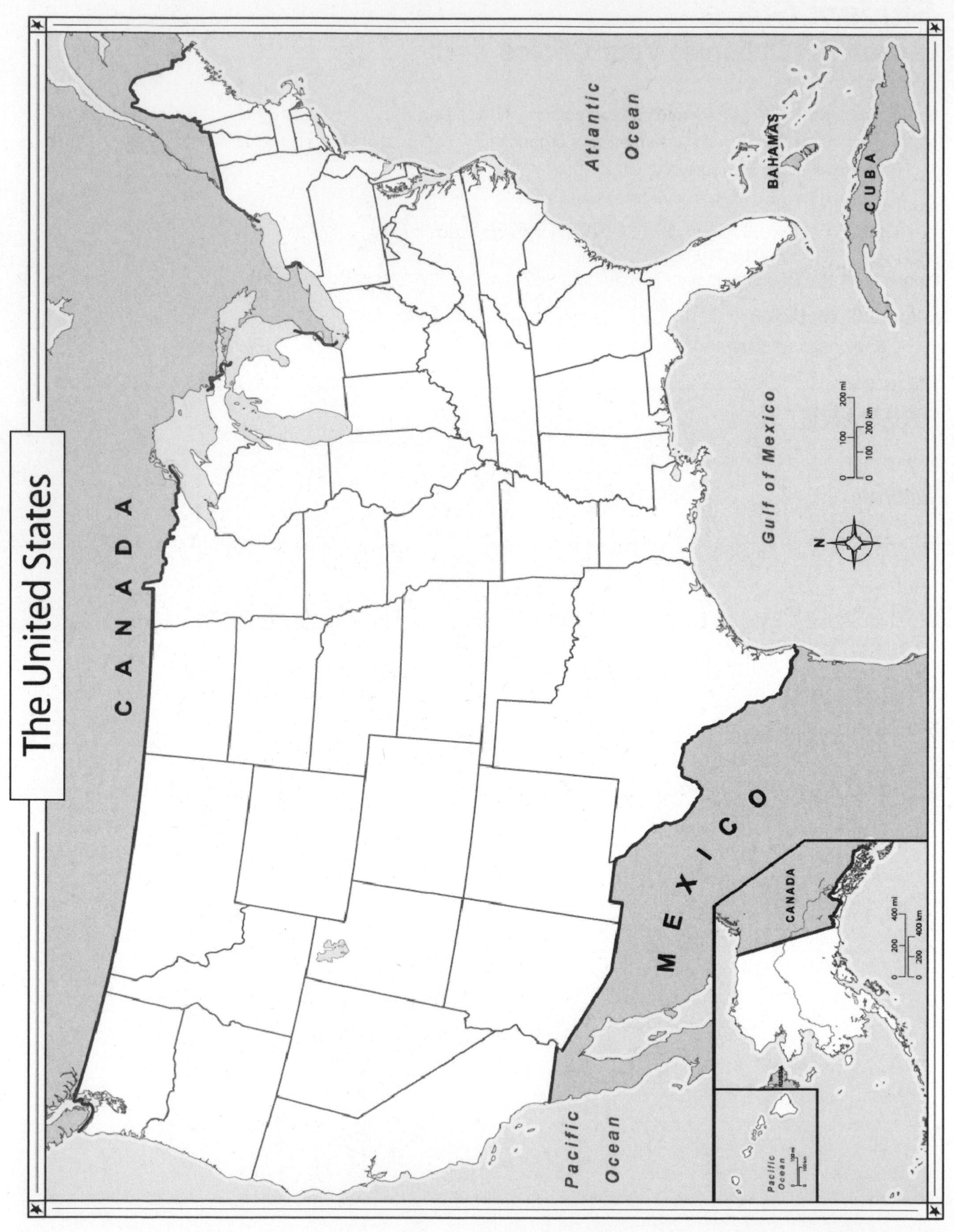
The United States
CANADA
Atlantic Ocean
BAHAMAS
CUBA
Gulf of Mexico
MEXICO
Pacific Ocean
N

Student Guide
Lesson 10: Completing the Essay Outline

You've researched and taken notes on the person you believe to have contributed the most to United States history from 1900 to 1940. The information is organized on the chart from the Notes and Thesis sheet. Now it's time to write the essay outline.

Lesson Objectives

- Write an outline in preparation for writing a thesis-based essay.

PREPARE

Approximate lesson time is 60 minutes.

Materials

For the Student

Essay Plan and Outline

LEARN

Activity 1: Completing the Essay Outline *(Offline)*

Instructions

Print the Essay Plan and Outline sheet and complete Part 1: Prepare an Outline. Preparing this outline will organize the information from your chart in the way you will use it in your essay.

Name Date

Essay Plan and Outline

Directions:

Before beginning to work on the outline, look at your thesis statement and the chart from the Notes and Thesis sheet. If you think you need more information to support the ideas expressed in your thesis, go online and do a little more research. Look for evidence to support your three main points. Add the new information to the chart.

Part 1: Prepare an Outline

Once you think you have enough supporting facts and details, it's time to organize the information from the chart in the way you will use it in your essay. Fill in the blank outline on pages 2-5. Your essay, and outline, will follow this format:

Paragraph 1 – Introduction that includes the thesis statement
Paragraph 2 – First reason you selected the individual
Paragraph 3 – Second reason you selected the individual
Paragraph 4 – Third reason you selected the individual
Paragraph 5 – Conclusion that summarizes the main ideas and restates the thesis

- **Introduction:** Your introduction will include the thesis statement for your essay. Write your thesis statement below Roman numeral I on the outline.
- **Main Topic:** Your outline will contain three main topics—the three reasons you chose the person you did. Main topics in an outline are represented by Roman numerals. The first main topic in your outline is the first reason. Write a topic sentence about the reason below Roman numeral II on your outline. For example (using the sample thesis from the Notes and Thesis sheet), the topic sentence might be something like "Franklin Roosevelt overcame many obstacles during his life."
- **Subtopics:** Now decide what pieces of information you will use to support your first main topic, and what order that information should be in. In an outline, these pieces of information are called subtopics, and they are represented by capital letters (A., B., C.). You may not need all the capital letters on the outline, or you may add more if you need them.

  Add the subtopics to your outline under the first main topic. You must list at least two subtopics under each main topic. One subtopic for the main topic given above might be "Roosevelt was successful even though he had been crippled by polio."

- **Specific Facts:** Now add some specific facts about the subtopics. Continuing with our example, a specific fact for the above subtopic might be, "Roosevelt only had partial use of his legs." In an outline, specific facts are represented by Arabic numerals (1., 2., 3.). List at least two facts under each subtopic.
- Finally, check your chart one last time. You will probably not use all the information you recorded, but be sure you have not left out anything you think is important to support your position. Remember, your essay will follow the outline exactly. When you have completed the section for the first main topic, follow the same procedure for the other two main topics.
- **Conclusion:** Your essay will contain a concluding paragraph that summarizes the main ideas and restates the thesis. Jot down a few ideas for the conclusion below Roman numeral V on the outline.

OUTLINE

I. Introduction: Thesis Statement

____

____

____

____

II. First Main Topic: First reason you selected the individual

Topic Sentence:

____

____

____

____

A. ____________________________________

1. __________________________________

2. __________________________________

B. ______________________________

1. ______________________________

2. ______________________________

C. ______________________________

1. ______________________________

2. ______________________________

D. ______________________________

1. ______________________________

2. ______________________________

III. Second Main Topic: Second reason you selected the individual

Topic Sentence:

____

____

____

____

A. ______________________________

1. ______________________________

2. ______________________________

B. ______________________________

1. ______________________________

2. ______________________________

C. ______________________________

1. ______________________________

2. ______________________________

D. ______________________________

1. ______________________________

2. ______________________________

IV. Third Main Topic: Third reason you selected the individual

Topic Sentence:

____

____

____

____

A. ______________________________

1. ______________________________

2. ______________________________

B. ______________________________

1. ______________________________

2. ______________________________

C. ______________________________

1. ______________________________

2. ______________________________

D. ______________________________

1. ______________________________

2. ______________________________

V. Conclusion:

____

____

____

____

Part 2: Write the First Draft

Now it's time to write the first draft of your essay. Keep your outline where you can refer to it and follow it exactly.

- Write the first paragraph. Use your thesis statement as the introduction to your essay. Add some general information or explanation before or after it if you wish. Be sure your introduction tells what you will be writing about and gets the reader's attention.
- Write the second paragraph:
    1. Use the first main topic sentence, Roman numeral II in your outline, to state the main idea of the paragraph.
    2. Explain the topic sentence using the information listed in the subtopics and specifics in that section of the outline.
    3. Write a concluding sentence that connects back to the topic sentence.
- Write the third and fourth paragraphs of your essay using the same procedure.
- Write a concluding paragraph of three or four sentences that summarizes the major ideas of your essay and restates your thesis statement in some way.

Part 3: Revise and Refine

- Read back through the whole essay.
    - ♦ Did you answer the essay question?
    - ♦ Are all your ideas clearly written?
    - ♦ Does each paragraph have a topic sentence?
    - ♦ Do all sentences in each paragraph relate to the topic sentence?

- Make any changes now, and then make sure your essay follows this format:

  Paragraph 1 – Introduction that includes the thesis statement
  Paragraph 2 – First reason you selected the individual
  Paragraph 3 – Second reason you selected the individual
  Paragraph 4 – Third reason you selected the individual
  Paragraph 5 – Conclusion that summarizes the main ideas and restates the thesis

- Correct any spelling, grammar, or punctuation mistakes you see. Reading your essay aloud will help you spot errors.
- Share your essay with an adult.

Student Guide
Lesson 11: Writing the First Draft

It's time to write the first draft of your essay. Follow the directions in Part 2 of the Essay Plan and Outline sheet.

Lesson Objectives

- Identify, in a well-developed essay, an American who contributed significantly to United States history from the period 1900 to 1940 and provide support to this claim.

PREPARE

Approximate lesson time is 60 minutes.

Student Guide

Lesson 12: Writing the Final Draft

Write the final draft of your essay by revising and refining your first draft. Follow the directions in Part 3 of the Essay Plan and Outline sheet.

An adult will assess your final draft.

Lesson Objectives

- Identify, in a well-developed essay, an American who contributed significantly to United States history from the period 1900 to 1940 and provide support to this claim.

PREPARE

Approximate lesson time is 60 minutes.

ASSESS

Lesson Assessment: Writing the Final Draft (*Offline*)

You will complete an offline assessment covering some of the main points of this lesson. Your assessment will be scored by the teacher.

Name Date

Essay Plan and Outline

Directions:

Before beginning to work on the outline, look at your thesis statement and the chart from the Notes and Thesis sheet. If you think you need more information to support the ideas expressed in your thesis, go online and do a little more research. Look for evidence to support your three main points. Add the new information to the chart.

Part 1: Prepare an Outline

Once you think you have enough supporting facts and details, it's time to organize the information from the chart in the way you will use it in your essay. Fill in the blank outline on pages 2-5. Your essay, and outline, will follow this format:

Paragraph 1 – Introduction that includes the thesis statement
Paragraph 2 – First reason you selected the individual
Paragraph 3 – Second reason you selected the individual
Paragraph 4 – Third reason you selected the individual
Paragraph 5 – Conclusion that summarizes the main ideas and restates the thesis

- **Introduction:** Your introduction will include the thesis statement for your essay. Write your thesis statement below Roman numeral I on the outline.
- **Main Topic:** Your outline will contain three main topics—the three reasons you chose the person you did. Main topics in an outline are represented by Roman numerals. The first main topic in your outline is the first reason. Write a topic sentence about the reason below Roman numeral II on your outline. For example (using the sample thesis from the Notes and Thesis sheet), the topic sentence might be something like "Franklin Roosevelt overcame many obstacles during his life."
- **Subtopics:** Now decide what pieces of information you will use to support your first main topic, and what order that information should be in. In an outline, these pieces of information are called subtopics, and they are represented by capital letters (A., B., C.). You may not need all the capital letters on the outline, or you may add more if you need them.

  Add the subtopics to your outline under the first main topic. You must list at least two subtopics under each main topic. One subtopic for the main topic given above might be "Roosevelt was successful even though he had been crippled by polio."

- **Specific Facts:** Now add some specific facts about the subtopics. Continuing with our example, a specific fact for the above subtopic might be, "Roosevelt only had partial use of his legs." In an outline, specific facts are represented by Arabic numerals (1., 2., 3.). List at least two facts under each subtopic.
- Finally, check your chart one last time. You will probably not use all the information you recorded, but be sure you have not left out anything you think is important to support your position. Remember, your essay will follow the outline exactly. When you have completed the section for the first main topic, follow the same procedure for the other two main topics.
- **Conclusion:** Your essay will contain a concluding paragraph that summarizes the main ideas and restates the thesis. Jot down a few ideas for the conclusion below Roman numeral V on the outline.

OUTLINE

I. Introduction: Thesis Statement

____

____

____

____

II. First Main Topic: First reason you selected the individual

Topic Sentence:

____

____

____

____

A. ____________________________________

1. ________________________________

2. ________________________________

B. ______________________________

1. ______________________________

2. ______________________________

C. ______________________________

1. ______________________________

2. ______________________________

D. ______________________________

1. ______________________________

2. ______________________________

III. Second Main Topic: Second reason you selected the individual

Topic Sentence:

____

____

____

____

A. ______________________________

1. ______________________________

2. ______________________________

B. ______________________________

1. ______________________________

2. ______________________________

C. ______________________________

1. ______________________________

2. ______________________________

D. ______________________________

1. ______________________________

2. ______________________________

IV. Third Main Topic: Third reason you selected the individual

Topic Sentence:

____

____

____

____

A. ______________________________

1. ______________________________

2. ______________________________

B. ______________________________

1. ______________________________

2. ______________________________

C. ______________________________

1. ______________________________

2. ______________________________

D. ______________________________

1. ______________________________

2. ______________________________

V. Conclusion:

___

___

___

___

Part 2: Write the First Draft

Now it's time to write the first draft of your essay. Keep your outline where you can refer to it and follow it exactly.

- Write the first paragraph. Use your thesis statement as the introduction to your essay. Add some general information or explanation before or after it if you wish. Be sure your introduction tells what you will be writing about and gets the reader's attention.
- Write the second paragraph:
    1. Use the first main topic sentence, Roman numeral II in your outline, to state the main idea of the paragraph.
    2. Explain the topic sentence using the information listed in the subtopics and specifics in that section of the outline.
    3. Write a concluding sentence that connects back to the topic sentence.
- Write the third and fourth paragraphs of your essay using the same procedure.
- Write a concluding paragraph of three or four sentences that summarizes the major ideas of your essay and restates your thesis statement in some way.

Part 3: Revise and Refine

- Read back through the whole essay.
    - ♦ Did you answer the essay question?
    - ♦ Are all your ideas clearly written?
    - ♦ Does each paragraph have a topic sentence?
    - ♦ Do all sentences in each paragraph relate to the topic sentence?

- Make any changes now, and then make sure your essay follows this format:

  Paragraph 1 – Introduction that includes the thesis statement
  Paragraph 2 – First reason you selected the individual
  Paragraph 3 – Second reason you selected the individual
  Paragraph 4 – Third reason you selected the individual
  Paragraph 5 – Conclusion that summarizes the main ideas and restates the thesis

- Correct any spelling, grammar, or punctuation mistakes you see. Reading your essay aloud will help you spot errors.
- Share your essay with an adult.

Student Guide
Lesson 13: (Optional) Your Choice

You may use today's lesson time to do one or more of the following:

- Complete work in progress.
- Prepare for your state standardized test.
- See if you can name and locate the state capitals in the U.S. State Capitals Quiz or on the outline map.
- Go on to the next lesson.

Please mark this lesson complete in order to proceed to the next lesson in the course.

Lesson Objectives

- Explore knowledge and skills taught in this course.

PREPARE

Approximate lesson time is 60 minutes.

Materials

For the Student

Map of the United States

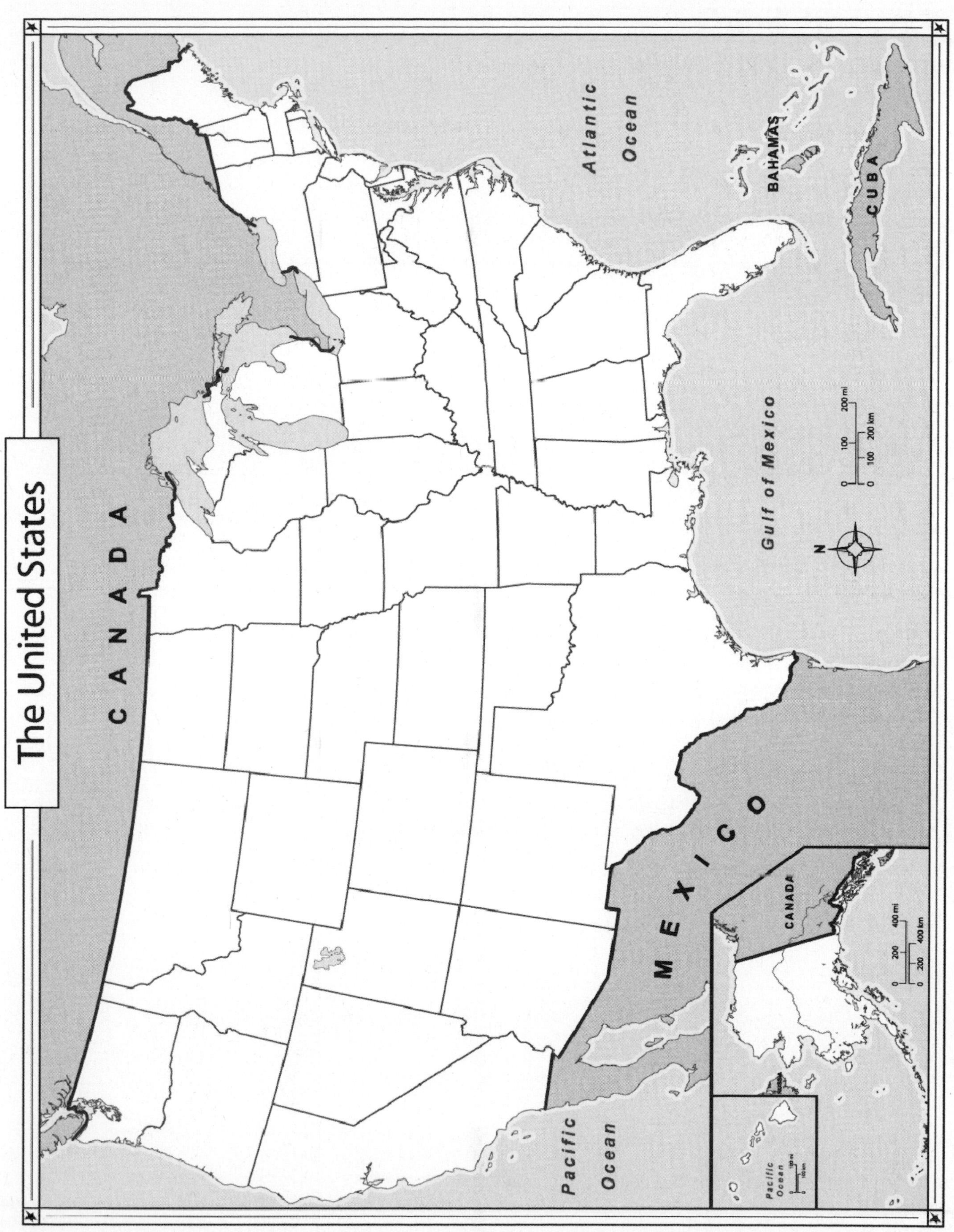
The United States
CANADA
Atlantic Ocean
BAHAMAS
CUBA
Gulf of Mexico
0 100 200 mi
0 100 200 km
N
MEXICO
Pacific Ocean
CANADA
0 200 400 mi
0 200 400 km
Pacific Ocean

Student Guide
Lesson 14: Unit Review

You have finished the unit! It's time to review what you've learned. You will take the Unit Assessment in the next lesson.

Lesson Objectives

- Demonstrate mastery of important knowledge and skills in this unit.

PREPARE

Approximate lesson time is 60 minutes.

Materials

For the Student

History Journal

LEARN

Activity 1: A Look Back *(Online)*

Review the information in the unit. Start by reviewing your History Journal. Then continue with the online activities.

Instructions

A. History Journal Review

Review what you've learned in this unit by going through your History Journal.

- Look at activity sheets you completed for this unit.
- Review unit keywords and definitions.
- Read through any writing assignments you did during the unit.
- Review the assessments you took.

B. Online Review

Review the following online activities:

- Relief, Recovery, and Reform
- Fireside Chat
- Roosevelt's Promise
- Code Breaker 1
- Code Breaker 2

Student Guide
Lesson 15: Unit Assessment

You've finished the unit! Now it's time to take the Unit Assessment.

Lesson Objectives

- Compare and contrast the political philosophies of Herbert Hoover and Franklin Roosevelt.
- Identify individuals (and their actions) who promoted or diminished the ideals of democracy during the 1930s.
- Give examples of the growing role of government during the Great Depression and how that continues today.
- Describe the weaknesses in the U.S. economy in the late 1920s that helped cause the Great Depression.
- Identify social, political, and economic problems the nation faced in 1933 and FDR's response to them.

PREPARE

Approximate lesson time is 60 minutes.

ASSESS

Unit Assessment: Hard Times (*Online*)

You will complete an online assessment covering the main points of this unit. Your assessment will be scored by the computer.

Student Guide

Unit 9: The Second World War
Lesson 1: Dictating Disaster

Dictators in Europe and Asia used hatred and violence to gain power and territory. The very existence of democracy was in peril. For two years, the United States stayed out of the fray, though FDR did everything he could to help Great Britain hold out against the enemy. But the Japanese attack on Pearl Harbor brought Americans into the war suddenly and completely, and unleashed the energy and determination of a "sleeping giant."

Adolf Hitler was a small man with a black mustache and a knack for playing on people's worst fears. Benito Mussolini was a pompous bully who picked on those who were weak. During the worldwide economic depression that followed the Great War, those men and others made a career of promoting fear and hatred among their countrymen. Under their leadership, nations turned into militant dictatorships bent on taking over the world.

Lesson Objectives

- Describe the problems in Germany that led to the rise of Adolf Hitler.
- Identify nations that became dictatorships during the 1930s and the dictators who led them.
- Recognize the difference between totalitarian and democratic states in terms of the importance of the state versus the importance of the people.

PREPARE

Approximate lesson time is 60 minutes.

Materials

For the Student

Dictating Disaster

A History of US (Concise Edition), Volume D (1929 to Present) by Joy Hakim

History Journal

Keywords and Pronunciation

Benito Mussolini (beh-NEE-toh moos-soh-LEE-nee)

communism : a political and economic system in which the people own goods and businesses in common, but the government manages and controls them

fascism (FA-shih-zuhm) : a political philosophy that values nation or race above the individual and promotes a centralized dictatorship

Hideki Tojo (hee-DEHK-ee TOH-joh)

nationalism : a philosophy that promotes one nation above all others and values that nation's culture and interests more than others

Nazism (NAHT-sih-zuhm) : the political and economic doctrines of the National Socialist German Workers' Party, which promoted totalitarian government, state control of industry, racial superiority of certain groups, and the supremacy of its leader

reparations : something done or given as amends or payment of damages

totalitarian (toh-TA-luh-TAIR-ee-uhn)

totalitarian state : a government that attempts to subject the citizen to an absolute state authority
Treaty of Versailles : the treaty ending World War I, which placed blame for the war and demands for financial reparations on Germany
Versailles (vuhr-SIY)

LEARN

Activity 1: More, More, More *(Offline)*

Instructions

A. Read *(Chapter 6, pages 24–29)*

- Answer Questions 2–3 on the Dictating Disaster sheet. Complete Question 1 when you review the Dictator Flash Cards later in the lesson. When you have finished, have an adult compare your answers with those in the Lesson Answer Key.
- Define the following terms and write the definitions in your History Journal. When you have finished, compare your definitions with those in the Keywords section.

communism
fascism (FA-shih-zuhm)
Nazism (NAHT-sih-zuhm)

B. Use What You Know

- Review the Dictator Flash Cards and complete Question 1 on the Dictating Disaster sheet.
- Then complete the online Code Breaker activities to compare the qualities of democratic and totalitarian governments.

ASSESS

Lesson Assessment: Dictating Disaster *(Online)*

You will complete an online assessment covering the main points of this lesson. Your assessment will be scored by the computer.

Name ______________________ Date ______________________

Dictating Disaster

1. The people listed below played a key role in the events described in this and the following chapters. Identify each person, where he is from, and what he did to increase global conflict.

   A. Adolf Hitler

   Country: ______________________

   Actions: ______________________

   B. Francisco Franco

   Country: ______________________

   Actions: ______________________

   C. Benito Mussolini

   Country: ______________________

   Actions: ______________________

   D. Joseph Stalin

   Country: ______________________

   Actions: ______________________

   E. Hideki Tojo

   Country: ______________________

   Actions: ______________________

2. Define the following terms and explain the relationship of each to the rise of Adolf Hitler:

A. Nazism

Definition: ______________________________

____

____

Relationship: ______________________________

____

____

B. Treaty of Versailles (vuhr-SIY)

Definition: ______________________________

____

____

Relationship: ______________________________

____

____

C. Reparations

Definition: ______________________________

____

____

Relationship: ______________________________

____

____

D. Nationalism

Definition: ______________________________

____

____

Relationship: ______________________________

____

____

E. Totalitarian (toh-TA-luh-TAIR-ee-uhn) state

Definition: ______________________________

____

____

Relationship: ______________________________

____

____

F. The Great Depression

Definition: ______________________________

____

____

Relationship: ______________________________

____

____

3. Learn from Maps

The Axis nations of German, Italy, and Japan began relentless campaigns of expansion during the 1920s and 1930s. Study the maps on page 29 and identify some of these expanded areas.

Germany: ____________________

Italy: ____________________

Japan: ____________________

Student Guide
Lesson 2: Hatred in Action

As economic depression ravaged Europe after the war, the German people looked around for someone to blame. Jews had been the target of hostility and discrimination for hundreds of years. Adolf Hitler used that anti-Semitism and people's fear to gain power. Whatever was wrong with Germany must be the fault of the Jews, he said. As Hitler began ruthlessly destroying Europe's Jews, racism within other nations kept the world largely silent.

Lesson Objectives

- Recognize the history and persistence of anti-Semitism and Hitler's use of anti-Semitism.
- Define *final solution* as it refers to Hitler's plan.
- Identify the purpose of Hitler's concentration camps.
- Recognize that groups other than Jews that Hitler deemed "undesirable" were also sent to concentration camps.
- Describe the controversy over letting large numbers of Jewish refugees enter the United States and the outcome of the controversy.

PREPARE

Approximate lesson time is 60 minutes.

Materials

For the Student

A History of US (Concise Edition), Volume D (1929 to Present) by Joy Hakim

History Journal

Keywords and Pronunciation

anti-Semitism (AN-tee-SEH-muh-tih-zuhm) : hostility toward or discrimination against Jews as a religious, ethnic, or racial group

Auschwitz (OWSH-vitz)

Kristallnacht (KRIHS-tahl-nahkt)

Maidanek (MIYDN-ehk)

refugee : a person who flees to another area, country, or power to escape danger or persecution

xenophobia (zee-nuh-FOH-bee-uh) : fear and hatred of strangers or foreigners or of anything that is strange or foreign

LEARN

Activity 1: When They Come for Me *(Offline)*

Instructions

A. Read (*Chapter 7, pages 30–37*)

- Answer the following questions in your History Journal. When you have finished, compare your answers to those in the Lesson Answer Key.

  1. What is anti-Semitism?
  2. What does the author suggest are some of the possible beginnings of anti-Semitism?
  3. What other groups that Hitler deemed "undesirable" were also sent to concentration camps?
  4. What was Hitler's "final solution" to anti-Semitism?
  5. Why did the United States block the entry of large numbers of Jewish refugees?

- Define the following terms. When you have finished, check your definitions against those in the Keywords section.

refugee
xenophobia (zee-nuh-FOH-bee-uh)

B. Making Connections

- View the online Art Gallery. These are images reflecting the situations and emotions of the people of the Holocaust.
- Pretend you live in the United States in the late 1930s. In your History Journal, write a letter to the editor of the newspaper explaining why the United States should accept the 20,000 children fleeing from Nazi persecution *(pages 34–37)*.

ASSESS

Lesson Assessment: Hatred in Action (*Online*)

You will complete an online assessment covering the main goals of this lesson. Your assessment will be scored by the computer.

LEARN

Activity 2. Optional: Hatred in Action *(Online)*

Student Guide
Lesson 3: Why War?

While Axis armies picked off one nation after another, democratic countries stood by, immobilized by fear and indecision. Most Americans thought they were safe, separated from Europe and Asia by two vast oceans. But as science and technology began to play a larger role in the war, Americans realized that the battleground was not overseas—it was right in their own backyard.

Lesson Objectives

- Recognize the role of science and scientists in determining the outcome of World War II.
- Summarize the arguments of isolationists, pacifists, and people like Billy Mitchell and FDR in the debate over U.S. policy in the 1930s.

PREPARE

Approximate lesson time is 60 minutes.

Materials

For the Student

A History of US (Concise Edition), Volume D (1929 to Present) by Joy Hakim

History Journal

Keywords and Pronunciation

Allies : the nations, led by Great Britain, the U.S., and the U.S.S.R., that united against the Axis powers in World War II

axis : the three powers--Germany, Italy, and Japan--that engaged the Allies in World War II

isolationist : a person who believes that his nation should stay out of world affairs

Lend-Lease : a program to lend equipment and raw materials to help the Allies fight the war in Europe

pacifist (PA-suh-fist) : a person who is opposed to the use of force under any circumstance

---

LEARN

Activity 1: The Science of War *(Offline)*

Instructions

A. Read *(Chapter 8, pages 38–39; Chapter 9, pages 40–43)*

- Answer the following questions. When you have finished, compare your answers to those in the Answer Key.

1. How did the flight of scientists from totalitarian nations affect the outcome of the war?
2. What are some of the countries that scientists left to go to the United States?
3. What was Einstein asked to do to support the Allied countries in the war?
4. Why did totalitarian leaders look down on democratic nations?
5. What role did isolationism and pacifism play when people in the United States debated whether the country should join the war?

6. What advice did Colonel Billy Mitchell give to the United States?
7. How did Americans receive his advice?
8. Where did FDR stand on the issue of a coming war?

- Define these terms. When you have finished, compare your definitions with those in the Keywords section.

Allies
Axis
isolationist
pacifist

B. Focus on Civics

In your History Journal, write a letter to the editor reacting to the court-martial of Billy Mitchell. Consider the following questions as you write. What was Mitchell's argument? Should he have been court-martialed for criticizing his bosses in public? Should the government have listened to him? Were his ideas "laughable," as some people said? Why do you think the government was willing to listen to Einstein but not to Mitchell?

ASSESS

Lesson Assessment: Why War? (*Online*)

You will complete an online assessment covering the main goals of this lesson. The assessment will be scored by the computer.

Student Guide
Lesson 4: War

In the early hours of December 7, 1941, Japanese planes rained bombs on a U.S. military base in Pearl Harbor, Hawaii, inflicting terrible damage on nearly the entire Pacific fleet in a surprise attack. With America's entry into the war, the battle against totalitarianism would touch nearly every continent.

Click the images of Winston Churchill and Franklin D. Roosevelt to listen to excerpts from two important speeches made during the war. In the first, Churchill, Britain's prime minister, rallies his country during its darkest hour. In the second, Roosevelt addresses Congress the day after Japan attacked Pearl Harbor.

Lesson Objectives

- Identify the German invasion of Poland in 1939 as the event that triggered World War II.
- Identify the Japanese attack on Pearl Harbor in 1941 as the cause of U.S. entry into World War II.
- Describe the background to and conduct of the war prior to December 7, 1941.

PREPARE

Approximate lesson time is 60 minutes.

Materials

For the Student

A History of US (Concise Edition), Volume D (1929 to Present) by Joy Hakim

History Journal

Keywords and Pronunciation

blitzkrieg (BLITS-kreeg) : German for "lightning war," a new type of warfare used by German forces in World War II in which troops, tanks, and artillery quickly sped across nations

---

LEARN

Activity 1: The United States Enters the War *(Offline)*

Instructions

A. Read *(Chapter 10, pages 44–48)*

As you read, take notes in your History Journal. Include the following:

1. Significant events that led to Britain and France entering the war.
2. The major events of the war before Japan attacked Pearl Harbor.
3. Events that led to the attack on Pearl Harbor and the United States entering the war.

B. Use What You Know

Americans learned what was happening in the war from newsreels, newspaper articles, and radio broadcasts. Click Germany's Lightning War to see some newsreels that chronicle Germany's blitzkrieg (BLITS-kreeg) across Europe.

Perhaps the best-known radio correspondent of World War II was Edward R. Murrow. In 1937, CBS sent Murrow to set up a network of correspondents to report on the gathering storm in Europe. He and his group of young reporters ended up reporting the entire war from the front lines. Listeners in America and around the world tuned their radios to listen to these amazing reports.

Write a short report to broadcast over the airwaves, highlighting the significant events leading up to the war and events of the war. Use the notes you took while reading the chapter to help you prepare your report. If you have a tape recorder, record your report when you've finished.

Check the Lesson Answer Key to make sure you included the most important events in your broadcast.

C. Focus on Geography

Click Hitler Is Appeased to see the territory taken by Hitler as a result of Europe's policy of appeasement. Then click Interactive Map: 1919–1945 to explore the European and Pacific theaters of war. Locate the areas that were under Axis control in 1942.

ASSESS

Lesson Assessment: War (*Online*)

You will complete an online assessment covering the main goals of this lesson. Your assessment will be scored by the computer.

LEARN

Activity 2. Optional: War *(Online)*

Student Guide
Lesson 5: Who Was Who?

Anyone who has ever read Hitler's writings knows what Hitler had in mind—he wanted to rule the world. After taking over two countries that neighbored Germany, he joined forces with Soviet leader Joseph Stalin to occupy a third. But Hitler never intended to share his power. Two years after signing a friendship pact with Stalin, he did something sneaky—he turned his army loose on the Soviet Union. This single act of betrayal was destined to change the world.

Lesson Objectives

- Demonstrate knowledge gained in previous lessons.
- Identify the major nations involved in World War II, their capitals, and their leaders as either Axis or Allied powers.
- Explain the factors that led to an alliance between the Allies and the Soviet Union.
- Identify nations that became dictatorships during the 1930s and the dictators who led them.
- Recognize the difference between totalitarian and democratic states in terms of the importance of the state versus the importance of the people.
- Recognize isolationism as a deterrent to U.S. participation in the war and its end with the attack at Pearl Harbor

---

PREPARE

Approximate lesson time is 60 minutes.

Materials

For the Student

Who Was Who?

A History of US (Concise Edition), Volume D (1929 to Present) by Joy Hakim

History Journal

Keywords and Pronunciation

ally (A-liy)

LEARN

Activity 1: An Unlikely Ally *(Offline)*

Instructions

A. Read *(Chapter 11, pages 49–53)*

As you read, complete the Who Was Who? sheet. Compare your answer with the answers in the Lesson Answer Key and place the completed sheet in your History Journal.

B. Discuss

Great Britain, the United States, and the Soviet Union became allies in the war despite shared hostility and a deep-seated mistrust. Many people thought the Allies should have tried to defeat Hitler without Stalin's help.

Discuss with an adult the ethics of allying with Stalin.

ASSESS

Lesson Assessment: Who Was Who? *(Online)*

You will complete an online assessment covering the main points of this lesson. Your assessment will be scored by the computer.

Name ______________________ Date ______________________

Who Was Who?

1. In 1939, Hitler and Stalin signed the Nazi-Soviet Pact. A pact is a treaty or an agreement. What did Hitler and Stalin agree to?

____

2. One of them broke the pact. Who was it?

____

3. What did he do?

____

4. Why did he do this?

____

5. After the pact was broken, who did Stalin join?

____

6. Complete the charts below.

Axis Powers in 1942

Capital	Country	Leader
Berlin		Adolf Hitler
	Japan	General Hideki Tojo
Rome		

Major Allies in 1942

Capital	Country	Leader
Washington, D.C.	United States	Franklin Roosevelt
London		

Student Guide
Lesson 6: Democracy Defended

Have you ever tried writing in code? During World War II, Axis and Allied forces made code writing into an art. Cryptographers created complex secret languages that helped troops communicate battle plans without letting the enemy know what they were up to. The war inspired many new inventions as well. Some were vehicles that could transport troops into difficult-to-reach locations. Others were weapons that made warfare deadlier than ever.

Lesson Objectives

- Describe ways in which the use of airpower changed warfare.
- Recognize the role of codes and code breakers in World War II.
- Give examples of technical innovations and scientific discoveries that came about because of the war's challenges.
- Summarize the difficulties of fighting a two-front war.

PREPARE

Approximate lesson time is 60 minutes.

Materials

For the Student

Necessity Is the Mother of Invention

A History of US (Concise Edition), Volume D (1929 to Present) by Joy Hakim

History Journal

Keywords and Pronunciation

amphibious (am-FIH-bee-uhs) : able to travel on land or in water

cryptography (krihp-TAH-gruh-fee) : making and using secret codes

front : a zone of conflict between armies

LEARN

Activity 1: A Global Conflict *(Offline)*

Instructions

A. Read *(Chapter 12, pages 54–57, and Chapter 13, pages 58–60)*

Answer the following questions as you read about how the war's challenges brought about technical innovations.

1. How did airpower change warfare?

____

____

2. What innovations and inventions came about as people tried to meet the challenges of fighting World War II?

____

____

3. What is cryptography (krihp-TAH-gruh-fee)? How was it used during the war? Which side had a code that no one was ever able to break? What was this code based on? (page 57)

____

____

____

4. What were two problems that fighting a two-front war posed to U.S. generals and admirals?

____

____

5. Who was the United States fighting in the Pacific Theater?

____

6. Who was the United States fighting in the European Theater?

____

7. What three naval battles did the United States win in the Pacific in 1942?

____

B. Use What You Know

Complete the Necessity Is the Mother of Invention sheet. Check your work and place the completed assignment in your History Journal.

C. Focus on Geography

Click the online Interactive Map: 1919–1945. Click World War II and explore the map of the Pacific Theater.

Use the Word Bank to answer the following questions:

1. Which battle took place near an island located northwest of the Hawaiian Islands? _______________

2. Which battle took place in the Solomon Islands? _______________

3. Which battle took place in the waters off the northeastern coast of Australia? _______________

Word Bank: Guadalcanal; Battle of the Coral Sea; Battle of Midway

ASSESS

Lesson Assessment: Democracy Defended (*Online*)

You will complete an online assessment covering the main objectives of this lesson. Your assessment will be scored by the computer.

Name Date

Necessity Is the Mother of Invention

Have you ever heard the expression "Necessity is the mother of invention"? The saying originated from the fact that when people are in need, they often invent something to fill that need. For example, the Midwestern meat industry needed a way to keep meat from spoiling so they could ship it to markets in the East. This necessity was the mother of an invention—refrigerated railroad cars.

People often invent things in times of war. After the war is over, civilians may end up using these inventions for peaceful purposes. Unfortunately, some inventions have no other purpose than to kill the enemy more effectively.

Below is a list of problems faced by those who fought World War II. Beside each problem, list innovations or inventions that people came up with to solve the problem.

Problem	Inventions/Innovations
1. How to get troops and equipment onto Pacific islands quickly	
2. How to destroy submarines	
3. How to travel places on rough roads, mountain passes, and rutted fields	
4. How to make blood and blood plasma available to wounded soldiers	
5. How to communicate with fighting units without letting the enemy know what you're saying	

Student Guide
Lesson 7: (Optional) Your Choice

You may use today's lesson time to do one or more of the following:

- Complete work in progress.
- Prepare for your state standardized test.
- Visit two websites to learn more about the homefront during World War II (Produce For Victory and The Perilous Fight).
- See if you can name and locate the state capitals in the U.S. State Capitals Quiz.
- Go on to the next lesson.

Please mark this lesson complete in order to proceed to the next lesson in the course.

Lesson Objectives

- Explore knowledge and skills taught in this course.

PREPARE

Approximate lesson time is 60 minutes.

Materials

For the Student

Map of the United States

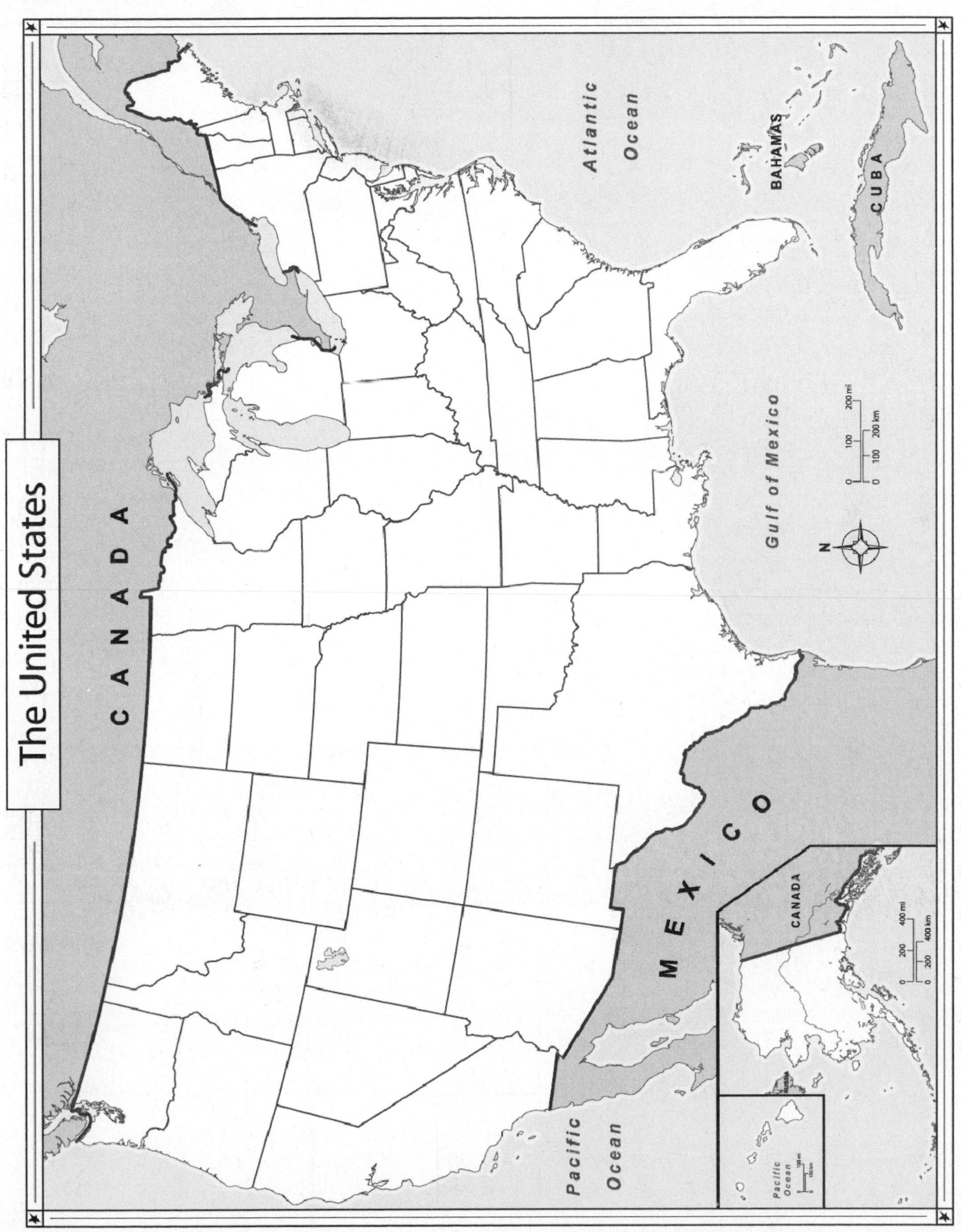
The United States
CANADA
MEXICO
Atlantic Ocean
Pacific Ocean
Gulf of Mexico
BAHAMAS
CUBA
N

Student Guide
Lesson 8: Democracy Denied

After the attack on Pearl Harbor, Americans began to fear everyone who was Japanese or of Japanese descent, afraid they were secretly supporting the enemy. The mistrust grew so great that, eventually, the government sent all Japanese Americans to detention camps. Forced to leave most of their possessions behind, they got by on the meager resources the camps provided. "They gave us a horse stable the size of our dining room with a divided door where the horse put his head out," said one Japanese-American girl. "That was our sleeping quarters."

Lesson Objectives

- Describe the causes and results of the detention of Japanese Americans, as well as the experiences of those who were detained.

PREPARE

Approximate lesson time is 60 minutes.

Materials

For the Student

A History of US (Concise Edition), Volume D (1929 to Present) by Joy Hakim

History Journal

Keywords and Pronunciation

habeas corpus (HAY-bee-uhs KOR-puhs) : the right of a citizen to obtain a legal order written by a court or judge as a protection against illegal imprisonment

Nisei (NEE-say) : a child of Japanese immigrants who was born in the United States

---

LEARN

Activity 1: Forgetting the Constitution *(Offline)*

Instructions

A. Read *(Chapter 14, pages 61–65)*

Read about how the American government denied democracy to approximately 120,000 Japanese and Americans of Japanese ancestry during World War II.

B. Use What You Know

General John DeWitt, the official in charge of the relocation of Japanese and Americans of Japanese ancestry made this statement:

"It makes no difference whether a Japanese is theoretically a citizen. He is still a Japanese. Giving him a scrap of paper won't change him."

Imagine you are a Nisei (NEE-say) serving in the "Go for Broke" 442nd Infantry Division fighting in Europe. In your History Journal, write a rebuttal to General DeWitt's statement.

A *rebuttal* is an argument that proves something is not true or contradicts and opposes something. In this case, your rebuttal should contradict DeWitt's statement. It should show that his statement is false.

C. Read On *(Chapter 15, pages 66–69; Chapter 16, pages 70–75)*
As you read, make a list in your History Journal of all the events that occurred in 1943 that will make an eventual Allied victory possible.

ASSESS

Lesson Assessment: Democracy Denied (*Online*)

You will complete an online assessment covering the main objectives of this lesson. Your assessment will be scored by the computer.

LEARN

Activity 2. Optional: Democracy Denied *(Online)*

Student Guide
Lesson 9: Strategies

The battle for Guadalcanal shattered Japanese illusions of military superiority. The U.S. victory at the remote tropical island of Guadalcanal changed the Pacific conflict into an offensive war aimed at breaking Japan's grip on Asia. Soon, the conflict in Europe began to change direction as well. Cracks began to appear in the Axis defense system, and German troops braced for an Allied invasion.

Lesson Objectives

- Recognize Guadalcanal as a strategic island, and the Battle of Guadalcanal as a turning point in terms of the Allies' move from defensive to offensive fighting.
- Use maps to evaluate the options for invading Nazi Germany.
- Recognize the events of 1943 that would make an eventual Allied victory possible.

PREPARE

Approximate lesson time is 60 minutes.

Materials

For the Student

Taking the Offensive

A History of US (Concise Edition), Volume D (1929 to Present) by Joy Hakim

History Journal

Keywords and Pronunciation

Guadalcanal (gwahd-l-kuh-NAL)

Pas-de-Calais (pahd-kah-LAY)

LEARN

Activity 1: Taking the Offensive *(Offline)*

Instructions

A. Check Your Reading *(Chapter 15, pages 66–69; Chapter 16, pages 70–75)*

Check your reading by completing the Taking the Offensive sheet.

B. Use What You Know

Japan's military leaders viewed Guadalcanal as a strategic island in the Pacific. From an airbase on this tropical island, Japan could directly threaten Australia and New Zealand. The United States also realized the strategic importance of Guadalcanal. U.S. military commanders decided to go on the offensive to keep Japan from completing an airbase there.

Imagine you are a war correspondent covering the Pacific Theater. Write an article about Guadalcanal that is at least two paragraphs long. Use the technique most journalists use and begin your article with a *lead*—a short paragraph that answers most or all of the questions *who, what, where, when,* and *why* ("the five W's"), as well as *how.* The purpose of the lead is to get the reader's attention and quickly state the most important facts of the story. The paragraphs following the lead should provide additional details.

Be sure your article explains the importance of Guadalcanal and the outcome of the battle there.

C. Beyond the Lesson

You might enjoy learning more about Guadalcanal by reading *Guadalcanal Diary* by Richard Tregaskis (Random House, 1984).

ASSESS

Lesson Assessment: Strategies (*Online*)

You will complete an online assessment covering the main objectives of this lesson. Your assessment will be scored by the computer.

Name Date

Taking the Offensive

Early in 1943, the Allies "reached the end of the beginning." Several things happened that year that set the stage for an eventual victory by the Allies. Complete the time line below by writing a newspaper headline for each major event described by the clue. Check your work with examples given in the Lesson Answer Key.

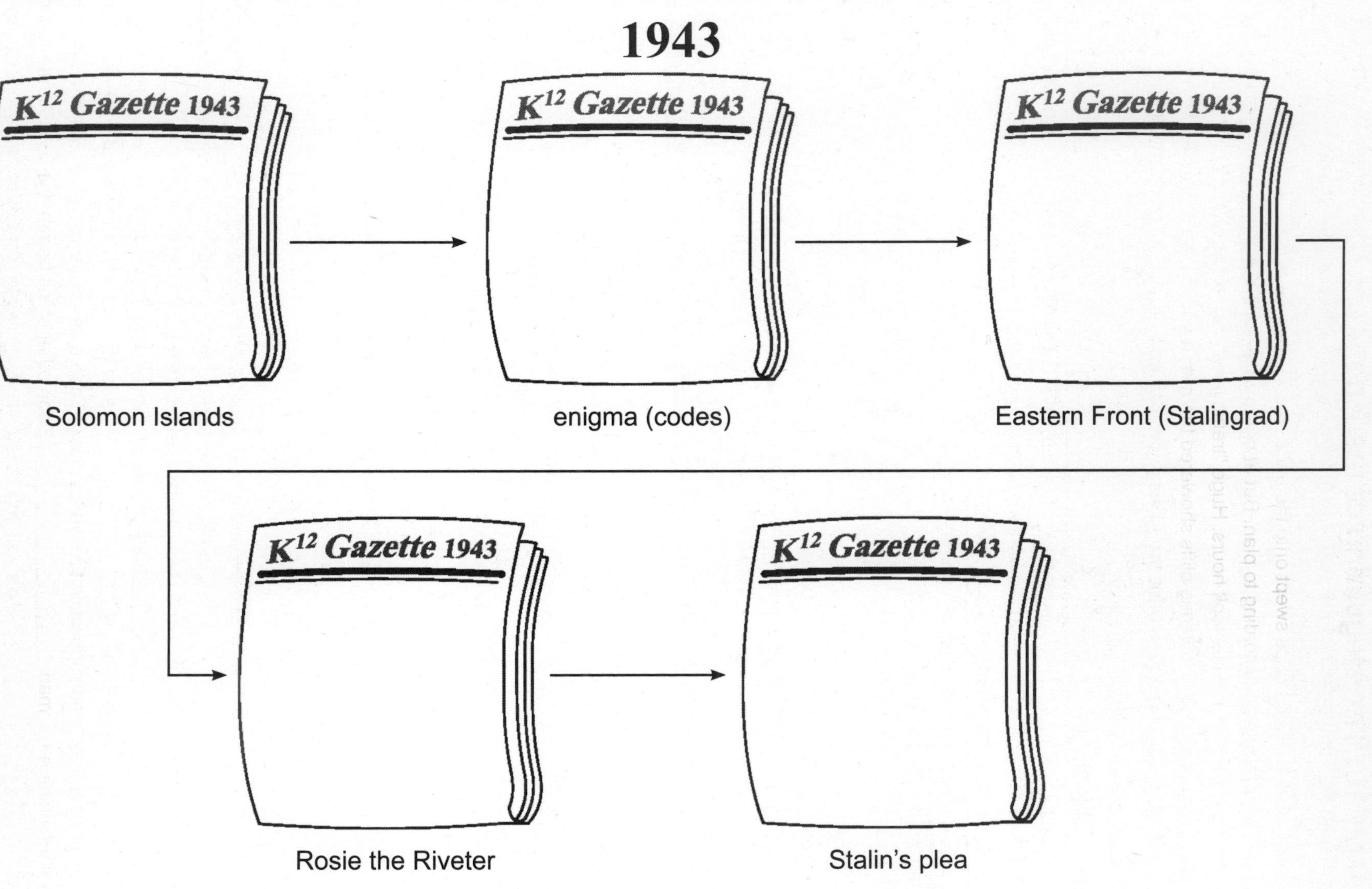

Student Guide
Lesson 10: The Beginning of the End

On June 6, 1944, Allied troops swept onto the mine-strewn beaches of northwestern France. In some places things went more or less according to plan. But at one beach—with the code name Omaha—the landing that was supposed to take minutes took hours. Huge "traffic jams" formed as soldiers and equipment tried to come ashore. Nazi gunners atop towering cliffs showered the men with a constant spray of bullets. By nightfall, thousands of soldiers were dead, but the Allies had taken the beaches. For the Axis, it was the beginning of the end.

Lesson Objectives

- Identify Dwight D. Eisenhower as the Supreme Allied Commander who was in charge of the invasion.
- Describe the D-Day invasion in terms of planning, strategy, and human sacrifice.

PREPARE

Approximate lesson time is 60 minutes.

Materials

For the Student

A History of US (Concise Edition), Volume D (1929 to Present) by Joy Hakim

History Journal

Keywords and Pronunciation

Pas-de-Calais (pahd-kah-LAY)

LEARN

Activity 1: D-Day *(Offline)*

Instructions

A. Read *(Chapter 17, from the beginning to "A Wartime Diary," pages 76–79)*
Imagine it's June 7, D-Day-plus-1. You are among the troops that took part in the landing at Omaha Beach. You have time to write a quick diary entry before your squad moves out. Complete the diary entry below by filling in the blanks.

June 7, 1944
I can't believe I'm alive! The fighting yesterday was the worst I've ever seen. Even though the weather was bad, General __________________, the Supreme Allied Commander who was in charge of the invasion, decided to go ahead with the attack. Our fleet was awesome! It was the largest __________________ ever assembled. At __________________ Beach, one of the two beaches where our guys landed, things didn't go well at all. There were a lot of __________________: most of our tanks sank, bombs missed their targets, and gliders dropped men and supplies in the wrong place. Then a destroyer came up near the beach and landed a shell right inside a German __________________. Soon other ships began shelling German gunners in the concrete __________________. This was the break we needed. We were finally able to move up and secure the beach.

B. Review

Use the following online activities to review for a future multi-lesson assessment:

- Get a Clue: Guadalcanal
- Get a Clue: An Unlikely Ally

C. Read On *(Chapter 17, "A Wartime Diary, pages 80–81)*

ASSESS

Lesson Assessment: The Beginning of the End (*Online*)

You will complete an online assessment covering the main objectives of this lesson. Your assessment will be scored by the computer.

Student Guide
Lesson 11: Closing In

The rapid-fire events of 1945 made it clear that the Axis didn't have a chance of winning the war. Yet neither Germany nor Japan would surrender. Instead they retreated to their home countries to wage a desperate fight to the finish.

Lesson Objectives

- Demonstrate knowledge gained in previous lessons.
- Identify the Atlantic Charter and the Yalta Conference as steps toward planning the post-war era.
- Identify Franklin Roosevelt as the only president to serve more than two terms.
- Describe FDR's goals for the end of the war.
- Describe the characteristics and experience Truman brought to the presidency.
- Identify the major nations involved in World War II, their capitals, and their leaders as either Axis or Allied powers.
- Explain the factors that led to an alliance between the Allies and the Soviet Union.
- Describe the causes and results of the detention of Japanese Americans, as well as the experiences of those who were detained.
- Recognize Guadalcanal as a strategic island, and the Battle of Guadalcanal as a turning point in terms of the Allies' move from defensive to offensive fighting.

PREPARE

Approximate lesson time is 60 minutes.

Materials

For the Student

A History of US (Concise Edition), Volume D (1929 to Present) by Joy Hakim

History Journal

Keywords and Pronunciation

Guadalcanal (gwahd-l-kuh-NAL)

LEARN

Activity 1: 1945 *(Offline)*

Instructions

A. Check Your Reading *(Chapter 17, "A Wartime Diary," pages 80–81)*

Summarize what you've read in "A Wartime Diary" by completing the following statements.

1. The German army's last offensive on the western front takes place in ________________ at the Battle of the ________________.
2. FDR is inaugurated for a fourth term. No other president has served more than ________ terms.
3. By February, thousands of Allied bombers are making bombing runs to ________________.

4. In February, Roosevelt meets with __________________ and __________________ to plan for the final battles of the war. They agree that the countries of the world should meet in April to form the ____________________________. Their meeting came to be known as the _________ conference.
5. General __________________________________ returns to the Philippines.
6. The air war takes an enormous toll on civilian populations as Allied bombers fly to cities in _____________ and _______________ dropping thousands of bombs.
7. In the face of obvious defeat, Germany and Japan refuse to __________________.

B. Read *(Chapter 18, pages 82–84; Chapter 19, pages 85–86)*

As you read, complete the following. Check your answers with the answers in the Lesson Answer Key.

1. FDR heads to Georgia for a much-needed break. He's concerned about the postwar world. Soon after the war started, he and Churchill signed a document called the __________________. It said that after the war, nations would have the right to _______-_______________.
2. Roosevelt wants to end the old, before-the-war _______________ ways. He believed that people should be free to _____________ themselves.
3. Roosevelt wanted the war to have meaning. He wanted to go beyond the defeat of Nazi Germany, to an end of not only World War II, but also an "end to the beginnings of all _____________."
4. Harry S. Truman became the president after FDR's death. Describe some of Truman's personal characteristics and political experiences he brought to the presidency.

C. Assessment

Complete the online assessment.

ASSESS

Lesson Assessment: Closing In (*Online*)

You will complete an online assessment covering the main points of this lesson. Your assessment will be scored by the computer.

Student Guide
Lesson 12: End of an Era

As Roosevelt entered his fourth term, he began mapping out plans for peace. But FDR never saw his ideas tested. His death thrust the job of ending the war and designing a peace into the lap of Harry Truman. Roosevelt's death triggered a mass outpouring of grief rivaled only by the tear-filled tribute paid to another wartime president—Abraham Lincoln.

Lesson Objectives

- Give examples of FDR's accomplishments as president from 1933 to 1945.
- Recognize concentration camps as examples of the evils of totalitarian government.

PREPARE

Approximate lesson time is 60 minutes.

Materials

For the Student

A History of US (Concise Edition), Volume D (1929 to Present) by Joy Hakim

History Journal

LEARN

Activity 1: A Nation Mourns *(Offline)*

Instructions

A. Read *(Chapter 20, pages 87–94)*

As you read, answer the following questions. Compare your answers with the answers in the Lesson Answer Key.

1. List at least four of FDR's achievements as president.
2. How did the Allies react as they discovered more and more concentration camps?
3. Approximately how many people died in the concentration camps?
4. In which concentration camp did Anne Frank die as a prisoner? How do we know so much about Anne Frank and her family?
5. What brought an end to the totalitarian leadership of Mussolini and Hitler in April 1945?

B. Use What You Know

Congress established the Franklin Delano Roosevelt Memorial Commission in 1955. Forty-two years later, on May 2, 1997, the memorial was dedicated in Washington, D.C.

Imagine you are a congressman in 1955, arguing for the creation of a memorial to FDR. List all the reasons you can think of for building a memorial. Review the chapter if you need help thinking of reasons.

When you have finished, compare your list with the one given in the Lesson Answer Key.

C. Beyond the Lesson ***(Optional)***

Check your library or local bookstore for *The Franklin Delano Roosevelt Memorial (Cornerstones of Freedom)*, by Anne Phillips (Children's Press, 2000). This book tells the story of the Washington, D.C., monument to one of America's greatest presidents. It includes a short biography of Roosevelt and many photographs.

ASSESS

Lesson Assessment: End of an Era (*Online*)

You will complete an online assessment covering the main objectives of this lesson. Your assessment will be scored by the computer.

Student Guide
Lesson 13: End of War

Within a month of Roosevelt's death, Germany had surrendered. The Allies pressured Japan to surrender as well, but the Japanese leaders dismissed the demand as "unworthy of public notice." In one of the most agonizing decisions in U.S. history, President Truman gave the go-ahead to use a new weapon that promised to be more deadly than any the world had ever seen.

Lesson Objectives

- Summarize the reasons for using the atomic bomb to end the war.
- Describe the destruction caused by the atomic bomb at Hiroshima.
- Recognize that the war in Europe ended before the war in the Pacific ended and before the atomic bomb had been tested.

PREPARE

Approximate lesson time is 60 minutes.

Advance Preparation

- Unit 13, Lesson 14, End of War, discusses the effects of the atomic bomb on Hiroshima. You may want to preview the lesson before you assign it to your student. The textbook contains graphic images and descriptions that may disturb some students. Be prepared to spend extra time discussing these difficult topics with your student.

Materials

For the Student

A History of US (Concise Edition), Volume D (1929 to Present) by Joy Hakim

History Journal

Keywords and Pronunciation

Hiroshima (hee-roh-SHEE-mah)

LEARN

Activity 1: Horrors of War *(Offline)*

Instructions

A. Read *(Chapter 21, pages 95–98)*

B. Use What You Know

Time Line: End of the War

Following up on what you've learned about the Second World War, place the events in the correct chronological order by numbering them 1–3 (with 1 being the event that occurred first).

____ The United States drops the atomic bomb on Japan.
____ The war in Europe ends.
____ The United States tests the atomic bomb.

When you have finished, check your answer with the Lesson Answer Key.

The Atomic Bomb

In your History Journal, list the reasons the United States gave for using the atomic bomb to end the war in the Pacific. Compare your reasons with the ones in the Lesson Answer Key.

C. Discuss

Discuss with an adult why the decision to use the atomic bomb was such a difficult one.

ASSESS

Lesson Assessment: End of War (*Online*)

You will complete an online assessment covering the main objectives of this lesson. Your assessment will be scored by the computer.

Student Guide
Lesson 14: A Beginning

By the middle of August 1945, Russian troops were closing in on Japan and the United States had dropped a second atomic bomb on the island nation. Faced with the choice of peace or the utter destruction of his country, Emperor Hirohito chose peace, and the world celebrated.

Lesson Objectives

- Describe the reaction of the American people to the end of the war and infer their hopes for the future.

PREPARE

Approximate lesson time is 60 minutes.

Materials

For the Student

End of War Picture Analysis

A History of US (Concise Edition), Volume D (1929 to Present) by Joy Hakim

History Journal

Keywords and Pronunciation

Hirohito (hihr-oh-HEE-toh)

LEARN

Activity 1: End of War *(Offline)*

Instructions

A. Read *(Chapter 22, pages 99–100)*

Read about Japan's surrender and the end of the war in the Pacific. As you read, think about how Americans felt about the end of the war and what they might want for the future.

B. Use What You Know

Print the End of War Picture Analysis sheet. Use it to help you analyze the bottom left photograph on page 100. Place your completed work in your History Journal.

ASSESS

Lesson Assessment: A Beginning *(Online)*

You will complete an online assessment covering the main points of this lesson. Your assessment will be scored by the computer.

Name Date

End of War Picture Analysis

Step 1. Observation

Look at the photograph on the bottom left of page 100. Study the photograph carefully. As you analyze it, what words come to mind?

Write down as many adjectives as you can think of that might describe the way Americans felt about the end of the war.

______

______

______

Step 2. Inference

Write a sentence that tells how Americans reacted to the end of the war.

______

______

______

Imagine that you were alive in 1945. You have lived through four years of U.S. involvement in the most destructive war in history. Thousands of soldiers will be coming home. You have seen people's reactions to the war's end. What are your hopes for the future?

______

______

______

Step 3. Questions

What questions, if any, does this photograph raise in your mind?

______

______

______

Student Guide
Lesson 15: (Optional) Your Choice

You may use today's lesson time to do one or more of the following:

- Complete work in progress.
- Prepare for your state standardized test.
- Visit two websites to learn more about the homefront during World War II (Produce For Victory and The Perilous Fight).
- See if you can name and locate the state capitals in the U.S. State Capitals Quiz.
- Go on to the next lesson.

Please mark this lesson complete in order to proceed to the next lesson in the course.

Lesson Objectives

- Explore knowledge and skills taught in this course.

PREPARE

Approximate lesson time is 60 minutes.

Materials

For the Student

Map of the United States

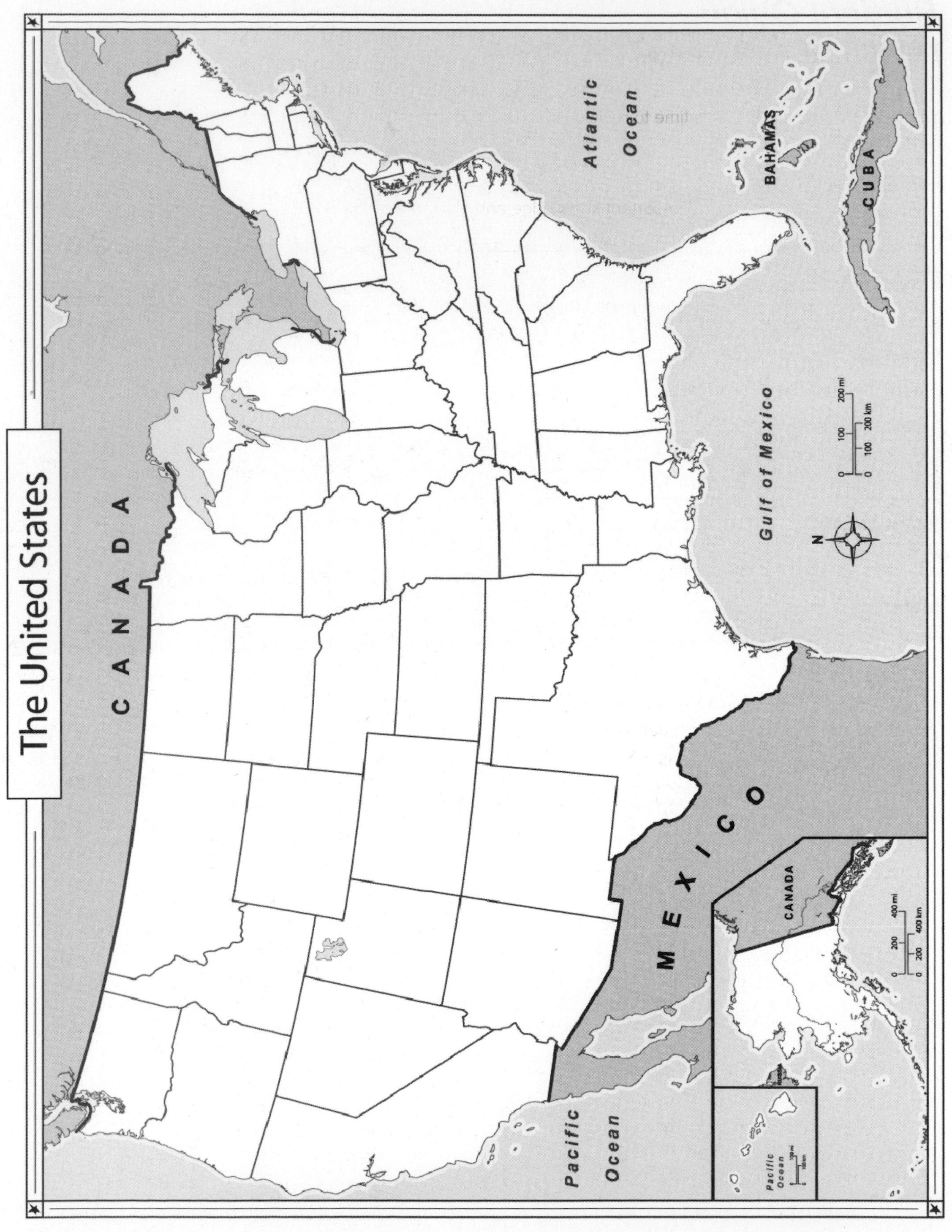
The United States
CANADA
MEXICO
Atlantic Ocean
Pacific Ocean
Gulf of Mexico
BAHAMAS
CUBA
N
0 100 200 mi
0 100 200 km
CANADA
0 200 400 mi
0 200 400 km
Pacific Ocean

Student Guide
Lesson 16: Unit Review

You have finished the unit! It's time to review what you've learned. You will take the Unit Assessment in the next lesson.

Lesson Objectives

- Demonstrate mastery of important knowledge and skills in this unit.

PREPARE

Approximate lesson time is 60 minutes.

Materials

For the Student

History Journal

LEARN

Activity 1: A Look Back *(Online)*

Instructions

A. History Journal Review

Review what you learned in this unit by going through your History Journal. You should:

- Look at activity sheets you completed for this unit.
- Review unit keywords and definitions.
- Read through any writing assignments you did during the unit.
- Review the offline assessments you took.

Don't rush through. Take your time. Your History Journal is a great resource for a unit review.

B. Online Review

Review the following online activities:

- Time Line: 1919–1945
- Interactive Map: 1919–1945
- Flash Cards: Dictators
- Democracy Denied
- Code Breaker 1: Democracy and Totalitarianism
- Code Breaker 2: Democracy and Totalitarianism
- Get A Clue: An Unlikely Ally
- Get A Clue: Guadalcanal

Student Guide
Lesson 17: Unit Assessment

You've finished the unit! Now it's time to take the Unit Assessment.

Lesson Objectives

- Describe Hitler's use of anti-Semitism and genocide.
- Recognize isolationism as a deterrent to U.S. participation in the war and its end with the attack at Pearl Harbor
- Identify major individuals and events of WWII.
- Describe the impact of WWII on life around the world and in the U.S.
- Assess the constitutional violations of the internment of Japanese Americans.
- Identify military, technical, and civilian strategies used to achieve victory in WWII.
- Assess decisions made on ending the war and building peace.
- Locate on a map the extent of Axis control and the major nations on the Allied and Axis sides of the conflict.

PREPARE

Approximate lesson time is 60 minutes.

ASSESS

Unit Assessment: The Second World War, Part 1 *(Online)*

Complete the computer-scored portion of the Unit Assessment. When you have finished, complete the teacher-scored portion of the assessment and submit it to your teacher.

Unit Assessment: The Second World War, Part 2 *(Offline)*

Complete the teacher-scored portion of the Unit Assessment and submit it to your teacher.

Student Guide

Unit 10: Recovery, Reaction, Reform
Lesson 1: New Challenges

Harry Truman led the nation through war's end. But peace wasn't easy. Much of Europe and Japan lay in ruins, communism seemed to threaten the nation, and fear led to a second Red Scare. The 1950s saw a nation yearning for calm, for family life, for rest. The country moved forward economically, but not everyone shared in the postwar prosperity. As television and rock and roll made their mark, so did a growing demand for civil rights.

The United States emerged from World War II as the richest, most powerful nation on earth. But the war's end did not bring lasting peace, as FDR had hoped. The second-most powerful country in the world—the Soviet Union—began to flex its muscles, and the rivalry between the two nations intensified into a war of nerves.

Lesson Objectives

- Identify ways in which the power of the U.S.S.R. influenced U.S. policies after World War II.
- Describe the difference between communist and capitalist economic systems in terms of government control, competition, and profit motive.

PREPARE

Approximate lesson time is 60 minutes.

Materials

For the Student

New Challenges

A History of US (Concise Edition), Volume D (1929 to Present) by Joy Hakim

History Journal

Keywords and Pronunciation

capitalism : an economic system in which individuals or corporations own goods and businesses, and public demand determines the prices, production, and distribution of most goods

communism : a political and economic system in which the people own goods and businesses in common, but the government manages and controls them

---

LEARN

Activity 1: Two Ideas, Two Rivals *(Offline)*

Instructions

A. Read *(Chapter 23, pages 102–104; and Chapter 24, pages 105–108)*

As you read today's assignment, complete the New Challenges sheet. Use the Lesson Answer Key to check your work.

B. Think

The Red Scare was the time after World War I when many Americans were afraid of communism. What happened during that time? How did the U.S. attorney general respond to Americans' fear of communism? Do you remember reading about the Palmer raids? What happened in regard to the First Amendment?

Now think about what you have just read and answer the following question in your History Journal.

How do you think Americans will react to the post-World War II communist threat?

C. Use What You Know

Complete the Two Ideas, Two Rivals online activity. Print the completed activity and place it in your History Journal.

ASSESS

Lesson Assessment: New Challenges (*Online*)

You will complete an online assessment covering the main objectives of this lesson. Your assessment will be scored by the computer.

Name ______________________________ Date ______________________________

New Challenges

Complete the sheet as you read Chapters 23 and 24, pages 102–108.

1. Two rival political systems that came into conflict after World War II were __________________ and __________________. Their opposing economic systems were __________________ and __________________. The Soviet Union had a __________________ form of government and an economic system based on __________________. The United States was a __________________ with an economic system based on __________________.

2. Fear of the U.S.S.R. and of communism had an effect on American policy after World War II. Describe two ways in which the U.S. reacted to growing Soviet power.

____

____

3. Complete the chart by writing "Yes" or "No" in each box.

	Communism	Capitalism
Control – Does the government control the economy?		
Competition – Is there a lot of competition in the marketplace?		
Motivation – Does profit motivate people to work hard?		

Student Guide
Lesson 2: New Leadership

Harry Truman had already made some of the toughest decisions a president has ever had to make, and now he faced another. Communism was spreading, and it was spreading to countries that did not welcome it. Should he try to stop it? Truman could have easily turned his back on the problem. After all, he had enough problems just running his own country. But Truman's past and his knowledge of history had prepared him to handle tough times. Once again, he rose to the challenge.

Lesson Objectives

- Describe Truman's background, including his job experiences and role models.
- Identify Winston Churchill as the prime minister of Great Britain during World War II.
- Identify *iron curtain* as the division between communist and non-communist Europe.
- Give evidence of dissatisfaction among people in communist countries.
- Identify the Truman Doctrine as the U.S. policy guaranteeing aid to any nation threatened by communism.

PREPARE

Approximate lesson time is 60 minutes.

Materials

For the Student

The Iron Curtain

A History of US (Concise Edition), Volume D (1929 to Present) by Joy Hakim

History Journal

LEARN

Activity 1: A Curtain of Iron *(Offline)*

Instructions

A. Read *(Chapter 25, pages 109–111; and Chapter 26, pages 112–115)*

Look for the answers to the following questions as you read today's assignment:

1. What jobs did Truman have before he became president?
2. Who were Truman's role models? Whom did he admire and respect?
3. What was the Truman Doctrine?

B. Use What You Know

Complete the Iron Curtain sheet by following these steps:

1. View the online Interactive Map: 1946–1969.
2. Click The Cold War, and then click Europe (the continent).
3. Use the information to help you complete the Iron Curtain sheet.

ASSESS

Lesson Assessment: New Leadership (*Online*)

You will complete an online assessment covering the main objectives of this lesson. Your assessment will be scored by the computer.

Name ______________________________ Date ______________________________

The Iron Curtain

Use the Interactive Map: 1946–1969 to help you complete this sheet.

1. What does *NATO* stand for? ______________________________
2. Name three *NATO* countries that existed in 1955.

   ____
3. What was the Warsaw Pact? ______________________________

   ____

   ____
4. Name three Warsaw Pact countries that existed in 1955.

   ____
5. Name two nations in Europe that were not aligned with NATO or the Warsaw Pact.

   ____
6. Which nations were communist—NATO or Warsaw Pact? ______________________________

   Which were noncommunist? ______________________________
7. Two Warsaw Pact nations tried to revolt against their communist masters in the U.S.S.R. Name the two countries and tell how the revolts ended.

   ____

   ____

   ____
8. Why do you think Winston Churchill used the term *iron curtain* to describe the division between communist and noncommunist Europe?

   ____

   ____

   ____

Student Guide
Lesson 3: Fighting Bad Ideas

Harry Truman knew how people feel after they've lost a war. His own Confederate ancestors had carried hatred in their hearts all their lives. He knew that the nations defeated in World War II needed help. But he also needed to focus on the troubles affecting his own country. Truman had a few ideas about how to attack both fronts. What he had in mind was something that had never been done before in the history of the world.

Lesson Objectives

- Identify the Marshall Plan as a program to aid European nations after World War II and to promote prosperity and democracy.
- Describe the result of the U.S. occupation of Japan, including Japan's transition to democracy.
- List ways in which Truman fought racism in the United States.

PREPARE

Approximate lesson time is 60 minutes.

Materials

For the Student

- Foreign Affairs Time Line
- Foreign Affairs Time Line Entry
- Foreign Affairs Time Line: Marshall Plan
- A History of US (Concise Edition), Volume D (1929 to Present) by Joy Hakim
- History Journal

LEARN

Activity 1: Truman's Foreign and Domestic Policies *(Offline)*

Instructions

A. Read *(Chapter 27, pages 116–121)*

As you read, look for ways in which Truman fought racism in the United States. List three in your History Journal. Compare your list with the one in the Lesson Answer Key.

B. Use What You Know

Not all Americans thought the United States should spend millions of dollars to help their former enemies. Many opposed the Marshall Plan.

Write and deliver a short speech as Truman defending the Marshall Plan. As you plan the speech, think about why Truman thought the Marshall Plan was needed. If necessary, review your reading.

Check the Lesson Answer Key to make sure you've included the most important points.

C. Focus on Foreign Affairs

The events of World War II shattered Americans' belief that the United States could stay isolated from the rest of the world. Countries around the globe were now more connected than ever before. The Marshall Plan signaled a new direction in U.S. foreign policy. Americans would soon learn about places many had never heard of before.

Today you will begin a time line of U.S. foreign affairs. You will add to the time line in subsequent lessons. The first entry on the time line—the Marshall Plan—is already completed to give you an example of how the time line works.

The topic of the second time line entry is the occupation of Japan after World War II. You will complete this entry on your own.

1. Print the following sheets:

    - Foreign Affairs Time Line
    - Foreign Affairs Time Line: Marshall Plan
    - Foreign Affairs Time Line Entry

2. Color the Foreign Affairs Time Line sheet and hang it on a wall, leaving space at the right to add more sheets.

3. Attach a length of colored string or yarn to the right side of the sheet.

4. Cut out the boxes from the Foreign Affairs Time Line: Marshall Plan sheet along the dotted lines. Affix them to an 8 1/2" × 11" sheet of white paper or construction paper.

5. Hang this sheet on the wall to the right of the Foreign Affairs Time Line sheet and attach the other end of the string or yarn to it.

6. Using the Marshall Plan sheet as a model, fill out the Time Line Entry sheet about the occupation of Japan.

7. Place this sheet to the right of the Marshall Plan sheet and join them with more string or yarn.

D. Assessment

Complete the online assessment.

E. Read On *(Chapter 28, pages 122–125)*
Truman took Mark Twain's words to heart: "Always do right." Truman did right by supporting the Marshall Plan to help rebuild Europe. And he did right by tackling a very explosive issue at home—civil rights. What happened when Truman decided to try to end lynchings, poll taxes, and segregation of the armed services?

As you read Chapter 28, look for the answer to this question:

Why did people think Truman would lose the 1948 presidential election?

ASSESS

Lesson Assessment: Fighting Bad Ideas (*Online*)

You will complete an online assessment covering the main objectives of this lesson. Your assessment will be scored by the computer.

Foreign Affairs Time Line

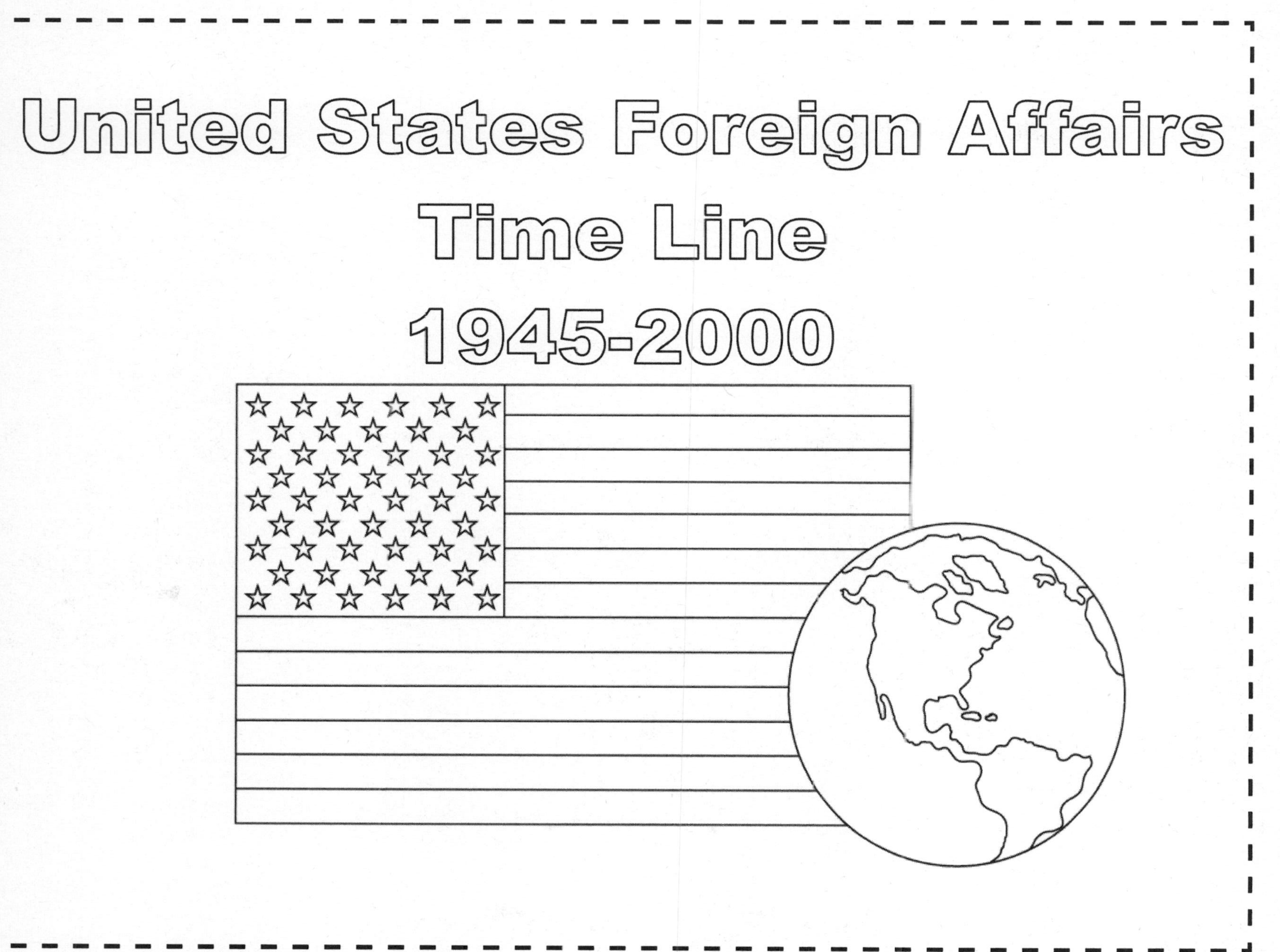

Name Date

Name Date

Foreign Affairs Time Line: Marshall Plan

1947

Year

Truman Launches Marshall Plan

Event (for example: U.S. Declares War on Japan)

Truman and Secretary of State George Marshall come up with a plan to send billions of dollars in aid and assistance to U.S. allies and former enemies in Europe.

Brief Overview of Event

FOR EUROPEAN RECOVERY
SUPPLIED BY THE
UNITED STATES OF AMERICA

Illustration or Drawing

Name Date

Foreign Affairs Time Line Entry

Year

Event (for example: U.S. Declares War on Japan)

Illustration or Drawing

Brief Overview of Event

Student Guide
Lesson 4: Despite the Polls

Everyone knew Truman wouldn't be reelected. But someone forgot to tell Truman!

Lesson Objectives

- Demonstrate knowledge gained in previous lessons.
- Explain why people expected Truman to lose the 1948 election.
- Identify Truman as the winner of the 1948 election.

PREPARE

Approximate lesson time is 60 minutes.

Materials

For the Student

History Journal

A History of US (Concise Edition), Volume D (1929 to Present) by Joy Hakim

---

LEARN
Activity 1: Headlines Say "Dewey" – Voters Say "Truman" *(Online)*
Instructions

A. Check Your Reading *(Chapter 28, pages 122–125)*

Watch a short video of the 1948 whistle stop tour. When the page has loaded, click Quicktime to watch the video.

After you've watched the video, answer the following questions in your History Journal. Write each answer as a complete sentence. When you've finished, click Answers to check your work.

1. What two candidates are shown in the video?
2. How did Truman campaign? Why did he choose this method for campaigning?
3. How did newspapers handle the election?
4. Who was predicted to win the 1948 election? Who actually won?

B. Use What You Know

Visit the Truman Library website and complete the 1948 Election Activity Sheet, which is located on the website.

ASSESS

Lesson Assessment: Despite the Polls *(Online)*

You will complete an online assessment covering the main points of this lesson. Your assessment will be scored by the computer.

LEARN

Activity 2: Read On *(Offline)*

The late 1940s was a prosperous time for lots of people, but it was also a time of fear. Many Americans were convinced that communism's influence was growing in the United States. Why did they believe this? Look for "evidence" as you read Chapter 30, pages 131–135.

Student Guide
Lesson 5: Seeing Red Again

Fear. Fear of communism. It was growing in the United States. The Soviet Union had control of Eastern Europe, and communism was starting to take hold in Asia. Disturbing new evidence proved that communist spies were living in the United States. They had even stolen top-secret information about the atomic bomb and sold it to the Soviets. No question about it—these were frightening times!

Lesson Objectives

- Explain that some people saw social-welfare programs and alleged spying incidents as evidence of communist influence in the United States.
- Describe the growth of communism in Asia and its effect on the United States.
- Identify nations that were major participants in the Korean War.

PREPARE

Approximate lesson time is 60 minutes.

Materials

For the Student

Focus on Geography: Korea

A History of US (Concise Edition), Volume D (1929 to Present) by Joy Hakim

History Journal

Keywords and Pronunciation

Pyongyang (pyuhng-YAHNG)

LEARN

Activity 1: Spies at Home, War in Korea *(Online)*

Instructions

A. Check Your Reading *(Chapter 30, pages 131–135)*

In an earlier lesson you were asked to look for "evidence" that convinced many Americans of a growing communist influence in the United States. What did you find?

Why were many Americans convinced that the influence of communism was growing in the United States?

You can view possible answers to these questions online by clicking The Red Menace button.

B. Focus on Geography ***(Online)***

Use the online map to help you answer the questions on the Focus on Geography: Korea sheet. When you have finished, check your answers against those in the Lesson Answer Key. Put the completed sheet in your History Journal. Click Interactive Map: 1946–1969. On the map, click Cold War, and then Korea (the country).

C. Use What You Know ***(Online)***

Political cartoonists in the late '40s and early '50s had a lot of material for their cartoons. Study the online cartoon and answer the on-screen questions.

ASSESS

Lesson Assessment: Seeing Red Again (*Online*)

You will complete an online assessment covering the main goals of this lesson. Your assessment will be scored by the computer.

LEARN

Activity 2: Read On *(Offline)*

Name _______________________ Date _______________________

Focus on Geography: Korea

Use the Interactive Map: 1946–1969 to answer the following questions:

1. What communist country lies just north of the Korean Peninsula?

   ____

2. Along what line of latitude was Korea divided after World War II? ____________

3. What happened in June of 1950?

   ____

4. In November 1950, the UN front line was north of the North Korean capital of Pyongyang (pyuhng-YAHNG). What began on November 26 that pushed the UN forces south?

   ____

   ____

5. Who were the major participants in the Korean War?

   ____

   ____

6. List two ways in which the growth of communism in Asia had an impact on the United States. Read the last paragraph on page 135 to help you answer the question.

   - ____
   - ____

Student Guide
Lesson 6: Hunting Reds

The nation was sick. It had a bad case of anticommunist hysteria that threatened the rights of all Americans.

Lesson Objectives

- Identify Joseph McCarthy as the U.S. senator who drew attention to himself by leading a hunt for communists in the United States.
- Name some ways in which the nation reacted to the fear of communism.
- Recognize similarities between the Red Scare of the 1950s and reactions to fears in other time periods.

PREPARE

Approximate lesson time is 60 minutes.

Materials

For the Student

- Document Analysis: Lyrics
- Witch Hunts
- A History of US (Concise Edition), Volume C (1865-1932) by Joy Hakim
- A History of US (Concise Edition), Volume D (1929 to Present) by Joy Hakim
- History Journal

Keywords and Pronunciation

lyricist (LIHR-uh-sist)

LEARN

Activity 1: McCarthy Hunts Communists *(Offline)*

Instructions

A. Check Your Reading *(Chapter 31, pages 136–140)*

Review the reaction in America to the growing fear of communism by clicking the America Reacts button.

B. Document Analysis: Lyrics

Complete the Document Analysis: Lyrics sheet. Compare your answers to those in the Lesson Answer Key.

C. Use What You Know

Was McCarthy's witch hunt the first one in history? Hardly. In the late 1600s, Puritan settlers in Salem, Massachusetts, went on a witch hunt. The target of their hunt? Fellow townsfolk whom they suspected of practicing witchcraft. The residents of Salem feared the unknown, and they ended up imprisoning and hanging innocent people.

Fear and hysteria have caused other witch hunts throughout history.

Review briefly the Red Scare after World War I (Volume C, *Chapter 53, pages 260–262)* and the forced internment of Japanese Americans during World War II *(Chapter 14, pages 61–65)*.

Complete the Witch Hunts sheet. Compare your answers with those in the Lesson Answer Key. Save this sheet in your History Journal.

ASSESS

Lesson Assessment: Hunting Reds (*Online*)

You will complete an online assessment covering the main goals of this lesson. Your assessment will be scored by the computer.

Name ______________________________ Date ______________________________

Document Analysis: Lyrics

These are lyrics from a song about the anticommunist crusade of the postwar era.

> The fascists came with chains and war
> To prison us in hate.
> And many a good man fought and died
> To save the stricken faith.
> And now again the madmen come
> And shall our victory fail?
> There is no victory in a land
> Where free men go to jail.

Step 1. Observation

A lyricist (LIHR-uh-sist) is a person who writes the words to songs. Lyricists often use language to stir up people's feelings and emotions. Read the lyrics above from a song written in the 1950s. Read them twice. What specific words from the verse do you think the lyricist included to stir up strong feelings and emotions?

Step 2. Inference

1. Whom do you think the lyricist is referring to in the first two lines? ____________________
2. What event do the second and third lines refer to? Keep in mind that the words were written in the 1950s. ____________________
3. Whom do you think the lyricist is referring to as "the madmen" in the fifth line?

   ____
4. Explain what you think the lyricist means in the last two lines.

   ____

   ____
5. Who do you think wrote these lyrics—a supporter of McCarthy or an opponent?

   ____

Step 3. Questions

6. What questions, if any, do these lyrics raise in your mind?

Name Date

Witch Hunts

Just how similar was the Red Scare of the 1950s to reactions to fear in other time periods? Complete the table by writing "Yes" or "No" in the appropriate boxes.

	Japanese Internment	Post-WWI Red Scare	Post-WWII Red Scare
The public was frightened because of real events.			
Innocent people were accused and convicted.			
Rights were ignored and abused.			
Most everyone accused was assumed to be guilty.			
The public thought they saw guilt everywhere.			
Certain types of people were suspect because of race, religion, political belief, occupation, etc.			
Accusations were almost always unjustified.			

Discuss

Discuss with an adult whether or not you think witch hunts like McCarthy's could happen, or are happening, today.

Student Guide
Lesson 7: (Optional) Your Choice

Lesson Objectives

- Explore knowledge and skills taught in this course.

PREPARE

Approximate lesson time is 60 minutes.

Materials

For the Student

Map of the United States

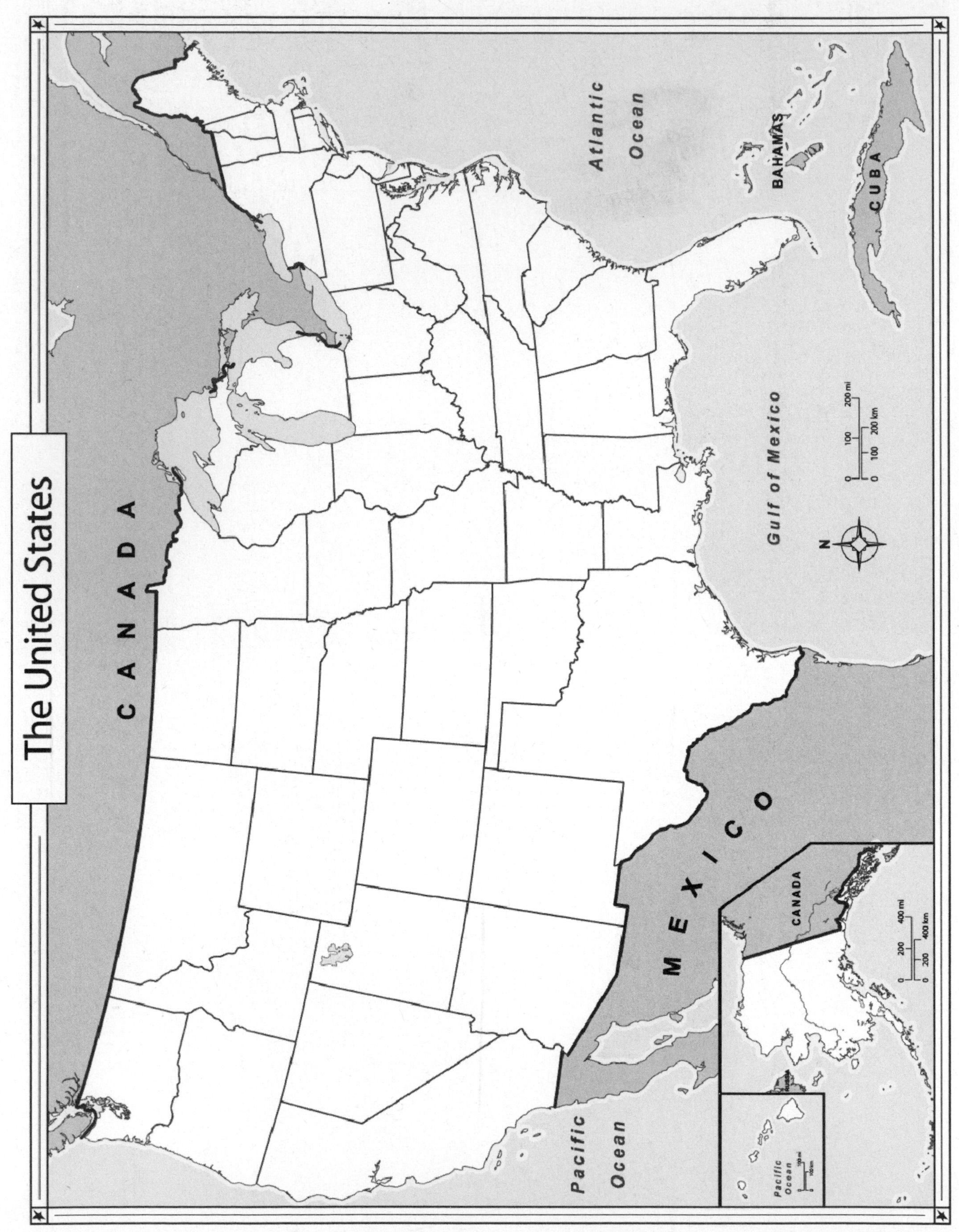
The United States
CANADA
MEXICO
Atlantic Ocean
BAHAMAS
CUBA
Gulf of Mexico
N
Pacific Ocean
CANADA
Pacific Ocean

Student Guide
Lesson 8: The Nifty Fifties

Consumer goods had been scarce during World War II, but after the war things changed. In the 1950s, people could buy almost anything they wanted—bicycles, TV sets, ballpoint pens, dishwashers—you name it. A stamp for a letter cost three cents. Five cents bought a Coke.

The '50s brought changes in government as well. Democrats had occupied the White House for 20 years, but now Americans were ready for something different. In 1952 they elected a Republican president—an army general named Dwight D. Eisenhower.

Lesson Objectives

- Describe ways in which the television changed American culture.
- Describe Eisenhower's style of leadership.
- Summarize Eisenhower's fears concerning an arms race.

PREPARE

Approximate lesson time is 60 minutes.

Materials

For the Student

- The 1950s—America Then and Now
- A History of US (Concise Edition), Volume D (1929 to Present) by Joy Hakim
- History Journal

Keywords and Pronunciation

arms race : a competition between two or more nations to see who can build the most or the deadliest weapons

vaccine (vak-SEEN) : a substance made of a weakened or dead bacteria or virus that is administered to a living creature to increase immunity to a particular disease

---

LEARN

Activity 1: The Nifty Fifties *(Online)*

Instructions

Click Start on the television to see some scenes from the '50s.

Activity 2: Happy Days – Grease – American Bandstand *(Offline)*

Instructions

A. Read (*Chapter 32, pages 141–145*)

As you read, answer the following questions and compare your answers to those in the Lesson Answer Key.

1. What style of leadership did Eisenhower think a president should have?
2. Summarize Eisenhower's fears concerning an arms race.
3. What issues was Eisenhower accused of ignoring?

Write definitions for these terms in your History Journal. When you have finished, compare your definitions to those in the Keywords section.

arms race

vaccine (vak-SEEN)

B. Use What You Know

Complete The 1950s—America Then and Now sheet.

ASSESS

Lesson Assessment: The Nifty Fifties *(Online)*

You will complete an online assessment covering the main points of this lesson. Your assessment will be scored by the computer.

Name Date

The 1950s—America Then and Now

In the column titled Then, fill in information about America in the 1950s. In the Now column, describe life in the United States today.

	Then	**Now**
Teen Life		
Family Life		
Entertainment		
Politics		
Science		
Inventions		

Answer the following question.

How did television change life in the United States in the 1950s?

Student Guide
Lesson 9: New Ways of Life

Drive-in restaurants, interstate highways, suburbs, and supermarkets. The face of America changed dramatically in the 1950s as the automobile transformed the way people lived, traveled, and ate. Everything seemed bigger, better, faster than before. It was the beginning of a new age in the United States.

Lesson Objectives

- Give examples of things in current American culture that were introduced in the 1950s, such as fast food and suburbs.
- Identify groups left out of the economic prosperity of the 1950s.
- Distinguish between fact and fiction in America of the 1950s.

PREPARE

Approximate lesson time is 60 minutes.

Materials

For the Student

On the Street Where You Live

A History of US (Concise Edition), Volume D (1929 to Present) by Joy Hakim

History Journal

Keywords and Pronunciation

baby boom : a marked increase in birthrate in the United States between 1946 and 1964

franchise (FRAN-chiyz) : the right or license granted to an individual or group to market a company's goods or services

G.I. Bill of Rights : a variety of bills that Congress enacted to give money to military veterans for college educations, home-buying loans, and other benefits

---

LEARN

Activity 1: New Ways of Life *(Onlinc)*

Instructions

Warm-Up

Begin the lesson by viewing the online slide show and imagine what life would be like without automobiles.

Activity 2: On the Street Where You Live *(Offline)*

Instructions

A. Read (*Chapter 33, pages 146–152*)

As you read, answer the following questions.

1. Why was Levitt's housing-development business so successful? To answer the question, think about Levitt's approach and the circumstances in which he was building.
2. How did Kemmons Wilson hope to attract the business of American travelers in the 1950s?

3. In the chapter feature titled "Ah, Suburbia, Happy Suburbia," what is the author's message?
4. How might the author's message be generalized to all of society?

Write a brief definition for each of the following terms in your History Journal. When you have finished, compare your definitions with those in the Keywords section of this lesson.

baby boom
franchise (FRAN-chiyz)
G.I. Bill of Rights

B. Use What You Know
Complete the On the Street Where You Live sheet.

ASSESS

Lesson Assessment: New Ways of Life *(Online)*

You will complete an online assessment covering the main points of this lesson. Your assessment will be scored by the computer.

Name Date

On the Street Where You Live

List the changes in American life that occurred with the growth of suburbs. Use the text and photos in the chapter as a reference.

Before Suburbs	After Suburbs

Answer the following questions:

1. Levittown, McDonald's, Holiday Inns, and drive-in theaters; what do they all have in common?

____

____

____

2. How was the success of McDonald's related to the economic condition of many Americans during the 1950s?

____

____

____

3. How did McDonald's and other businesses take advantage of Americans' new dependence on the automobile?

____

____

____

4. If someone wrote a book called *America in the 1950s*, what topics might you find in a chapter called "Trouble in Paradise"?

____

____

____

Student Guide
Lesson 10: Trouble Abroad

Shortly after World War II, a Vietnamese man named Ho Chi Minh began a personal mission to free his country from foreign rule. The conflict that followed would become an international nightmare.

Lesson Objectives

- Identify the Philippines, India, and Vietnam on a map.
- Recognize similarities in the post-war situation of the Philippines, India, and Vietnam, and explain how these countries dealt with the situation in different ways.
- Explain the beginnings of U.S. involvement in Vietnam and Eisenhower's reluctance to be involved.

PREPARE

Approximate lesson time is 60 minutes.

Materials

For the Student

- Foreign Affairs Time Line Entry
- Trouble Abroad
- A History of US (Concise Edition), Volume D (1929 to Present) by Joy Hakim
- wall map, world
- History Journal

Keywords and Pronunciation

colonialism : control by one power or nation over another area or people

domino theory : the theory that if communism takes over one nation, it will take over the neighboring nations as well

dove : an opponent of a war or warlike policy

hawk : a supporter of a war or warlike policy

imperialism : the policy of expanding national power or influence by taking other lands

---

LEARN

Activity 1: Revolution *(Offline)*

Instructions

A. Read *(Chapter 34, pages 153–156)*

As you read, complete the Trouble Abroad sheet. When you have finished, compare your answers with those in the Lesson Answer Key.

Write a brief definition for each of these words in your History Journal. When you have finished, compare your definitions with those in the Keywords section of this lesson.

colonialism
domino theory
doves
hawks
imperialism

B. Focus on Foreign Affairs
Continue to track international events by adding to the Foreign Affairs Time Line.

- Estimate how many time line entries you'll need to mark important events that took place in the Philippines, Vietnam, India, and Korea.
- Print several copies of the Foreign Affairs Time Line Entry Sheet. You'll need one sheet for each entry.
- Fill out each entry sheet. **You do not need to include the exact dates of events in these countries. Just write the name of each important event and a brief overview.**
- Add the new time line entries to your collection on the wall.
- Review the online flash cards before you complete the assessment online.

ASSESS

Lesson Assessment: Trouble Abroad (*Online*)

You will complete an online assessment covering the main goals of this lesson. Your assessment will be scored by the computer.

Name ______________________________

Trouble Abroad

As you read *(Chapter 34, pages 153–156)*, answer the following questions:

1. On the map, label the Philippines, India, and Vietnam.

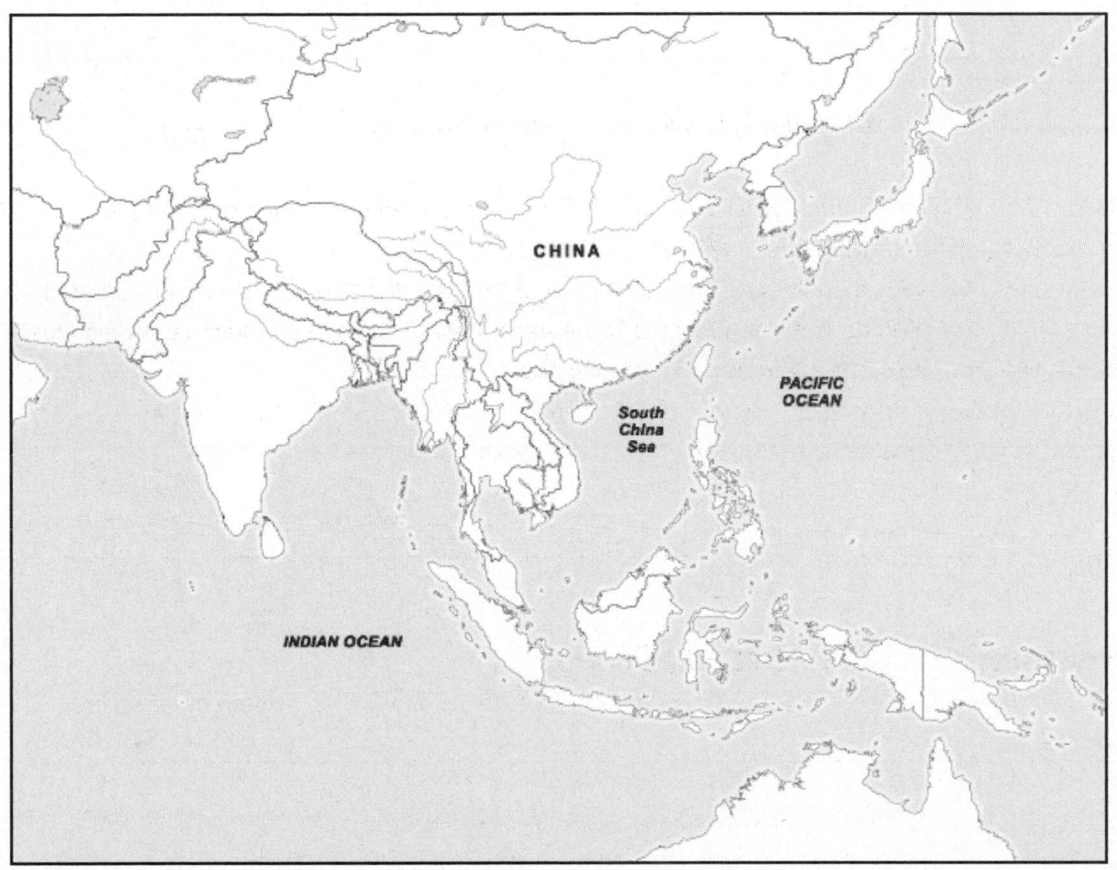

2. Think about the early days of the Cold War. The Truman Doctrine, the Marshall Plan, and the Korean War were all part of the policy of containment that President Truman initiated. What was the goal of that policy? (Look back on page 134 if you need help.)

____

____

____

____

3. What did the Philippines, India, and Vietnam have in common in the days before World War II?

4. How did the Philippines gain independence? How did India? Vietnam?

5. What role did the United States play in the struggle between the Vietminh and the French?

6. Explain what Eisenhower meant when he compared Vietnam to the first in a row of dominoes.

7. Why did Eisenhower resist the pressure to fight in Vietnam?

Name Date

Foreign Affairs Time Line Entry

Year

Event (for example: U.S. Declares War on Japan)

Brief Overview of Event

Illustration or Drawing

Name Date

Foreign Affairs Time Line Entry

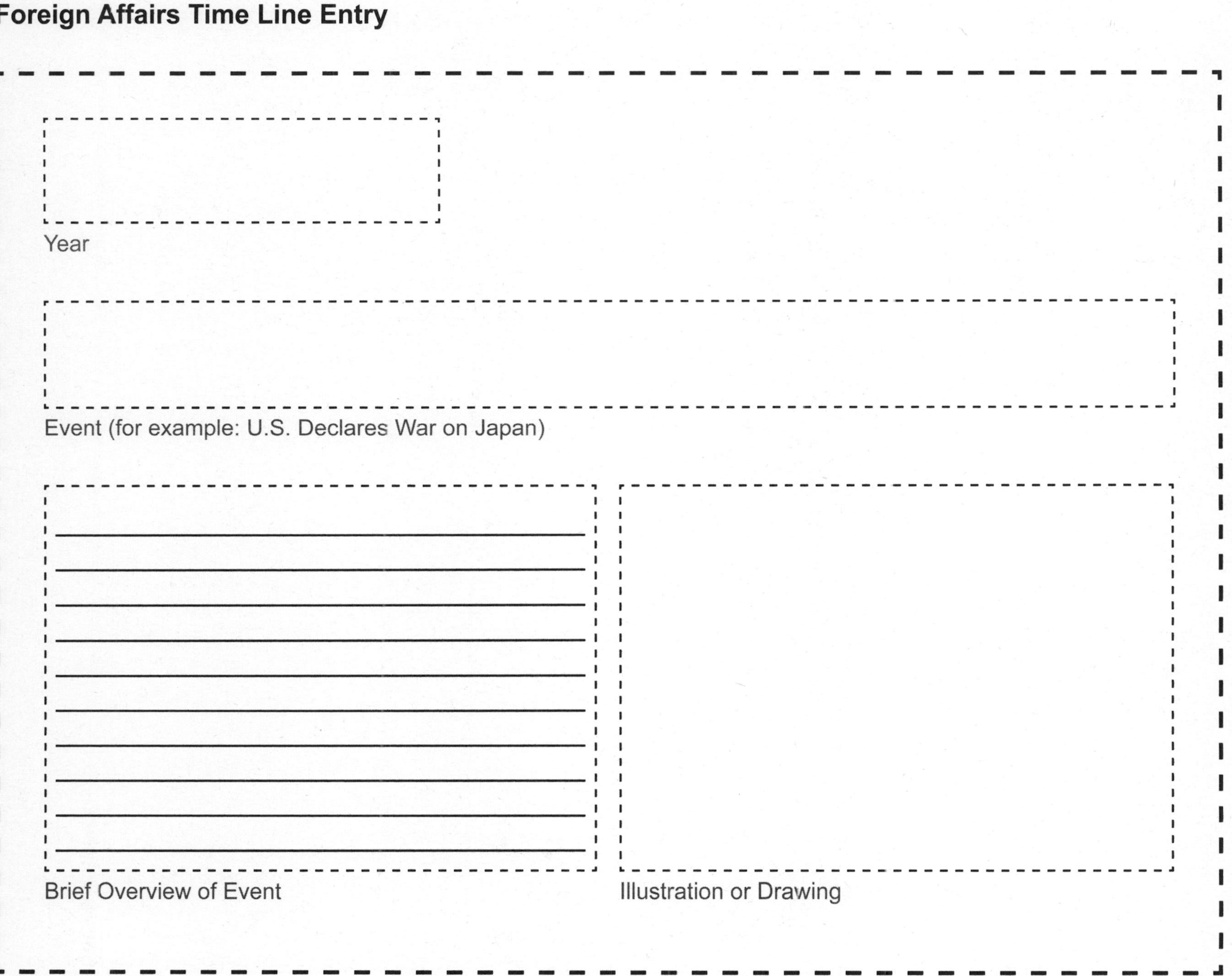

Name Date

Foreign Affairs Time Line Entry

Year

Event (for example: U.S. Declares War on Japan)

Illustration or Drawing

Brief Overview of Event

Name Date

Foreign Affairs Time Line Entry

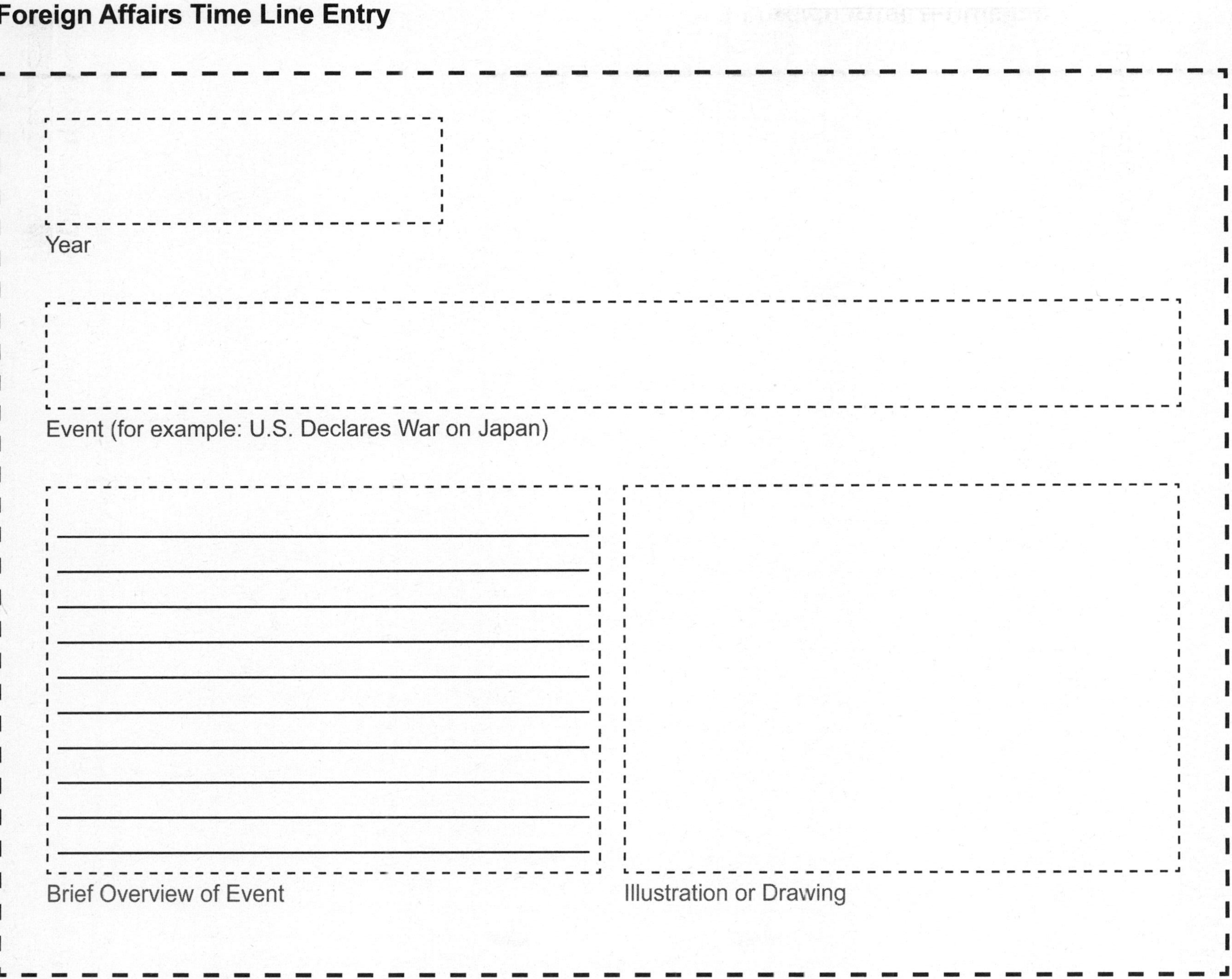

Student Guide
Lesson 11: Playing for Change

In 1947, Jackie Robinson broke baseball's color barrier by becoming the first African American to play professionally in the major leagues. He endured the racist reactions of many white baseball fans as well as rejection by teammates. But Robinson persevered. Learn how his talent and determination changed the the nation's pastime and inspired others.

Lesson Objectives

- Explain the meaning of *Jim Crow*.
- Summarize Jackie Robinson's role in breaking racial barriers in the United States.

PREPARE

Approximate lesson time is 60 minutes.

Materials

For the Student

Profile

A History of US (Concise Edition), Volume D (1929 to Present) by Joy Hakim

History Journal

LEARN

Activity 1: Breaking the Color Barrier *(Offline)*

Instructions

A. Read *(Chapter 29, pages 126–130)*

As you read, answer the following questions. When you have finished, compare your answers with those in the Lesson Answer Key.

1. Define the term *Jim Crow*. What does it mean to live in a Jim Crow nation?
2. What did the phrase "separate but equal" mean to many people during Jim Crow segregation and did those words ring true?
3. Who was Branch Rickey? What was his goal for baseball?
4. Why did Rickey choose Jackie Robinson as the player to integrate the Brooklyn Dodgers?
5. Describe how Jackie Robinson won the affection and respect of some baseball fans and his fellow ballplayers.
6. How do you think Jackie Robinson played a role in breaking racial barriers in the United States?

B. Use What You Know

Use the information in today's reading and the Profile sheet to write a Profile of Courage for Jackie Robinson. You can also view the following websites for additional information on Jackie Robinson.

- The Official Site of Jackie Robinson
- Baseball and Jackie Robinson
- Jackie Robinson, Civil Rights Advocate

ASSESS

Lesson Assessment: Playing for Change *(Online)*

You will complete an online assessment covering the main points of this lesson. Your assessment will be scored by the computer.

Name ______________________ Date ______________________

Profile of ______________________

Place Picture Here

Student Guide
Lesson 12: Breaking Barriers

The Supreme Court's decision in *Plessy v. Ferguson* set segregation and Jim Crow firmly in place. Nearly 60 years later, the court took a different stand in *Brown v. Board of Education,* declaring that segregating public schools was unconstitutional. The new ruling was a huge victory for minorities, but the battle wasn't over. Laws have to be enforced, and some Americans were determined not to enforce this one.

Lesson Objectives

- Identify people who worked against Jim Crow.
- Describe the varying reactions to the decision in *Brown v. Board of Education.*
- Recognize that people interpret the Constitution in different ways at different times.
- Summarize the Supreme Court's decision in *Brown v. Board of Education.*

PREPARE

Approximate lesson time is 60 minutes.

Materials

For the Student

A History of US (Concise Edition), Volume D (1929 to Present) by Joy Hakim

History Journal

Keywords and Pronunciation

dissenting opinion : a justice's written opinion disagreeing with the majority opinion of the court

integrate : to bring together different racial and ethnic groups

---

LEARN

Activity 1: Struggling Against Segregation *(Offline)*

Instructions

A. Read (*Chapter 35, pages 157–165*)

As you read, answer these questions in your History Journal. When you have finished, compare your answers with those in the Lesson Answer Key.

1. What did the 1896 court decision in *Plessy v. Ferguson* say about the 14th Amendment?
2. What was the connection between Topeka, Kansas; Clarendon County, South Carolina; and Farmville, Virginia?
3. What arguments did Thurgood Marshall and NAACP lawyers use against segregation in *Brown v. Board of Education*?
4. Who wrote in 1954, "separate educational facilities are inherently (essentially) unequal"?
5. Why was it important that the Supreme Court's decision on segregation be almost unanimous?
6. How did most Southern communities react to the decision and why didn't more people speak out against the reaction? Did the same reaction occur everywhere?

Write a brief definition for each of these terms in your History Journal. When you have finished, compare your definitions with those in the Keywords section.

dissenting opinion
integrate

B. Use What You Know
Use the information in today's reading to complete the online Flash Cards Maker activity. Create flash cards for four of the following people. You may also use the Grolier's *New Book of Knowledge* in the Help section to find more information about these people.

1. Charles Houston
2. Justice Marshall Harlan
3. Linda Brown
4. Thurgood Marshall
5. Chief Justice Earl Warren

ASSESS

Lesson Assessment: Breaking Barriers (*Online*)

You will complete an online assessment covering the main goals of this lesson. Your assessment will be scored by the computer.

Student Guide
Lesson 13: Champions of Change

How do you deal with injustice? You can turn away from it, which is the easiest thing to do. You can fight it with weapons and fists, which is harder, and sometimes produces more injustice. Or, you can fight it with nonviolence, which means standing up to evil with calm, unflinching courage. In the 1950s, Martin Luther King, Jr., Rosa Parks, and other African Americans fought injustice with nonviolence and won the battle.

Lesson Objectives

- Summarize the influence of Gandhi and Thoreau on King's philosophy.
- Identify the key events and people involved in the Montgomery Bus Boycott, and the outcome of the boycott.
- Give examples of the power of the boycott.

PREPARE

Approximate lesson time is 60 minutes.

Materials

For the Student

- Perseverance
- Profile
- A History of US (Concise Edition), Volume D (1929 to Present) by Joy Hakim
- History Journal

Keywords and Pronunciation

boycott (BOY-kaht) : to join together in refusing to buy, sell, or use something or to have any dealings with someone

civil disobedience : opposing a law or practice by refusing to obey it

civil rights movement : a movement that sought fair treatment for all Americans regardless of race

Henry David Thoreau (thuh-ROH)

Mohandas Gandhi (MOH-huhn-dahs GAHN-dee)

NAACP : the National Association for the Advancement of Colored People, an organization of blacks and whites formed to fight racial injustice

---

LEARN

Activity 1: Struggling Against Segregation *(Offline)*

Instructions

A. Read (*Chapter 36, pages 166–168; and Chapter 37, pages 169–173*)

Write a brief definition for each of these terms in your History Journal. When you have finished, compare your definitions with those in the Keywords section of this lesson.

boycott	NAACP
civil disobedience	nonviolence
civil rights movement	

B. Use What You Know

Complete the Perseverance chart.

C. Profile of Courage

- View the online Bus Boycott Gallery.
- Print the image of Rosa Parks.
- Write a Profile of Courage for Rosa Parks using the Profile sheet.

ASSESS

Lesson Assessment: Champions of Change *(Online)*

You will complete an online assessment covering the main points of this lesson. Your assessment will be scored by the computer.

LEARN

Activity 2: Champions of Change *(Online)*

Instructions

You may follow the instructions on the screen to learn more about the Montgomery Bus Boycott.

Name ______________________ Date ______________________

Perseverance

1. Define *perseverance*: ______________________

2. Complete the table below by filling in ways in which the people in each column showed perseverance in the struggle for civil rights.

Gandhi	Martin Luther King, Jr.	Community of Montgomery

3. What role did the black church play in the segregated South?

4. How was Martin Luther King, Jr., influenced by the ideas of Mohandas Gandhi and Henry David Thoreau?

5. Identify the key events and people involved in the Montgomery Bus Boycott, and the outcome of the boycott.

People: ______________________________

____

____

Events: ______________________________

____

____

Outcome: ______________________________

____

____

6. Give two examples of the power of the boycott.

____

____

____

____

Name _______________ Date _______________

Profile of _______________

Place Picture Here

Student Guide
Lesson 14: Child Champions

Three years after the Supreme Court ruled to end segregation in the classroom, states in the Deep South still banned blacks from all-white schools. It took nine courageous boys and girls from Little Rock, Arkansas, to wake up the nation and challenge segregation in the South.

Lesson Objectives

- Define civil rights movement.
- Explain the reasons for segregation at Central High School and elsewhere in the South long after the Supreme Court ordered desegregation.
- Describe the atmosphere and hardships black students faced in trying to attend Central High School.
- Recognize the roles of political leaders and the military in integrating the school.

PREPARE

Approximate lesson time is 60 minutes.

Materials

For the Student

A History of US (Concise Edition), Volume D (1929 to Present) by Joy Hakim

History Journal

Keywords and Pronunciation

civil rights movement : a movement that sought fair treatment for all Americans regardless of race

National Guard : a military force whose job is to defend the public during civil emergencies and maintain peace within a country or state

---

LEARN

Activity 1: The Little Rock Nine *(Offline)*

Instructions

A. Read (*Chapter 38, pages 174–176*)

As you read, answer the following questions. When you have finished, compare your answers with those in the Lesson Answer Key.

1. Why was Central High School still segregated three years after the Supreme Court ruled that schools must integrate?
2. What role did the Arkansas governor play in the crisis at Little Rock?
3. Describe the atmosphere at Central High School in the fall of 1957, both inside and outside the school.
4. How was Central High School finally integrated?

Write a brief definition for each of these terms in your History Journal. When you have finished, compare your definitions with those in the Keywords section of this lesson.

civil rights movement
National Guard

B. Use What You Know

Show what you learned in this lesson. Use the online Flash Card Maker to create your own flash cards for the people listed below. Describe each person's role in the crisis at Little Rock.

- National Guard
- Governor Orval Faubus
- Desegregation Activists
- The Little Rock Nine
- Newspaper Reporters
- President Eisenhower

ASSESS

Lesson Assessment: Child Champions (*Online*)

You will complete an online assessment covering the main objectives of this lesson. Your assessment will be scored by the computer.

LEARN

Activity 2. Optional: Child Champions *(Online)*

Instructions

You may follow the directions online to learn more about the LIttle Rock Nine.

Student Guide
Lesson 15: (Optional) Your Choice

Lesson Objectives

- Explore knowledge and skills taught in this course.

PREPARE

Approximate lesson time is 60 minutes.

Materials

For the Student

Map of the United States

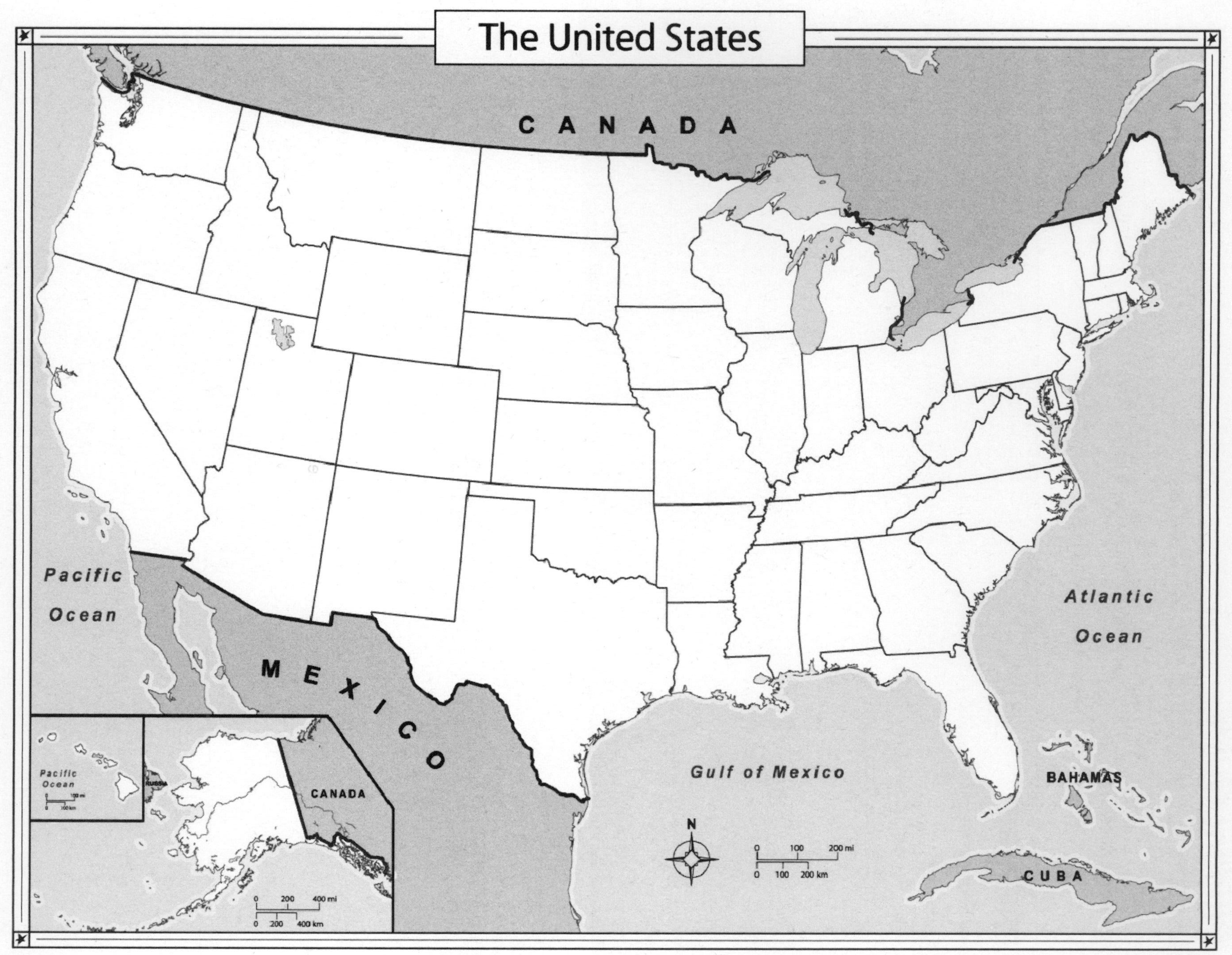
The United States
CANADA
MEXICO
Pacific Ocean
Atlantic Ocean
Gulf of Mexico
BAHAMAS
CUBA
N
0 100 200 mi
0 100 200 km
CANADA
0 200 400 mi
0 200 400 km
Pacific Ocean

Student Guide
Lesson 16: Unit Review

You have finished the unit! It's time to review what you've learned. You will take the Unit Assessment in the next lesson.

Lesson Objectives

- Demonstrate mastery of important knowledge and skills in this unit.

PREPARE

Approximate lesson time is 60 minutes.

Materials

For the Student

History Journal

Keywords and Pronunciation

franchise (FRAN-chiyz) : the right or license granted to an individual or group to market a company's goods or services
G.I. Bill of Rights : a variety of bills that Congress enacted to give money to military veterans for college educations, home-buying loans, and other benefits
hawk : a supporter of a war or warlike policy
Henry David Thoreau (thuh-ROH)
imperialism : the policy of expanding national power or influence by taking other lands
integrate : to bring together different racial and ethnic groups
Mohandas Gandhi (MOH-huhn-dahs GAHN-dee)
NAACP : the National Association for the Advancement of Colored People, an organization of blacks and whites formed to fight racial injustice
National Guard : a military force whose job is to defend the public during civil emergencies and maintain peace within a country or state
nonviolent protest : peaceful protest that avoids the use of physical violence
Pyongyang (pyuhng YAHNG)
vaccine (vak-SEEN) : a substance made of a weakened or dead bacteria or virus that is administered to a living creature to increase immunity to a particular disease

LEARN

Activity 1: A Look Back *(Online)*

Instructions

A. History Journal Review

Review what you learned in this unit by going through your History Journal. You should:

- Look at activity sheets you completed for this unit.
- Review unit keywords and definitions.
- Read through any writing assignments you did during the unit.
- Review the flash cards you created for the unit.
- Review the assessments you took.

Don't rush through. Take your time. Your History Journal is a great resource for a unit review.

Student Guide

Lesson 17: Unit Assessment

You've finished the unit! Now it's time to take the Unit Assessment.

Lesson Objectives

- Demonstrate familiarity with landmark Supreme Court cases including *Plessy v. Ferguson* and *Brown v. the Board of Education.*
- Describe the cultural and political shifts of the post-war era.
- Identify the role of individuals, the media, and the Supreme Court in promoting civil rights in the 1950s.
- Recognize the origins and key policies of the Cold War.
- Identify the causes and results of military conflict in Korea and Vietnam.
- Describe ways in which the television changed American culture.
- Give examples of things in current American culture that were introduced in the 1950s, such as fast food and suburbs.
- Identify major political and reform leaders of the 1950s and the actions or policies associated with them.
- Identify individuals or practices that restricted the rights of citizens in the 1950s.

PREPARE

Approximate lesson time is 60 minutes.

ASSESS

Unit Assessment: Recovery, Reaction, Reform, Part 1 *(Online)*

Complete the computer-scored portion of the Unit Assessment. When you have finished, complete the teacher-scored portion of the assessment and submit it to your teacher.

Unit Assessment: Recovery, Reaction, Reform, Part 2 *(Offline)*

Complete the teacher-scored portion of the Unit Assessment and submit it to your teacher.

Student Guide

Unit 11: A Turbulent Time
Lesson 1: JFK

The Peace Corps, the space race, the war on poverty—all challenged Americans to do their best. But Americans also faced fear, anger, and violence. Cold War crises threatened the nation's sense of security and thousands were protesting war in Vietnam. Blacks, Chicanos, Native Americans, women, and others were demanding change.

Some Americans thought John F. Kennedy's youth and religion would be roadblocks to his election. But in a very close vote, he became the youngest man and the first Catholic to win the presidency. JFK urged thousands to leave their jobs and join government service or go overseas to help those less fortunate. From day one, he was determined to be an active president, a good president, a president who would inspire the nation. Click Student Activity to hear excerpts from JFK's inaugural speech.

Lesson Objectives

- Describe John F. Kennedy when he was elected president.
- Give examples of Kennedy's ability to inspire others.
- Analyze excerpts of Kennedy's inaugural speech.

PREPARE

Approximate lesson time is 60 minutes.

Materials

For the Student

New Hope for the Future

A History of US (Concise Edition), Volume D (1929 to Present) by Joy Hakim

History Journal

Keywords and Pronunciation

bipartisan (biy-PAHR-tuh-zuhn) : involving or relating to two political parties

ecology : the scientific study of the interrelationships between living things and the environment

Peace Corps : a volunteer agency that would let Americans share their experience and knowledge with people of less fortunate nations

---

LEARN

Activity 1: A Golden Age of Poetry and Power *(Offline)*

Instructions

A. Warm-Up

Begin the lesson by listening to excerpts from John F. Kennedy's inaugural speech.

B. Read *(Chapter 39, pages 178–181)*

As you read, answer the following questions in your History Journal.

1. What characteristics did John F. Kennedy bring to the presidency?
2. What did he ask Americans to do in his inaugural address?

C. Use What You Know

Complete the New Hope for the Future sheet. Compare your answers with the ones in the Lesson Answer Key.

D. Assessment

Complete the online assessment.

E. Read On *(Chapter 40, pages 182–185)*

As you read, answer the following questions in your History Journal.

1. In what parts of the world were U.S. foreign affairs very tense?
2. How did the missile crisis end?

ASSESS

Lesson Assessment: JFK (*Online*)

You will complete an online assessment covering the main goals of this lesson. Your assessment will be scored by the computer.

LEARN

Activity 2. Optional: JFK *(Online)*

Name Date

New Hope for the Future

Read the excerpts from John F. Kennedy's inaugural address and answer the questions.

Excerpt 1

Let every nation know, whether it wishes us well or ill, that we shall pay any price, bear any burden, meet any hardship, support any friend, oppose any foe to assure the survival and the success of liberty.

This much we pledge—and more.

1. Do you think this could have been a warning? If so, whom was he warning?

Excerpt 2

. . . to those nations who would make themselves our adversary, we offer not a pledge but a request: that both sides begin anew the quest for peace, before the dark powers of destruction unleashed by science engulf all humanity in planned or accidental self-destruction.

2. What does JFK mean by "dark powers of destruction unleashed by science"?

Excerpt 3

Let both sides explore what problems unite us instead of belaboring those problems which divide us.

Let both sides, for the first time, formulate serious and precise proposals for the inspection and control of arms—and bring the absolute power to destroy other nations under the absolute control of all nations.

Let both sides seek to invoke the wonders of science instead of its terrors. Together let us explore the stars, conquer the deserts, eradicate disease, tap the ocean depths and encourage the arts and commerce.

3. Whom do you think JFK was referring to in his inaugural address when he said "both sides"?

Excerpt 4

In the long history of the world, only a few generations have been granted the role of defending freedom in its hour of maximum danger. I do not shrink from this responsibility—I welcome it. I do not believe that any of us would exchange places with any other people or any other generation. The energy, the faith, the devotion which we bring to this endeavor will light our country and all who serve it—and the glow from that fire can truly light the world.

4. What threat was JFK referring to when he spoke of "defending freedom in its hour of maximum danger"?

____

____

5. How might the "glow from that fire" [energy, faith, devotion] "light the world"?

____

____

Excerpt 5

And so, my fellow Americans: ask not what your country can do for you—ask what you can do for your country.

6. Rewrite this sentence in your own words.

____

____

Student Guide
Lesson 2: Crises

Both the United States and Russia had weapons that could destroy the world. Cold War fears of communism dominated U.S. foreign policy. What did Kennedy do when he faced tough decisions about communists in Cuba and Vietnam?

Lesson Objectives

- Locate Cuba on a map and explain the significance of its location relative to the United States.
- Explain the rise of John F. Kennedy's popularity after the Bay of Pigs disaster.
- Describe the actions John F. Kennedy took in regard to Vietnam.
- Summarize the crisis in Cuba in 1962.

PREPARE

Approximate lesson time is 60 minutes.

Materials

For the Student

Foreign Affairs Time Line Entry

A History of US (Concise Edition), Volume D (1929 to Present) by Joy Hakim

History Journal

World wall map

LEARN
Activity 1: JFK Fights Communism *(Offline)*

Instructions

A. Check Your Reading *(Chapter 40, pages 182–185)*

Review the reading assignment and answer the following questions in your History Journal.

1. President Harry Truman had a plaque on his desk in the Oval Office. It said, "The Buck Stops Here." How does that saying apply to JFK's handling of the Bay of Pigs disaster?
2. How did President Kennedy handle the missile crisis?
3. Name two decisions Kennedy made about Vietnam.

B. Focus on Foreign Affairs

Print two Foreign Affairs Time Line Entry sheets and add the Bay of Pigs and Cuban Missile Crisis to the Foreign Affairs Time Line. You may need to do some online research to include the date for each event.

C. Focus on Geography

Use your wall map to locate Cuba in the Caribbean Sea. Answer the following questions in your History Journal. When you have finished, compare your answers with those in the Answer Key.

1. How far is Cuba from the United States?
2. Why was the location of Cuba relative to the United States so important?

D. Assessment

Complete the online assessment.

E. Beyond the Lesson

When Russia's leader, Nikita Khrushchev, decided to put nuclear missiles in Cuba, the Joint Chiefs of Staff of the United States wanted President Kennedy to bomb Cuba. What do you think JFK should have done? Should he have launched a preemptive attack? Talk to an adult about JFK's decision to negotiate with Russia for the removal of the missiles from Cuba.

ASSESS

Lesson Assessment: Crises (*Online*)

You will complete an online assessment covering the main goals of this lesson. Your assessment will be scored by the computer.

Name Date

Foreign Affairs Time Line Entry

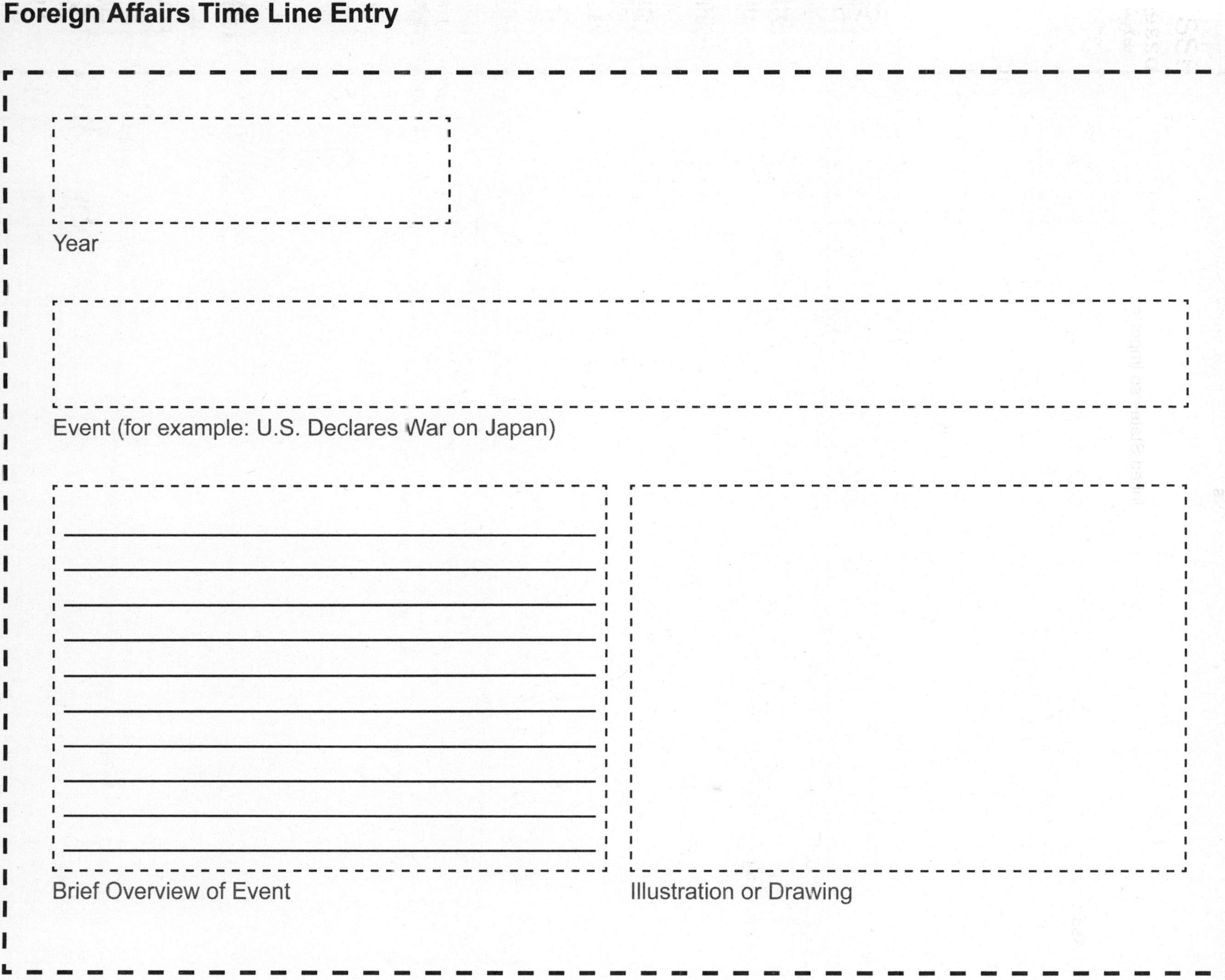

Name Date

Foreign Affairs Time Line Entry

Year

Event (for example: U.S. Declares War on Japan)

Brief Overview of Event

Illustration or Drawing

Student Guide
Lesson 3: Time to Act

The civil rights movement was gaining momentum in the South. Media coverage of police brutality was winning support for the demonstrators' goals. A rally in Washington, D.C., might convince Congress to pass a civil rights bill—but how many people would come? A few hundred? A few thousand? How many people would care enough to make the trip?

Lesson Objectives

- Analyze portions of Martin Luther King's speech.
- Explain how the television coverage of events in the South helped the civil rights movement.
- Explain that there were differences in the methods and approaches to the civil rights movement of different organizations.
- Summarize the goals of the civil rights movement of the 1960s.

PREPARE

Approximate lesson time is 60 minutes.

Materials

For the Student

Martin Luther King's Dream

A History of US (Concise Edition), Volume D (1929 to Present) by Joy Hakim

History Journal

Keywords and Pronunciation

CORE : Congress for Racial Equality

NAACP : the National Association for the Advancement of Colored People, an organization of blacks and whites formed to fight racial injustice

SCLC : Southern Christian Leadership Conference

Sit-in : tactic used by protesters who sat down in segregated establishments and refused to leave

SNCC : Student Nonviolent Coordinating Committee

LEARN

Activity 1: Wanted: Freedom and Equality for All *(Offline)*

Instructions

A. Read *(Chapter 41, pages 186–189; Chapter 42, pages 190–193)*

While you are reading, answer the following questions in your History Journal:

1. Why did moderate whites in Birmingham and elsewhere stay quiet in the face of injustice toward blacks?
2. What did blacks in Birmingham and elsewhere want?
3. What happened to the protesters?

4. Look at the pictures on pages 188 and 189. How do you think seeing those pictures might influence television viewers who knew very little about conditions in the South?
5. Use page 190 to make a chart of four major civil rights organizations in your History Journal. For each organization, chart the methods it used and identify individuals or the kinds of people who participated in the group. You will need this chart in future lessons.

Organization	Methods	People
NAACP		
SCLC		
SNCC		
CORE		

6. How many people participated in the March on Washington?

B. Use What You Know

The speech Martin Luther King delivered at the March on Washington captured the spirit of the civil rights movement. Complete the Martin Luther King's Dream sheet.

C. Assessment

Complete the online assessment.

ASSESS

Lesson Assessment: Time to Act (*Online*)

You will complete an online assessment covering the main goals of this lesson. Your assessment will be scored by the computer.

LEARN

Activity 2. Optional: Time to Act *(Online)*

Instructions

You may wish to go to the library or online to take a closer look at the nonviolent ways that Martin Luther King, Jr., and Southern blacks used in demonstrations.

Name Date

Martin Luther King's Dream

Read the excerpts from Martin Luther King's 'I Have a Dream' speech and translate the quotes into your own words and look for meaning.

Excerpt 1
I have a dream that my four children will one day live in a nation where they will not be judged by the color of their skin but by the content of their character.

Excerpt 2
I have a dream that one day… little black boys and black girls will be able to join hands with little white boys and white girls and walk together as sisters and brothers.

Student Guide
Lesson 4: A Tragic Transition

Kennedy was enjoying the respect and admiration of the people, and his ideas were finally being heard. Congress was starting to pass his New Frontier bills. Life was good in "Camelot" until a terrible thing happened...

Lesson Objectives

- Demonstrate knowledge gained in previous lessons.
- Describe the goals of John F. Kennedy's New Frontier.
- Identify Lyndon B. Johnson's background and his goals as president.
- Recognize the effect of John F. Kennedy's assassination.

PREPARE

Approximate lesson time is 60 minutes.

Materials

For the Student

One Term, Two Presidents

A History of US (Concise Edition), Volume D (1929 to Present) by Joy Hakim

History Journal

Keywords and Pronunciation

New Frontier : Kennedy's program to improve the economy and guarantee equality to all Americans.

ZIP code : Zone Improvement Program number that tells the post office what area or place to deliver the mail

---

LEARN

Activity 1: Tragedy in Texas *(Offline)*

Instructions

A. Read *(Chapter 43, pages 194–196; Chapter 44, pages 197–198)*

As you read, answer these questions. When you have finished, compare your answers with those in the Lesson Answer Key.

1. List five aspects of the New Frontier program President Kennedy wanted Congress to enact as law.
2. Why did Kennedy's New Frontier program meet resistance at first?
3. Describe the ways people reacted to Kennedy's assassination.
4. Who became president after JFK's death? Why?

B. Use What You Know

Print the One Term, Two Presidents sheet. Compare the backgrounds of John F. Kennedy and Lyndon B. Johnson, their goals, and their strengths as president. You may have to look in earlier chapters of your book or refer to your History Journal to find some of the information.

C. Assessment (online)

D. Beyond the Lesson

Interview a person born before 1953 about his or her memories of John F. Kennedy's assassination. Take notes in your History Journal during the interview.

To help organize your interview, you may want to create a list of interview questions. The list might include, but not be limited to, questions like:

1. How old were you when the event happened?
2. Where were you when you found out?
3. Who was with you when you found out?
4. How did you find out?
5. What were your first thoughts?
6. How did you feel?
7. How did other people around you react?
8. What did you do the rest of that day? The rest of the week?
9. How often did you think about it?
10. Looking back now, do you think or feel differently?
11. Did it have a lasting effect on you in any way?
12. Are there any other thoughts or feelings you'd like to share about this?

ASSESS

Lesson Assessment: A Tragic Transition (*Online*)

You will complete an online assessment covering the main goals of this lesson. Your assessment will be scored by the computer.

Name Date

One Term, Two Presidents

Compare John F. Kennedy's and Lyndon B. Johnson's backgrounds, goals, and strengths as president. You may need to look back through your book or History Journal to find some of the information you'll need.

	Kennedy	Both	Johnson
Background			
Goals			
Strengths			

Student Guide
Lesson 5: The Great Society

The big man from the big state of Texas had big goals: He wanted to wipe out poverty in the United States. As a congressman, he'd approached national politics like a sprinter and he wasn't about to slow down when he reached the White House.

Lesson Objectives

- Identify how the escalating cost of conflict in Vietnam affected LBJ's Great Society programs.
- Analyze the phrase "War on Poverty."
- Describe the experience and strengths Johnson brought to the presidency.
- Identify programs of the Great Society.

PREPARE

Approximate lesson time is 60 minutes.

Materials

For the Student

The Great Society

A History of US (Concise Edition), Volume D (1929 to Present) by Joy Hakim

History Journal

Keywords and Pronunciation

deficit : spending more money than the government is bringing in from taxes, import duties, etc.

Great Society : Lyndon Johnson's program to improve the lives of Americans

war on poverty : Lyndon Johnson's plan to end poverty in the United States

---

LEARN

Activity 1: The Big Texan Goes to War *(Offline)*

Instructions

A. Read *(Chapter 45, pages 199–201; Chapter 46, pages 202–204)*

As you read, answer these questions. When you have finished, compare your answers with those in the Lesson Answer Key.

1. List three personal traits or experiences that prepared Lyndon Johnson for being president
2. Why do you think President Johnson used the phrase "declares unconditional war on poverty"? In what ways might poverty be considered an enemy?
3. What challenges did Johnson face in the war in Vietnam?
4. What challenges did LBJ face with the black community?
5. How much money did the United States spend on the war in Vietnam in 1967 and how did that affect Johnson's Great Society program?

B. Use What You Know

Complete the Great Society sheet. Write a brief description of some of President Johnson's most noteworthy Great Society programs.

ASSESS

Lesson Assessment: The Great Society (*Online*)

You will complete an online assessment covering the main goals of this lesson. Your assessment will be scored by the computer.

LEARN

Activity 2. Optional: The Great Society *(Online)*

Name Date

The Great Society

Write a brief description for each of President Johnson's more noteworthy Great Society programs.

Programs	Descriptions
*Project Head Start	
*The Job Corps	
*Upward Bound	
The Neighborhood Youth Corps	
The Teacher Corps	
*Medicare	
*Medicaid	

* still in existence

Student Guide
Lesson 6: Still Not Equal

How crazy was this? One minute Martin Luther King, Jr., was in jail and the next minute he was being awarded the Nobel Peace Prize. Let's take a look at how it happened!

Lesson Objectives

- Identify Martin Luther King, Jr., as the youngest recipient of the Nobel Peace Prize and explain why he won it.
- Identify Malcolm X as a militant leader who preached separatism until he converted to orthodox Islam and softened his views.
- Describe the events in Selma and the role television played.
- Summarize the restrictions on black voting rights in the South.

PREPARE

Approximate lesson time is 60 minutes.

Materials

For the Student

Still Not Equal

A History of US (Concise Edition), Volume D (1929 to Present) by Joy Hakim

History Journal

LEARN
Activity 1: We Shall Overcome! *(Offline)*
Instructions

A. Read *(Chapter 47, pages 205–208; Chapter 48, pages 209–211)*

As you read, answer these questions. When you have finished, compare your answers with those in the Lesson Answer Key.

1. Why did Alfred Nobel establish the Nobel Prizes?
2. Why was Martin Luther King, Jr., given the Nobel Peace Prize? What record in the history of the prize does he hold?
3. What kept blacks in the South from registering to vote?
4. How did Malcolm X's beliefs about separation of the races and violent protest change? Why did they change?
5. What do you think would have happened if the people marching from Selma to Montgomery had reacted to the police violence with violence of their own?
6. How did television play a part in the success of the march from Selma to Montgomery?

B. Use What You Know

Complete the Still Not Equal sheet. Put the major events in order, and then write a brief description of each event.

ASSESS

Lesson Assessment: Still Not Equal (*Online*)

You will complete an online assessment covering the main goals of this lesson. Your assessment will be scored by the computer.

LEARN

Activity 2. Optional: Still Not Equal *(Online)*

Name Date

Still Not Equal

Write a description for each of the events listed.

Event	Description
1. A state trooper beats Cager Lee.	
2. First Selma to Montgomery march (Bloody Sunday)	
3. James Reeb eats in a black café.	
4. Second Selma to Montgomery march (Turnaround Tuesday)	Martin Luther King, Jr. attempted to lead a second march to Montgomery, but turned around and went back to Selma to avoid violent confrontation.
5. Lyndon Johnson sends the voting rights bill to Congress.	
6. Third Selma to Montgomery march	

Student Guide
Lesson 7: (Optional) Your Choice

Lesson Objectives

- Explore knowledge and skills taught in this course.

PREPARE

Approximate lesson time is 60 minutes.

Materials

For the Student

Map of the United States

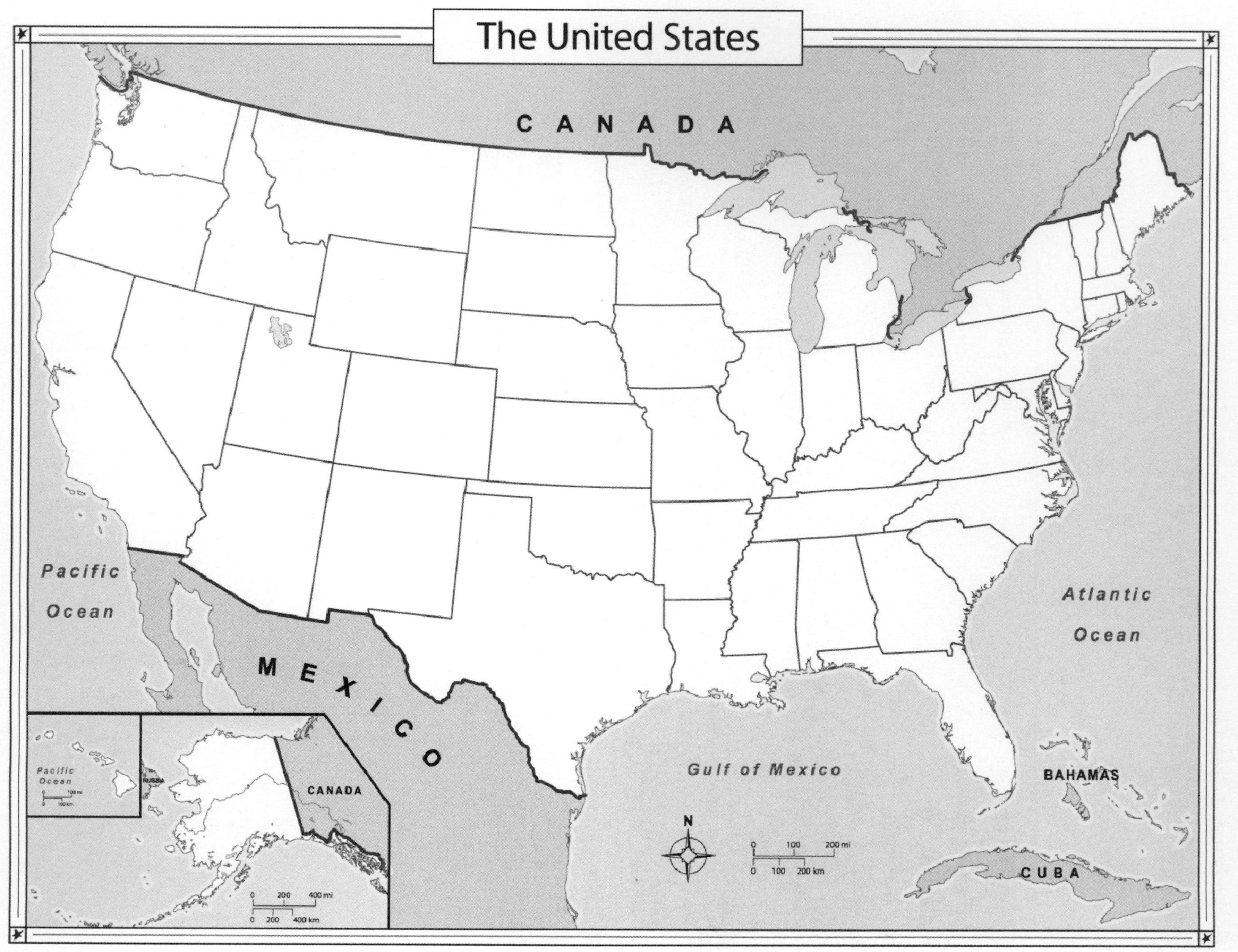
The United States
CANADA
Pacific Ocean
MEXICO
Atlantic Ocean
Gulf of Mexico
BAHAMAS
CUBA
N
0 100 200 mi
0 100 200 km
Pacific Ocean
RUSSIA
CANADA
0 200 400 mi
0 200 400 km

Student Guide
Lesson 8: More Guns Than Butter

The Vietnam War was costing the United States billions of dollars and thousands of lives. What were we fighting for?

Lesson Objectives

- Summarize the goals of U.S. participation in the Vietnam conflict.
- Identify the factors that kept the United States from achieving its goals during the Vietnam conflict.

PREPARE

Approximate lesson time is 60 minutes.

Advance Preparation

- Unit 11, Lesson 8, More Guns than Butter, discusses the Vietnam War. On page 216 there is a picture that may disturb some students. You may want to preview the chapter before you assign it and be prepared to discuss it with your student.

Materials

For the Student

Foreign Affairs Time Line Entry

U.S. Involvement in Vietnam Grows

A History of US (Concise Edition), Volume D (1929 to Present) by Joy Hakim

History Journal

Keywords and Pronunciation

guerrilla : a soldier who fights by using surprise tactics to bring down the enemy

napalm : jellied-gasoline explosives

LEARN

Activity 1: Lives Lost, Money Spent, and Still There's War *(Offline)*

Instructions

A. Read *(Chapter 49, pages 212–217)*

As you read, fill out the U.S. Involvement in Vietnam Grows sheet. When you have finished, compare your answers with those in the Lesson Answer Key.

B. Focus on Foreign Affairs

Complete the Foreign Affairs Time Line Entry sheet by adding the Gulf of Tonkin Resolution event. Add this sheet to your Foreign Affairs Time Line.

ASSESS

Lesson Assessment: More Guns Than Butter (*Online*)

You will complete an online assessment covering the main goals of this lesson. Your assessment will be scored by the computer.

Name ______________________________ Date ______________________________

U.S. Involvement in Vietnam Grows

Fill in the blanks in the paragraph below.

The Vietnamese were involved in a civil war. The North Vietnamese were receiving money and supplies from ________________ and ________________. That made the Americans very nervous. They feared the spread of ________________. The United States had not studied Southeast Asian history and didn't know that the ________________ and the ________________ did not get along. Presidents ________________, ________________, and ________________ and most of their advisers believed that the United States should stand up to ________________ anywhere.

Answer the following questions.

1. Why did presidents in both parties continue to send troops and supplies to fight in Vietnam?

2. How did President Johnson get congressional support for the Gulf of Tonkin Resolution? What happened as a result of the resolution?

3. Why was it so difficult to fight against guerrilla warriors in Vietnam?

4. How did the North Vietnamese treat American prisoners of war?

5. The author says that the United States did not understand what the war in Vietnam was about. Explain.

The author compares the problems the United States faced in Vietnam to the problems the British faced during the American Revolution. For each of the following statements about the American Revolution, write a comparable statement about the war in Vietnam.

6. Great Britain was the most powerful country in the world in 1776 and the new United States was a rural nation of farmers.

7. It was expensive and sometimes difficult for Great Britain to supply soldiers and equipment to a place thousands of miles away.

8. The people of the colonies wanted to be left alone to make their own choices.

9. Great Britain had many issues to deal with at home and abroad while the colonies were focused on the war.

10. The colonists knew the land and could fight and then disappear into the forests and hills.

11. The colonists got money and supplies from Britain's greatest enemy.

12. Advisers to the British government encouraged officials to send more troops and more weapons even though they were not winning the war.

Name ____________________ Date ____________________

Foreign Affairs Time Line Entry

Year

Event (for example: U.S. Declares War on Japan)

Brief Overview of Event

Illustration or Drawing

Student Guide
Lesson 9: Conflict Within Conflict

In the late 1960s many Americans were angry and frustrated—tired of waiting for change. Thousands of Americans took to the streets demanding "Equality now" and "No more war" and "Equal pay for equal work." Some marched in peaceful protests. Others turned to rioting and other violence. Many Americans feared the country would fall apart. Whatever had happened to Johnson's Great Society?

Lesson Objectives

- Describe the causes of civil unrest in the United States in the 1960s.
- Give examples of civil unrest in the United States in the 1960s and identify the groups who participated.

PREPARE

Approximate lesson time is 60 minutes.

Materials

For the Student

A History of US (Concise Edition), Volume D (1929 to Present) by Joy Hakim

History Journal

Keywords and Pronunciation

My Khe (MEE-khair)
My Lai (MEE-liy)

LEARN

Activity 1: Taking It to the Streets *(Offline)*

Instructions

A. Read *(Chapter 50, pages 218–221)*
As you read, answer these questions. When you have finished, compare your answers with those in the Lesson Answer Key.

1. How did Lyndon Johnson's actions lead to more and more antiwar demonstrations?

2. What role did television play in forming the opinion ordinary Americans had about the war?

3. Name at least four of the groups protesting in the 1960s.

4. How did the protests of the 1960s change over time?

5. Who was Thurgood Marshall?

B. Discuss

In the 1960s, many Americans participated in some form of protest. Would you protest government policy if you disagreed with it? What if you knew the president was lying to the public (as the media proved Lyndon Johnson was)? Would you protest? What of the dangers—remember the dogs and fire hoses in Selma? What about going to jail? What form of protest would you choose? Talk with an adult about your thoughts and feelings about the protest movements.

ASSESS

Lesson Assessment: Conflict Within Conflict (*Online*)

You will complete an online assessment covering the main goals of this lesson. Your assessment will be scored by the computer.

LEARN

Activity 2. Optional: Conflict Within Conflict *(Online)*

Student Guide
Lesson 10: Women Speak Out

Women of the 1950s and 1960s were portrayed on television as having perfect, idyllic lives. On TV, women loved taking care of their homes, husbands, and children. They felt fulfilled. In real life not all women wanted that role, but women didn't have a lot of options. Many wanted opportunities to develop and use their talents outside the home. Others believed traditional roles were best and that the new women's movement held potential for disaster.

Lesson Objectives

- Describe the role of the middle-class white woman as depicted by television of the 1950s and 1960s and in reality.
- Identify women who supported or opposed societal changes for women.
- Recognize that the women's movement of the 1960s was part of an ongoing demand for equal rights.
- Recognize the arguments for and against societal changes for women.
- Recognize the arguments for and against societal changes for women.

PREPARE

Approximate lesson time is 60 minutes.

Materials

For the Student

- Two Very Different Women
- What Am I?
- A History of US (Concise Edition), Volume D (1929 to Present) by Joy Hakim
- History Journal

LEARN

Activity 1: Friedan, Schlafly, and Friends *(Offline)*

Instructions

A. Read *(Chapter 51, pages 222–227)*

B. Use What You Know

Complete the following sheets:

- Two Very Different Women
- What Am I?

C. Profiles of Achievement

Betty Friedan and Phyllis Schlafly had very different views about the role of women in society and what the Equal Rights Amendment would mean for women.

1. Decide whose view you most agree with—Friedan's or Schlafly's.
2. Write a Profile of Achievement for the woman you chose. (You may use previously printed Profiles in your History Journal for reference.)
3. Then write a paragraph explaining why you would have supported that woman's views if you had lived during that time.

D. Focus on Economics

Study the table below. It compares the wages that men and women received for full-time work at similar jobs in two different years.

The numbers in the column labeled "Diff" show, for 1983, how women's salaries compared to men's as a percentage. For example, in *Service* occupations, women earned 81% of what men earned.
You need to calculate the percentages for 2000 and add them to the chart. To do that, divide the number in the "Women" column by the number in the "Men" column and multiply the answer by 100. Using *Service* occupations as an example: (314 ÷ 357) X 100 = 88 (rounded to nearest whole number). So in 2000, women earned 88% of what men earned.

Median Weekly Earnings						
	1983			**2000**		
Occupation	Men	Women	Difference	Men	Women	Difference
Executive/ Administrative/ Managerial	$530.00	$340.00	64%	$1,014.00	$686.00	
Sales Occupations	$389.00	$205.00	53%	$684.00	$407.00	
Administrative Support & Clerical	$362.00	$249.00	69%	$563.00	$449.0	
Service	$218.00	$176.00	81%	$357.00	$314.00	
Machine Operators/ Assemblers	$320.00	$202.00	63%	$495.00	$355.00	

1. What generalization can you make about women's pay compared to men's pay?

2. Do you see a change from 1983 to 2000? Explain.

ASSESS

Lesson Assessment: Women Speak Out (*Online*)

You will complete an online assessment covering the main goals of this lesson. Your assessment will be scored by the computer.

LEARN

Activity 2. Optional: Women Speak Out *(Online)*

Name Date

Two Very Different Women

Identify the views and beliefs of Betty Friedan and Phyllis Schlafly by copying the descriptions in the Description Bank into the appropriate box below.

Description Bank

- Was part of the conservative "New Right"
- Wrote *The Feminine Mystique*
- Supported ERA (Equal Rights Amendment)
- Believed that a career took away from the role as a wife and mother
- Believed that all people have the natural right to develop their potential
- Wanted women to have the same choices and opportunities as men
- Opposed ERA
- National leader of Stop ERA
- Wanted women to be equal partners in American society
- Emphasized the differences between men and women

Betty Friedan	Phyllis Schlafly

Name ______________________ Date ______________________

What Am I?

Use the Word Bank to answer the following questions.

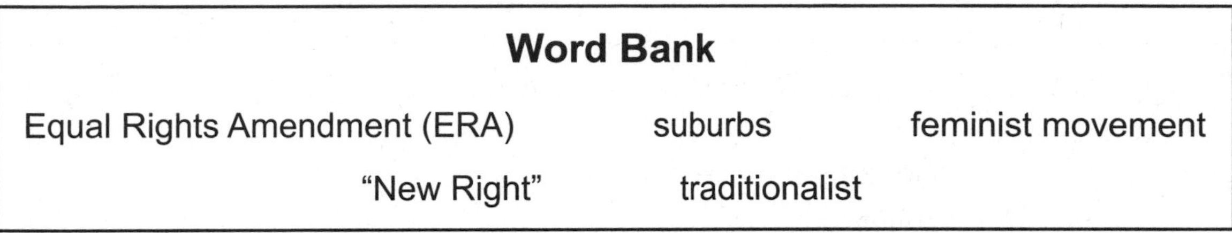

Word Bank

Equal Rights Amendment (ERA) suburbs feminist movement
"New Right" traditionalist

1. I am where many 1950s middle-class white women lived. What am I?

   ____

2. I believed that a woman's primary role was as a wife and mother. What am I?

   ____

3. I am the political force that developed in response to the turmoil of the times. What am I?

   ____

4. Some people wanted me added to the U.S. Constitution, but I was never ratified. What am I?

   ____

5. I am the political movement that wanted women to have the same opportunities as men did to develop their talents. What am I?

   ____

Student Guide
Lesson 11: Migrants

Imagine moving from place to place, picking crops from early morning to night, living in tents or one-room buildings without indoor plumbing, and never making enough money to get ahead. That's what migrant workers and their families had to face—until one migrant worker decided to do something about it.

Lesson Objectives

- Describe the hardships Mexican migrant workers faced in the United States.
- Identify César Chávez and the means he used to organize farm workers.

PREPARE

Approximate lesson time is 60 minutes.

Materials

For the Student

Profile

A History of US (Concise Edition), Volume D (1929 to Present) by Joy Hakim

History Journal

Keywords and Pronunciation

César Chávez (SAY-sahr CHAHV-ez)

LEARN

Activity 1: A Man Wanting to Help Others *(Offline)*

Instructions

A. Read (*Chapter 52, pages 228–232)*

As you read, answer the following questions.

1. What service do most migrant workers provide?
2. Where do most Mexican migrant workers find work?
3. Why did the owners of many large farms want to hire the migrant workers?
4. What hardships did Mexican migrant workers face in America?
5. What tactics did César Chávez (SAY-sahr CHAHV-ez) use to win recognition of his union?

B. Use What You Know

Use the information in today's reading and the Profile sheet to write a Profile of Courage for César Chávez. You can also view the following websites for additional information on César Chávez.

- America's Story: César Chávez
- American Hero: César Chávez
- United Farm Workers: The Story of César Chávez

ASSESS

Lesson Assessment: Migrants (*Online*)

You will complete an online assessment covering the main goals of this lesson. Your assessment will be scored by the computer.

Name Date

Profile of ______________________

Place Picture Here

Student Guide
Lesson 12: Hope and Hatred

During the '60s and '70s many people dreamed of ending poverty, discrimination, and what they considered an unjust war. They spilled into the streets calling for change. They became more insistent, louder, and more violent. Did the protests do any good?

Lesson Objectives

- Describe the differences between the problems in the South and in the North in the 1960s.
- Identify Robert F. Kennedy as a senator, an attorney general, and an activist who worked for civil rights and against poverty.
- Recognize the major goals of the Native American movement.
- Explain that Lyndon B. Johnson chose not to seek a second term as president.
- Describe how the life of Martin Luther King, Jr., ended.

PREPARE

Approximate lesson time is 60 minutes.

Materials

For the Student

Profile of Courage

A History of US (Concise Edition), Volume D (1929 to Present) by Joy Hakim

History Journal

LEARN

Activity 1: The Struggle to End Poverty *(Offline)*

Instructions

A. Read *(Chapter 53 pages 233–237; Chapter 54, pages 238–241)*

As you read, answer the following questions. Compare your answers to the ones in the Lesson Answer Key.

1. How did the problems Martin Luther King, Jr., addressed in the South differ from the problems he hoped to solve in the North?
2. Who was Robert (Bobby) Kennedy and how were his beliefs similar to those of César Chávez and Dr. King?
3. List at least two goals of the Native American rights movement.
4. What was the televised announcement that President Johnson made the night before Dr. King was to go back to Memphis?

B. Discuss

Discuss with an adult the lessons we can learn from Dr. King's final days.

C. Use What You Know

What did Robert F. Kennedy, Lyndon B. Johnson, and Martin Luther King, Jr., have in common? They wanted to end poverty in America. They wanted all people to be treated as equal citizens. They were courageous men who dedicated their lives to the struggle to end poverty and provide civil rights for all people.

These men deserve to be included in the Profiles in American History in your History Journal. Choose two of the men, and write a summary about them by completing two Profile of Courage sheets. Be sure to include each man's courageous efforts to guarantee civil rights and to end poverty in the United States. As you write your summaries, you may find it helpful to review the reading assignments from previous lessons.

ASSESS

Lesson Assessment: Hope and Hatred (*Online*)

You will complete an online assessment covering the main goals of this lesson. Your assessment will be scored by the computer.

Name Date

Profile of ______________________

Place Picture Here

Name Date

Profile of

Place Picture Here

Student Guide
Lesson 13: Victories and Violence

As Martin Luther King's funeral was taking place, riots broke out in cities across the nation. More people were killed. But everyone didn't turn to violence. Some found creative ways to bring about change.

Lesson Objectives

- Describe the reactions to Dr. King's assassination.
- Summarize major cultural, political, and economic achievements of blacks in the 1960s.
- Describe Malcolm X's experience with the power of words.
- Explain the description of Robert F. Kennedy, "Born the son of wealth, he died a champion of outcasts of the world," in terms of his background and goals.

PREPARE

Approximate lesson time is 60 minutes.

Materials

For the Student

A History of US (Concise Edition), Volume D (1929 to Present) by Joy Hakim

History Journal

LEARN

Activity 1: A Chain Reaction *(Offline)*

Instructions

A. Read *(Chapter 55, pages 242–246)*

As you read, answer the following questions.

1. How did Americans respond to King's death?
2. How did blacks gain cultural, political, and economic power in the years following Dr. King's death?
3. What did Malcolm X do in prison that helped him turn his life around and become a powerful speaker?
4. Describing Robert F. Kennedy, a historian wrote, "Born the son of wealth, he died a champion of outcasts of the world." Based on what you read about Robert Kennedy, what do you think the historian meant?

Activity 2: Notable People *(Online)*

Instructions

B. Use What You Know

Review what you've learned about some black writers by completing the online Flash Cards activity. You can also use *Grolier's Encyclopedia* online to find additional information for your Flash Cards.

ASSESS

Lesson Assessment: Victories and Violence (*Online*)

You will complete an online assessment covering the main goals of this lesson. Your assessment will be scored by the computer.

Student Guide
Lesson 14: Unit Review

You have finished the unit! It's time to review what you've learned. You will take the Unit Assessment in the next lesson.

Lesson Objectives

- Demonstrate mastery of important knowledge and skills in this unit.

PREPARE

Approximate lesson time is 60 minutes.

Materials

For the Student

History Journal

LEARN

Activity 1: A Turbulent Time *(Online)*

Instructions

A. History Journal Review

Review what you've learned in this unit by going through your History Journal. You should:

- Look at activity sheets you've completed for this unit.
- Review unit keywords.
- Read through any writing assignments you did during the unit.
- Review the assessments you took.

Don't rush through; take your time. Your History Journal is a great resource for a unit review.

Student Guide
Lesson 15: Unit Assessment

You've finished the unit! Now it's time to take the Unit Assessment.

Lesson Objectives

- Identify major political and reform leaders of the 1960s and their accomplishments and failings.
- Recognize major foreign policy events of the 1960s including Cuba and Vietnam as threats to world peace and domestic policies and peace.
- Assess the importance of geographic location in the Cuban crisis.
- Describe the domestic problems the nation faced in the 1960s and the ways the government addressed those problems.
- Describe the role of the media in disseminating information and forming public opinion.
- Identify individuals and groups who expanded the ideals of democracy.
- Give examples of the tactics used by environmental, social, and economic reformers.
- Describe the causes and results of the escalation of U.S. involvement in Vietnam in the 1950s and 60s.
- Recognize the relationship between poverty and other societal ills.
- Identify the causes and results of the black migration of the post-war era.

PREPARE

Approximate lesson time is 60 minutes.

ASSESS

Unit Assessment: A Turbulent Time, Part 1 *(Online)*

Complete the computer-scored portion of the Unit Assessment. When you have finished, complete the teacher-scored portion of the assessment and submit it to your teacher.

Unit Assessment: A Turbulent Time, Part 2 *(Offline)*

Complete the teacher-scored portion of the Unit Assessment and submit it to your teacher.

Student Guide

Unit 12: Not So Long Ago
Lesson 1: Marching to a Different Beat

Who could ever have imagined the changes that rocked the United States at the end of the twentieth century? Immigrants with dreams of freedom and opportunity streamed in from Central and South America, Asia, and Oceania. The country changed as Americans challenged their leaders. And, as communism crumbled, the United States emerged from the Cold War as the only superpower. Greater power meant greater responsibility, and the nation met threats to democracy by sending troops to many lands.

They took to the streets singing “We Shall Overcome” and demanding equality. They gathered on campuses chanting “No! No! We won’t go” and protesting the war in Vietnam. Many of the young people of the '60s often wore colorful clothing, and had long hair and strange habits. Many experimented with dangerous drugs. They rejected traditional music and listened to rock—the throbbing, pulsing new music that merged black and white musical traditions. They rebelled against society’s values and were convinced they could make a difference. Did they?

Lesson Objectives

- Describe the ideas, accomplishments, and failings of the 1960s counterculture.
- Identify at least two individuals that influenced the music of the '60s.
- Analyze music of the '60s to understand its meaning.

PREPARE

Approximate lesson time is 60 minutes.

Materials

For the Student

A History of US (Concise Edition), Volume D (1929 to Present) by Joy Hakim

History Journal

Keywords and Pronunciation

commune : a group of people who live together and share money and responsibilities
counterculture : a culture with values that are very different from those of established society
hippies : young people of the 1960s who rebelled against traditional values

---

LEARN

Activity 1: Times Are A-Changin' *(Offline)*

Instructions

A. Read *(Chapter 56, pages 248–252)*

As you read, answer the following questions. Compare your answers with those in the Lesson Answer Key.

1. Describe some of the actions and beliefs of young people in the '60s.
2. How was the rock music of the '60s different from earlier music?
3. Why did Bob Dylan become one of the most influential musicians of the Vietnam era?

4. Why was John Hammond important to American music?
5. Who were some of the other important people in rock music at that time?

Write a brief definition for each of these terms in your History Journal. When you have finished, compare your definitions with those in the Keywords section of this lesson.
counterculture
commune
hippies

B. Use What You Know

You are a writer for a historical magazine. You have been asked to write an article about the counterculture of the '60s. The counterculture was very controversial. Americans applauded some of the activities of the young hippies and condemned others. As you write your article in your History Journal, be sure to describe the positive and negative activities of the youth, drug abuse, and rock music of the '60s.

When you have finished your article, read it to an adult. Discuss any opinions, misunderstandings, or questions you may have about the information you read in today's lesson.

ASSESS

Lesson Assessment: Marching to a Different Beat (*Online*)

You will complete an online assessment covering the main goals of this lesson. Your assessment will be scored by the computer.

Student Guide
Lesson 2: The Nixon Era

In November 1972 Richard Nixon won a second term in a landslide victory. Twenty-one months later he had to resign in disgrace. What happened?

Lesson Objectives

- Describe the strengths and weaknesses Nixon brought to the presidency and their consequences.
- Summarize the major events of the Nixon presidency.

PREPARE

Approximate lesson time is 60 minutes.

Materials

For the Student

- Foreign Affairs Time Line Entry
- Nixon's Peaks and Valleys

A History of US (Concise Edition), Volume D (1929 to Present) by Joy Hakim

History Journal

LEARN

Activity 1: The Nixon Years *(Offline)*

Instructions

A. Warm-Up

You should begin the lesson online by listening to what Richard Nixon had to say at the end of his presidency before you begin today's reading.

B. Read *(Chapter 57, pages 253–259)*

As you read, answer the following questions in your History Journal. Compare your answers with those in the Answer Key.

1. What were the two sides of Richard Nixon's personality?
2. How did the two sides show themselves during his first term as president?
3. What caused Nixon's downfall?

C. Use What You Know

Complete the Nixon's Peaks and Valleys sheet. When you have finished, compare your answers with those in the Lesson Answer Key.

D. Focus on Foreign Affairs

Nixon's intelligent, reasonable side helped him lead the nation in a new foreign-policy direction. Nixon understood that the world was changing and that it was time to try to work with the communist nations. Today you will add Nixon's visit to China to your Foreign Affairs Time Line. Complete the Time Line Entry sheet about Nixon's visit to China. Place this sheet to the right of your last time line sheet, joining them with more string or yarn.

ASSESS

Lesson Assessment: The Nixon Era (*Online*)

You will complete an online assessment covering the main goals of this lesson. Your assessment will be scored by the computer.

LEARN

Activity 2. Optional: The Nixon Era *(Online)*

Name Date

Nixon's Peaks and Valleys

President Nixon's term in office included great peaks (when Americans were extremely proud) and deep valleys (when Americans were deeply divided or disillusioned). Identify the high and low points during Nixon's administration by describing major events that had either a positive or negative effect on the nation.

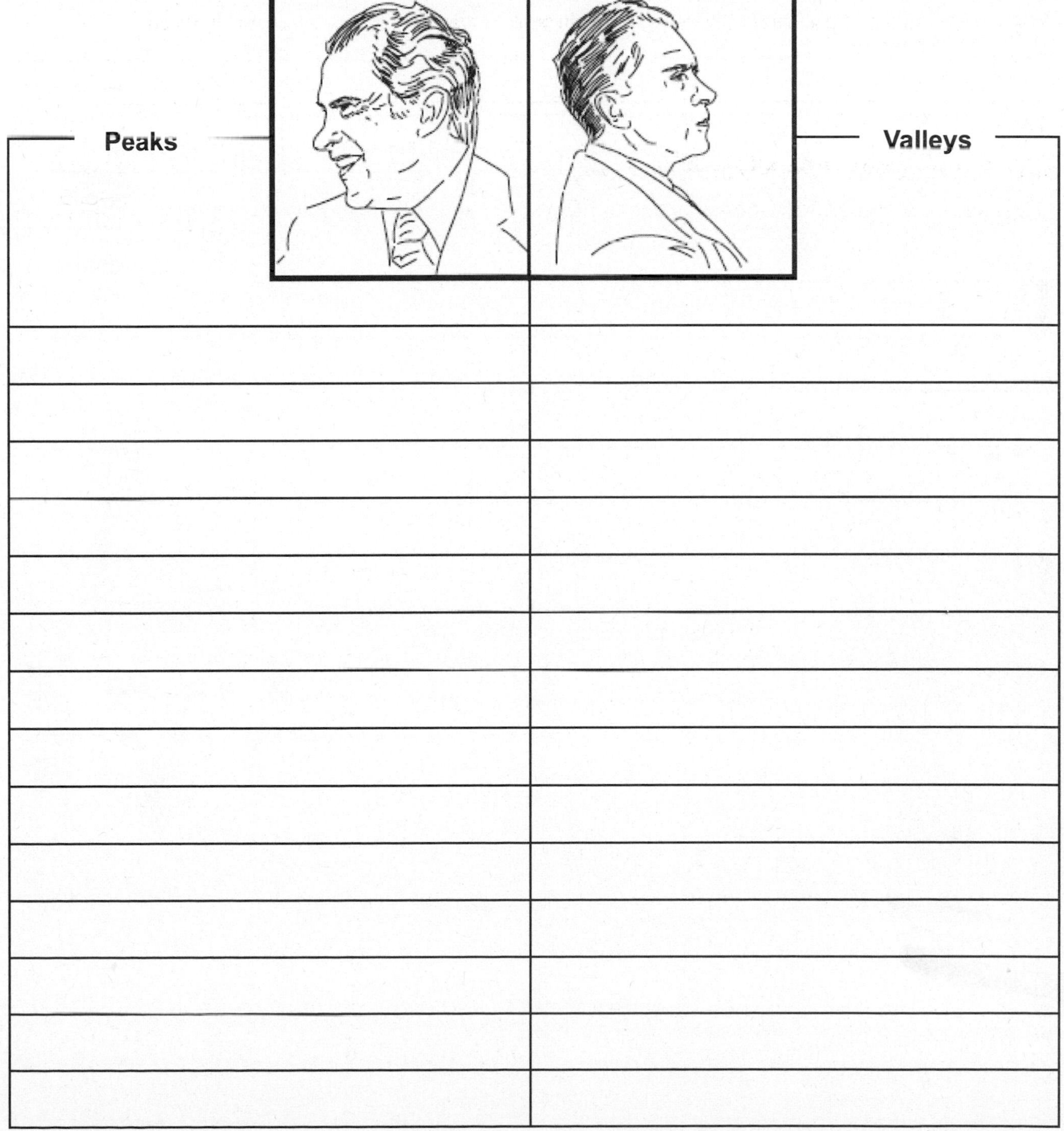

1. What unlawful acts that Nixon and his staff committed led to the Watergate scandal?

2. Why did Nixon resign?

3. Explain how the constitutional process helped solve the Watergate crisis.

Name Date

Foreign Affairs Time Line Entry

Year

Event (for example: U.S. Declares War on Japan)

Illustration or Drawing

Brief Overview of Event

Student Guide
Lesson 3: Writing Wrongs

Some people call the press a fourth branch of government. What does that mean? What kind of real power does the press have in a democracy? How much does a democracy need a free press? When *Washington Post* reporters delved into a story about a burglary at the offices of the Democratic National Committee and the trial that followed, they unleashed information that would lead to a congressional investigation, a flood of confessions, and evidence that implicated President Nixon. What happened when Congress drew up articles of impeachment?

Lesson Objectives

- Identify the impeachment process under the Constitution.
- Recognize how the press played a significant role in exposing the Watergate affair.

PREPARE

Approximate lesson time is 60 minutes.

Materials

For the Student

- Chain of Events
- How Does Impeachment Work?
- Profile in Courage
- History Journal

LEARN

Activity 1: Chain of Events *(Online)*

ASSESS

Lesson Assessment: Writing Wrongs (*Online*)

You will complete an online assessment covering the main goals of this lesson. Your assessment will be scored by the computer.

LEARN

Activity 2. Optional: Writing Wrongs *(Online)*

Name Date

Chain of Events

Summarize the sequence of events of the Watergate scandal. Start with the Washington Post's report of the break-in and end with Nixon's resignation.

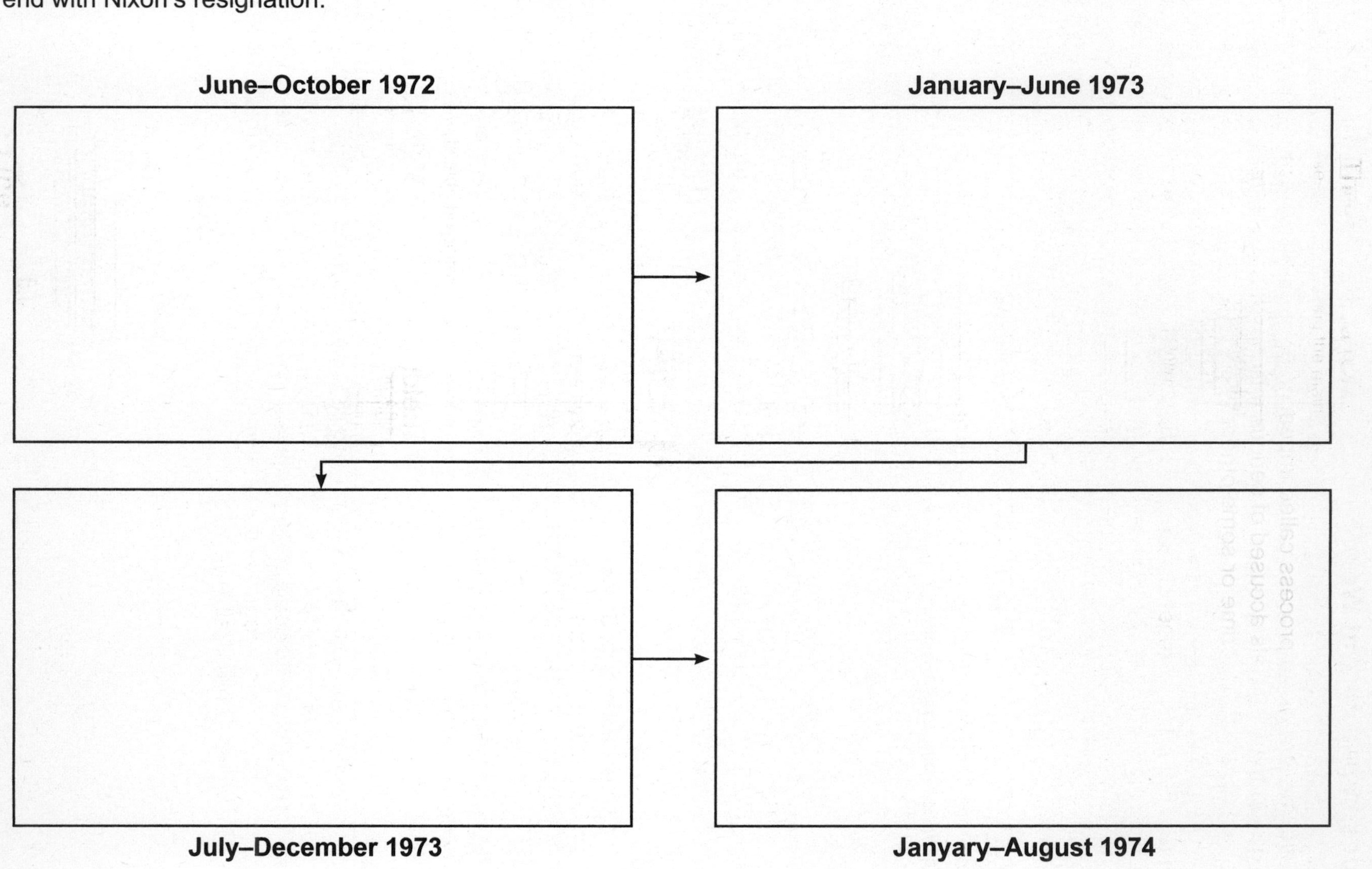

Name Date

How Does Impeachment Work?

The Constitution includes a process called impeachment that allows Congress to bring to trial U.S. government officials accused of serious misconduct. To impeach someone means to charge him or her with a crime or some other misdeed.

The Founders included the impeachment process in the Constitution so the American people would have a way to remove officials who break the law or abuse their power in a serious way. Congress has the power to impeach presidents, vice presidents, cabinet officers, federal judges, or any other civilian U.S. official —except members of Congress. It's not easy to impeach someone, though. It's a long, complicated process. Let's see how the basics work.

Step 1
Only the U.S. House of Representatives has the power to begin the impeachment process against a U.S. official. So first House members must debate whether or not the official deserves to be charged with crimes or serious misconduct.

Step 2
After debate, the House votes on whether or not to bring charges. If a majority of the House members vote yes, then the official is said to be "impeached." That is, the official has been accused of crimes or serious misconduct, and now must stand trial.

Step 3
Next the process moves to the U.S. Senate, where the trial takes place. The Senate sits as a jury and hears the charges against the impeached official. During the trial, senators listen to evidence and arguments about whether the official should be found guilty of the charges.

Step 4
At the end of the trial, the senators vote on whether the evidence proves that the official is guilty of the charges. If two-thirds of the senators vote guilty, then the official is convicted.

Step 5
Someone who is impeached and convicted doesn't go to jail or pay a fine. The punishment is that they're removed from office. The Senate may also prohibit that person from ever again holding office in the U.S. government. He or she may also be tried in a regular court of law. If convicted there, the punishment could involve a fine or jail time.

Name ______________________ Date ______________________

Profile of ______________________

Place Picture Here

Student Guide
Lesson 4: One-Term Presidents

When Gerald Ford took office, he faced the challenging job of healing the nation from the "long national nightmare" created by Watergate and the Vietnam War. Did he succeed?
Jimmy Carter, a Democrat from Georgia, took over the presidency next. Although Carter had some good ideas, he couldn't get Congress to cooperate. Why did he have so much trouble?

Lesson Objectives

- Identify U.S. presidents who served between the years 1974 and 2000.
- Recognize some of the major events associated with presidents Ford, Carter, Reagan, Bush, and Clinton.
- Explain how Gerald Ford became president without an election.
- Explore the possibilities of President Carter's reelection.
- Identify the major events associated with president Ford.
- Identify the major events associated with president Carter.

PREPARE

Approximate lesson time is 60 minutes.

Materials

For the Student

Presidential Time Line

A History of US (Concise Edition), Volume D (1929 to Present) by Joy Hakim

History Journal

LEARN

Activity 1: Presidents Ford and Carter *(Online)*

Instructions

A. Read *(Chapter 58, pages 260–262)*

As you read, answer the following questions and compare your answers with those in the Lesson Answer Key.

1. Gerald Ford became president of the United States, but he was never elected. How did that happen?
2. What political experience did Ford have before becoming president?
3. What two major issues did President Ford have to deal with when he became president, and what action did he take to clear up these issues?
4. First Lady Betty Ford was known for speaking out on controversial issues. What were some of those issues?
5. Why was President Jimmy Carter's administration unsuccessful in getting things done?

6. What were some of the major issues Carter faced while he was president?
7. What were some of Carter's accomplishments as president?
8. Explain why you think President Carter didn't get reelected.

B. Research

Complete the Presidential Time Lines for Presidents Ford and Carter by doing research online.

ASSESS

Lesson Assessment: One-Term Presidents (*Online*)

You will complete an online assessment covering the main goals of this lesson. Your assessment will be scored by the computer.

LEARN

Activity 2. Optional: One-Term Presidents *(Online) A*

Name ______________________ Date ______________________

Presidential Time Line

If you can find a picture of this president, attach it here.

Name: ______________________

Years in Office: _____ – _____

Number of Terms: ______

Vice president: ______________________

First Lady: ______________________

__________ President

☆☆☆☆☆☆☆☆☆☆☆☆☆☆☆☆☆

Name ______________________ Date ______________________

Presidential Time Line

If you can find a picture of this president, attach it here.

Name: ______________________

Years in Office: ______ – ______

Number of Terms: ______

Vice president: ______________________

First Lady: ______________________

______ President

☆☆☆☆☆☆☆☆☆☆☆☆☆☆☆☆☆

Student Guide
Lesson 5: The Great Communicator

Which U.S. president was a former movie star? He was boyish, easygoing, likable, and friendly, and he knew how to use television as no president had before him.

Let's find out more!

Lesson Objectives

- Identify major events that occurred during President Reagan's administration.
- Describe with examples Ronald Reagan's domestic philosophy and policies.
- Explain Reagan's strategy in dealing with the Soviet Union.
- Assess Reagan's greatest successes and failures.
- Identify major events that occurred during President Bush's administration.

PREPARE

Approximate lesson time is 60 minutes.

Materials

For the Student

Presidential Time Line

A History of US (Concise Edition), Volume D (1929 to Present) by Joy Hakim

History Journal

LEARN

Activity 1: His Presidential Role *(Offline)*

Instructions

A. Read *(Chapter 59, pages 263–269)*

As you read, answer the following questions and then compare your answers with those in the Lesson Answer Key.

1. Give examples of how Reagan executed his philosophy and policies on government during his presidency.
2. Describe conditions in the United States by the end of the '80s, after Reagan had implemented some of his philosophy and policies.
3. What was Reagan's strategy to balance the national budget? Was his strategy successful? Explain.
4. What was the Reagan administration's theory behind reducing big government? What were some of the results in reducing big government?
5. Explain Reagan's strategy in dealing with the Soviet Union.

B. Research

Research President Ronald Reagan online. Collect information about him from *The New Book of Knowledge,* Grolier's online encyclopedia, and from other websites.

Complete the Presidential Time Line sheet for Reagan and be sure to include the following information:

- Personal Characteristics/Background
- Major Contributions
- Major Failures
- Domestic Policies/Activities
- Foreign Policies/Activities

If you need more space to write, use extra paper or the back of the Presidential Time Line sheet.

ASSESS

Lesson Assessment: The Great Communicator (*Online*)

You will complete an online assessment covering the main goals of this lesson. Your assessment will be scored by the computer.

Name ______________________ Date ______________________

Presidential Time Line

If you can find a picture of this president, attach it here.

Name: ______________________

Years in Office: ____ – ____

Number of Terms: ______

Vice president: ______________________

First Lady: ______________________

__________ President

☆☆☆☆☆☆☆☆☆☆☆☆☆☆☆☆☆

Student Guide
Lesson 6: (Optional) Your Choice

Lesson Objectives

- Explore knowledge and skills taught in this course.

PREPARE

Approximate lesson time is 60 minutes.

Materials

For the Student

Map of the United States

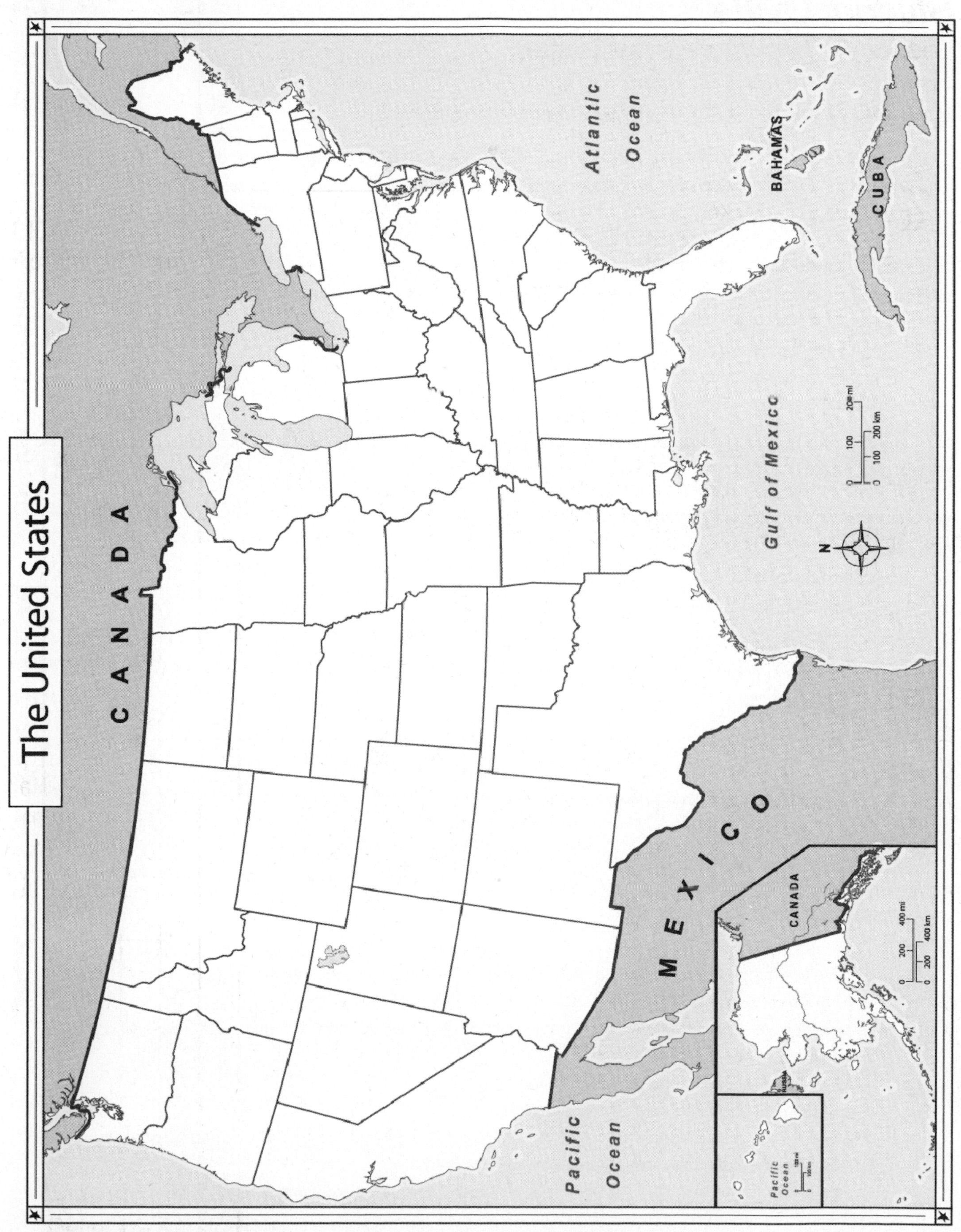
The United States
CANADA
Atlantic Ocean
BAHAMAS
CUBA
Gulf of Mexico
MEXICO
Pacific Ocean
CANADA
N

Student Guide
Lesson 7: Two More Presidents

Which U.S. president was a World War II Navy pilot and a genuine war hero?

Which president of the United States played the saxophone and at one time had considered a career as a musician? This same president was a Rhodes scholar, a Yale graduate, and a former governor.

Let's find out more about our 41st and 42nd presidents!

Lesson Objectives

- Identify major events that occurred during President Bush's administration.
- Recognize what is meant by "the end of the Cold War."
- Identify the causes and results of the Gulf War.
- Describe with examples Bill Clinton's achievements and failures.
- Explain the purpose and process of impeachment.

PREPARE

Approximate lesson time is 60 minutes.

Materials

For the Student

- Presidential Clues
- Presidential Time Line

A History of US (Concise Edition), Volume D (1929 to Present) by Joy Hakim

History Journal

LEARN

Activity 1: Economic Prosperity *(Offline)*

Instructions

A. Read *(Chapter 60, pages 270â273; Chapter 61, pages 274â276)*

As you read, answer the following questions. When you have finished, compare your answers with those in the Lesson Answer Key.

1. The title of Chapter 60 is "The End of the Cold War." What do you think is the meaning of the phrase "end of the Cold War"?
2. As president, George Bush promised not to raise taxes. Then why did he make an agreement with Congress to raise taxes?
3. What were the causes and results of the Gulf War?
4. Why did Bush send American forces into Somalia?
5. Give some examples of goals that President Bill Clinton achieved during his presidency, goals that he was unable to achieve, and failures of his presidency.
6. Explain the purpose and the process of impeachment. Bill Clinton was impeached, but he was not removed from the office of president. Why?

B. Research

Research online Presidents George H.W. Bush and William Clinton. Collect information from *The New Book of Knowledge*, Grolier's online encyclopedia, and from other websites (A good source would be the presidential libraries).

Complete a Presidential Time Line sheet for each president. Be sure to include the following information:

- Personal Characteristics/Background
- Major Contributions
- Major Failures
- Domestic Policies/Activities
- Foreign Policies/Activities

If you need more space to write, you may use extra paper or the back of the Presidential Time Line sheet.

C. Use What You Know

Complete the Presidential Clues sheet. Let's see how much you remember about the presidents who served between 1974 and 2000. Check your answers against those in the Lesson Answer Key.

ASSESS

Lesson Assessment: Two More Presidents (*Online*)

You will complete an online assessment covering the main goals of this lesson. Your assessment will be scored by the computer.

Name Date

Presidential Time Line

If you can find a picture of this president, attach it here.

Name: ____________________

Years in Office: _____ – _____

Number of Terms: ______

Vice president: ____________________

First Lady: ____________________

________ President

Name Date

Presidential Time Line

If you can find a picture of this president, attach it here.

Name: ________________

Years in Office: ____ – ____

Number of Terms: ____

Vice president: ________________

First Lady: ________________

________ President

Name Date

Presidential Clues

Fold the paper along the dotted line so the clues are behind this page and you cannot see them. Read each statement and check the correct president or presidents. Unfold the page to get a clue if you are not sure of the answer. If you need additional help, refer to your Presidential Time Lines.

	Ford	Carter	Reagan	Bush	Clinton	Question	Clue
1.						I built a 40-nation coalition under the United Nations to force Iraq to withdraw after it invaded Kuwait in1990.	I also served as vice president under Ronald Reagan.
2.						My greatest contribution was negotiating a treaty with the Soviet Union banning intermediate-range nuclear forces (INF) and easing tensions between our two countries.	I had a successful career acting in more than 50 movies and on television, and was the oldest person to be elected president.
3.						I worked to bring about a peace agree-ment between the leaders of Israel and the Palestinian Liberation Organization (PLO).	My country enjoyed prosperity and peace during my administration, but I was impeached and acquitted.
4.						We served as governors from our home states before we became president.	Our home states are Georgia, California, and Arkansas.
5.						My greatest contributions included the Salt II Arms Limitation Treaty with the Soviet Union and the Israeli-Egyptian peace treaty.	I resigned my military commission to run the family peanut business.
6.						We served in the House of Representatives before we became president.	Our home states are Michigan and Texas.
7.						I granted Richard Nixon an unconditional pardon for wrongdoings against the United States.	I am the only president who was not elected to the presidency or the vice presidency.
8.						We authorized the bombing of Iraq when Iraq violated United Nations agreements and refused to allow inspections of weapons facilities.	We are the 41st and 42nd presidents of the United States.

Student Guide
Lesson 8: Where in the World?

The world changed dramatically during the last quarter of the twentieth century. Many new nations formed and one reunited. The United States, in its role of superpower, sent troops to troubled areas. Where in the world did it all happen? Let's take a closer look.

Lesson Objectives

- Use maps to locate areas that have experienced major political changes since 1975.
- Identify areas of major U.S. military involvement since 1975.

PREPARE

Approximate lesson time is 60 minutes.

Materials

For the Student

- Fall of Communism
- U.S. Military Involvement
- World wall map

LEARN

Activity 1: Global Quest *(Online)*

Activity 2. Optional: Where in the World? *(Online)*

Name Date

Fall of Communism

A. Explore

Use the Europe and Asia, 1975, and Europe and Asia, 2003, maps and map call-outs to answer the following questions:

Soviet Union

1. How many states were part of the U.S.S.R in 1975?

2. Why were people in the countries of Eastern Europe increasingly dissatisfied with communism by the late 1980s?

3. How many of the countries that were once part of the U.S.S.R. had a communist government in 2003?

Germany

1. Germany was divided into two countries after World War II. Which of the two countries did democratic nations, including the United States, support and how?

2. Who built the Berlin Wall in 1961 and why?

3. What form of government did the reunited Germany have in 2003?

Yugoslavia

1. What led to the fall of communism in Yugoslavia?

2. How many countries are on the 2003 map where communist Yugoslavia used to be?

3. Name two reasons for civil unrest in the region that was once Yugoslavia.

B. Think About It

Write two or three sentences to summarize the changes and reasons for change in Europe in the last quarter of the twentieth century.

Name Date

U.S. Military Involvement

Using your wall map, locate each country where the U.S. military was involved between 1975 and 2000. Place a check mark in the right column after you locate each one.

President	Country Where U.S. Military Was Involved and Details About the Involvement	Check Here
Gerald Ford	Brought home the last troops from **Vietnam**	✓
Ronald Reagan	Sent Marines to **Lebanon** Sent Marines to **Grenada** Bombed military targets in **Libya** Protected **Kuwait's** oil tankers in the Persian Gulf	
George Bush	Sent troops to oust **Panama** dictator Manuel Noriega Sent Marines to **Somalia** to ensure that relief supplies got to starving Somalians Authorized new air strikes against **Iraq** for violating U.N. agreements	
Bill Clinton	Sent peacekeeping troops to **Bosnia** Sent troops to **Haiti** to help restore Jean-Bertrand Aristide to office Bombed **Iraq** when Saddam Hussein stopped U.N. inspections for evidence of nuclear, chemical, and biological weapons	

Student Guide
Lesson 9: Who Are We Now?

Every day, people from all over the world arrive in the United States with the dream of becoming part of this great nation. Why do so many people want to become Americans?

Lesson Objectives

- Identify the democratic beliefs and ideals that unite diverse peoples as Americans.
- Identify major reasons people give for immigrating to the United States.
- Analyze maps to gain information on U.S. demographics.

PREPARE

Approximate lesson time is 60 minutes.

Materials

For the Student

Modern Immigration Trends

A History of US (Concise Edition), Volume D (1929 to Present) by Joy Hakim

History Journal

LEARN

Activity 1: Common Threads *(Offline)*

Instructions

A. Read *(Chapter 62, pages 277–285)*

As you read, answer the following questions and compare your answers with the answers in the Lesson Answer Key.

1. From where did most of the first settlers, who settled the region that became the United States, come?
2. Why was the United States like a magnet for lots of different people?
3. From where did most of the immigrants come in the late nineteenth century and early twentieth century? Why were the earliest immigrants worried about the new immigrants?
4. From where did most of the immigrants come near the end of the twentieth century?
5. The United States counts its citizens every 10 years. What is this called?
6. Complete the following according to the 2010 census:
   Population:
   Largest cities:
   Fastest growing city:
   Percentage of regional population growth:
7. What did we learn about urban growth from information collected in 2000?
8. How can shifting populations make a political difference?

B. Use What You Know

Complete the Modern Immigration Trends sheet. Compare your answers with those in the Lesson Answer Key.

ASSESS

Lesson Assessment: Who Are We Now? (*Online*)

You will complete an online assessment covering the main goals of this lesson. Your assessment will be scored by the computer.

Name Date

Modern Immigration Trends

The map below depicts immigration to the United States in 1996. Examine the map and answer the questions that follow.

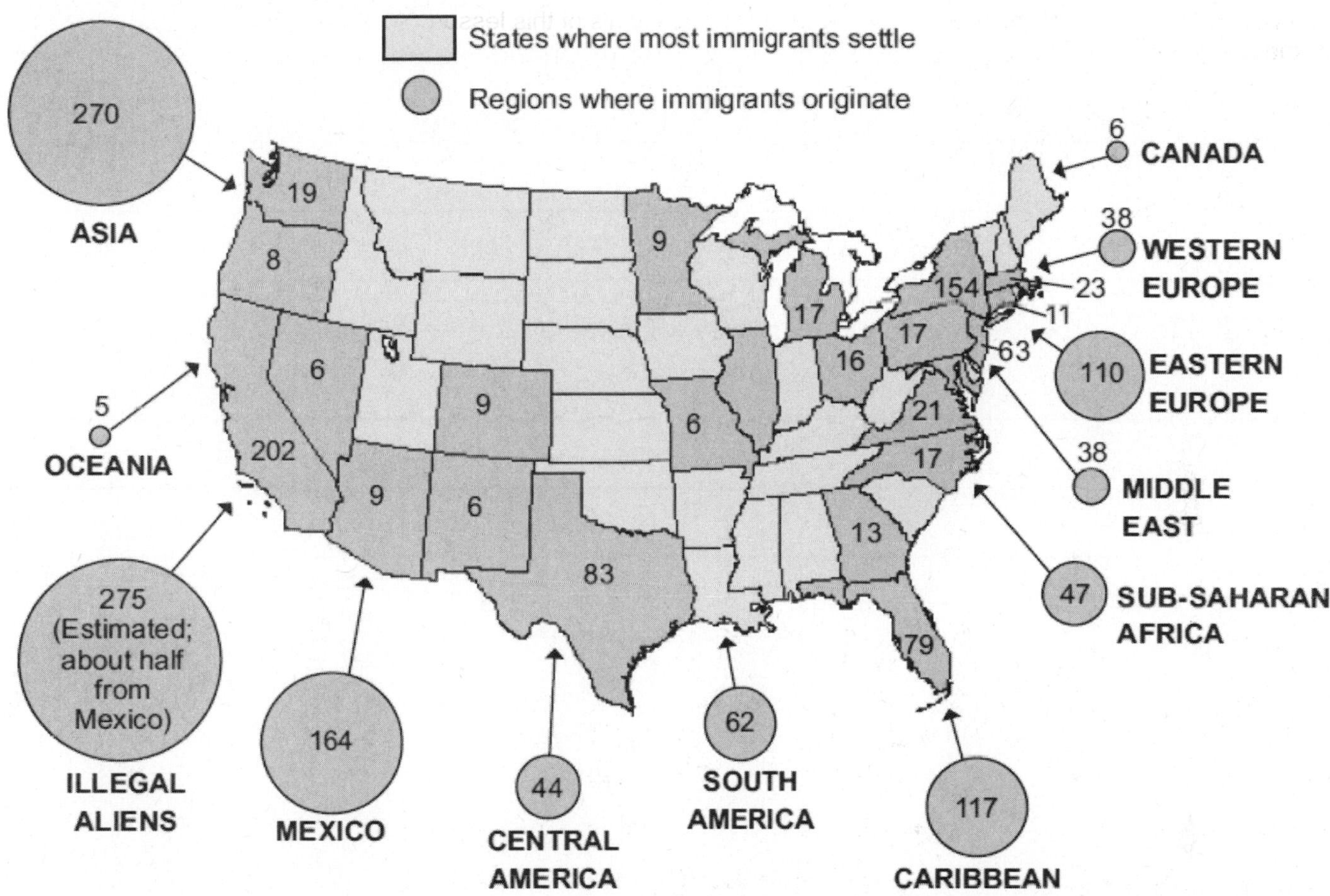

Numbers on the states = thousands of immigrants.
Numbers in circles = thousands of immigrants.

1. From which two regions—Asia/Oceania, Europe, Africa, and the Americas—did most immigrants come in 1996? How many immigrants came from each of these two areas?

____

____

2. How does this differ from immigration in the early twentieth century?

____

____

____

3. Which were the top five states in number of immigrants?

____

____

____

4. Based on your reading, what draws people to the United States?

____

____

____

5. What effects do you think this immigration will have on the American people?

____

____

____

Student Guide
Lesson 10: (Optional) Your Choice

Lesson Objectives

- Explore knowledge and skills taught in this course.

PREPARE

Approximate lesson time is 60 minutes.

Materials

For the Student

Map of the United States

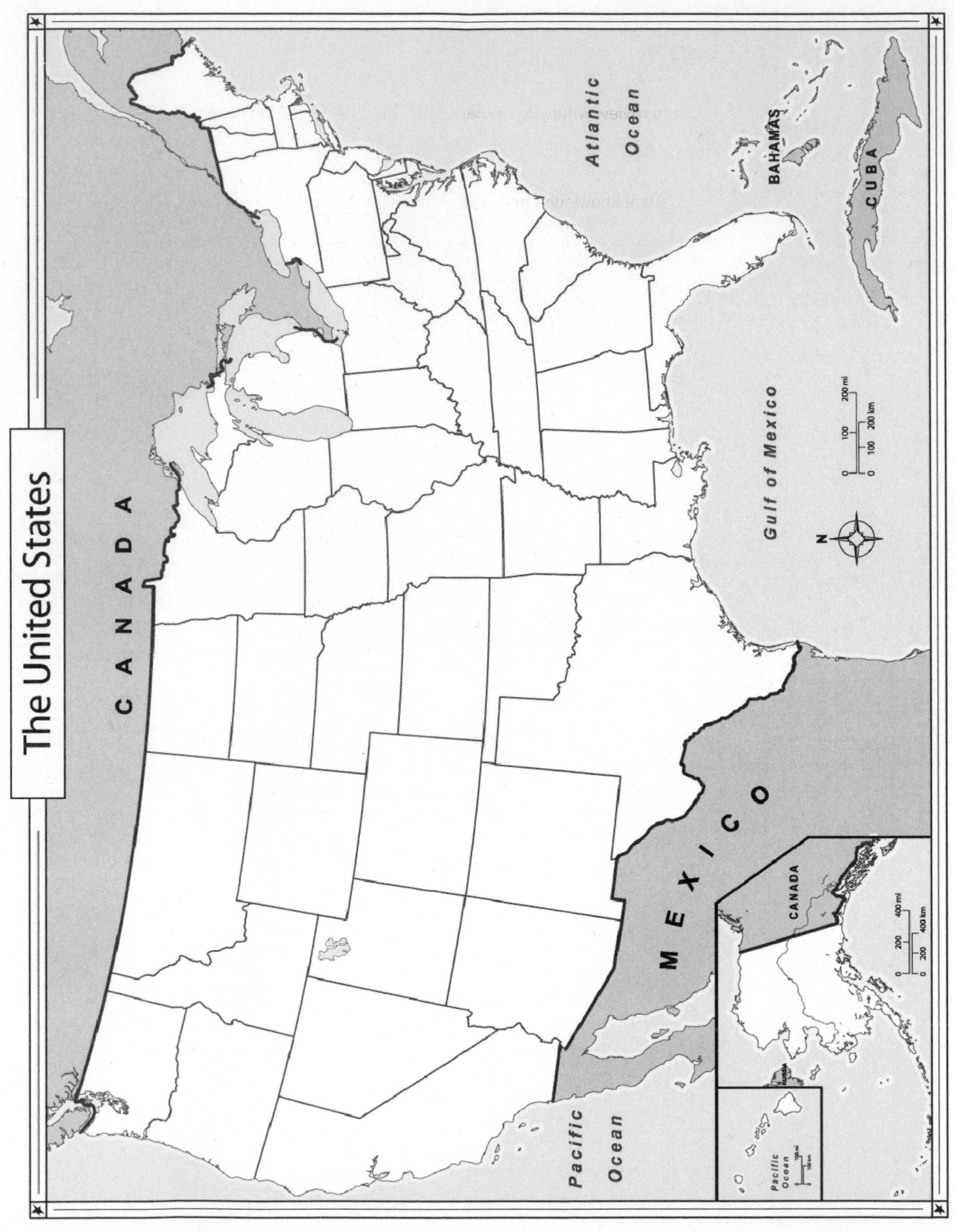
The United States
CANADA
MEXICO
Atlantic Ocean
BAHAMAS
CUBA
Gulf of Mexico
Pacific Ocean
N
0 100 200 mi
0 100 200 km
CANADA
0 200 400 mi
0 200 400 km
Pacific Ocean

Student Guide
Lesson 11: Unit Review

You have finished the unit. It's time to review what you've learned. You will take the Unit Assessment in the next lesson.

Lesson Objectives

- Demonstrate mastery of important knowledge and skills in this unit.

PREPARE

Approximate lesson time is 60 minutes.

Materials

For the Student

A History of US (Concise Edition), Volume D (1929 to Present) by Joy Hakim

History Journal

LEARN

Activity 1: A Look Back *(Offline)*

Instructions

A. History Journal Review

Review what you learned in this unit by going through your History Journal. You should:

- Look at activity sheets you completed for this unit.
- Review unit Keywords.
- Read through any writing assignments you did during the unit.
- Review the assessments you took.

Don't rush through. Take your time. Your History Journal is a great resource for a unit review.

B. Online Review

Now go online and use the following to review this unit:

- Unit Review
- Fall of Communism map
- Time Line

Student Guide
Lesson 12: Unit Assessment

You've finished the unit! Take the Unit Assessment.

Lesson Objectives

- Identify areas of major U.S. military involvement since 1975.
- Identify the presidents from Nixon to Clinton and their accomplishments and failings.
- Describe significant cultural movements of the 1960s and 1970s.
- Recognize the power of the free press in a democratic society.
- Recognize recent trends in immigration and the reasons for those trends.
- Identify political changes in Europe since 1980.

PREPARE

Approximate lesson time is 60 minutes.

ASSESS

Unit Assessment: Not So Long Ago *(Online)*

You will complete an online assessment covering the main points of this unit. Your assessment will be scored by the computer.

Student Guide

Unit 13: Into the Twenty-First Century
Lesson 1: A Complicated Election

What do Elizabeth Peratrovich, Cesar Chavez, Betty Friedan, and Martin Luther King, Jr., have in common? They all fought for equal rights. Although each one focused on a particular segment of the population, they all realized that the struggle for equality for *all* Americans was worth fighting for.
Did their efforts pay off? How successful were the equal rights movements of the 1950s and 1960s?

On November 7, 2000, Americans went to the polls to elect the country's first president of the twenty-first century. The Republican candidate was George W. Bush, son of former president George H.W. Bush. His Democratic rival was Albert Gore, Clinton's vice president. It had been the longest and most expensive campaign in the history of the nation up to that time. Al Gore won the popular vote, but he lost the election to George Bush. Learn how the Electoral College made that possible.

Lesson Objectives

- Explain the presidential election process in the United States.
- Assess the impact of the Electoral College system on the election of 2000.

PREPARE

Approximate lesson time is 60 minutes.

Materials

For the Student

Election of 2000

A History of US (Concise Edition), Volume D (1929 to Present) by Joy Hakim

History Journal

LEARN

Activity 1: Election of 2000 *(Offline)*

Instructions

A. Read *(Chapter 63, pages 286–290)*

As you read, answer the following questions and compare your answers with the answers in the Lesson Answer Key.

1. How is the president of the United States chosen?
2. How was the Electoral College established? What determines the number of electors a state may have? In most states, what determines how many electoral votes a candidate receives?
3. What was the outcome of the 2000 presidential election? What role did the U.S. Supreme Court play in this election?

B. Use What You Know

The Electoral College

Imagine that you are a television news anchor on the evening news and you have been directed to explain to the audience the process used in the United States to elect presidents—the Electoral College. You will include at least one visual aid.

Analyze the Election of 2000 Map
Complete the Election of 2000 sheet using the Election of 2000 map in the chapter. Compare your answers with those in the Lesson Answer Key.

ASSESS

Lesson Assessment: A Complicated Election (*Online*)

You will complete an online assessment covering the main goals of this lesson. Your assessment will be scored by the computer.

Name Date

Election of 2000

Use the Election of 2000 map to answer the following questions.

1. If U.S. presidents were elected based solely on the popular vote, who would have won the 2000 presidential election?

2. Why would a presidential candidate spend a lot of time and money campaigning in states like California, New York, Florida, and Texas?

3. Before Florida's electoral votes were decided, how many electoral votes did George W. Bush have? How many did Gore have? At this point, who would have won the election?

4. If, in 2000, Florida had only had a total of 19 representatives and senators in Congress, who would have won the election (provided that all of Florida's electors had voted for Bush)? Explain your answer.

5. If a recount had been allowed in Florida, and it had been found that Gore had won the popular election (and Florida's 25 electoral votes), who would have won the presidency? Explain your answer.

6. When George Bush was elected president in 2000, he became the fourth president in U.S. history to take office without defeating his opponent in the popular vote. Considering all of this, do you think the Electoral College is the best way to elect a president? Why or why not?

7. Why might large states want to continue using the Electoral College? Why might small states want to continue it?

8. Who might want to amend the Constitution to do away with the Electoral College?

Student Guide
Lesson 2: Terrible Challenges

On September 11, 2001, the United States suddenly came under attack. Terrorists targeted the World Trade Center in New York City and key government buildings in and around Washington, D.C., but millions of people around the world felt the effects. During this time of shock and fear, people everywhere showed compassion and selflessness in helping the victims and their survivors. Do you have questions about what happened that day?

Lesson Objectives

- Trace the events of 9/11/01.
- Identify Osama bin Laden and al-Qaeda as those responsible for the attacks.
- Recognize al Qaeda's distorted beliefs.
- Identify Afghanistan on a map and the reasons for the U.S. attack.

PREPARE

Approximate lesson time is 60 minutes.

Materials

For the Student

About Afghanistan

A History of US (Concise Edition), Volume D (1929 to Present) by Joy Hakim

History Journal

LEARN

Activity 1: A Nation Responds *(Offline)*

Instructions

A. Read *(Chapter 64, pages 291–295; Chapter 65, pages 296–299)*

As you read, answer the following questions and compare your answers with those in the Lesson Answer Key.

1. Prior to September 11, 2001, why were Americans so complacent?
2. Describe the events that took place on September 11, 2001.
3. What did President George W. Bush have to say about the attack on September 11?
4. What terrorist group was responsible for the attacks on September 11? What were the group's feelings about the U.S. and other free nations?
5. Why were the terrorists' message a perversion of Islam and a smokescreen?
6. Who was Osama bin Laden? Why did many Muslim leaders reject Osama's beliefs and al-Qaeda's actions?

B. Use What you Know

Complete the About Afghanistan sheet and compare your answers with the answers in the Lesson Answer Key.

ASSESS

Lesson Assessment: Terrible Challenges (*Online*)

You will complete an online assessment covering the main goals of this lesson. Your assessment will be scored by the computer.

Name ______________________________ Date ______________________________

About Afghanistan

1. Identify Afghanistan on the map below by coloring it in and labeling it.

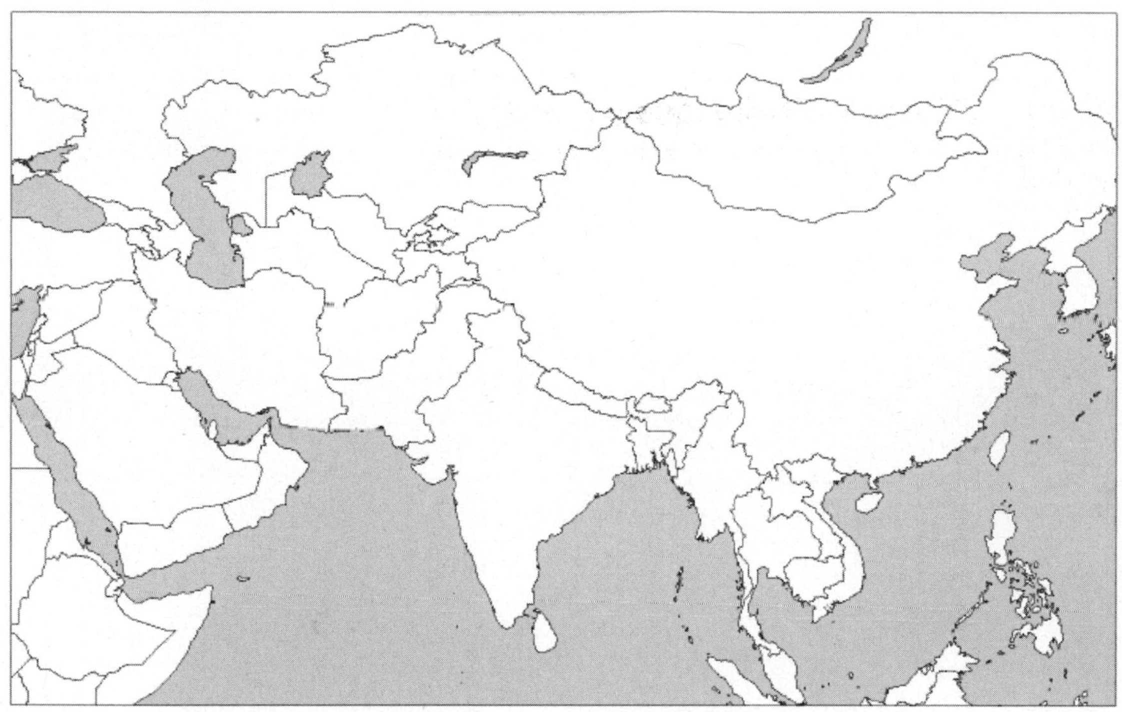

Use the map of Afghanistan in Chapter 65 to answer questions 2–4.

2. What countries surround Afghanistan?

____

3. With what country does Afghanistan share its longest border?

____

4. What is the capital of Afghanistan?

____

5. By 2000, what group controlled most of Afghanistan?

____

6. Who fled to Afghanistan after the 9/11 terrorist attacks?

____

7. Why did the United States attack Afghanistan?

____

Student Guide
Lesson 3: (Optional) Your Choice

Lesson Objectives

- Explore knowledge and skills taught in this course.

PREPARE

Approximate lesson time is 60 minutes.

Materials

For the Student

Map of the United States

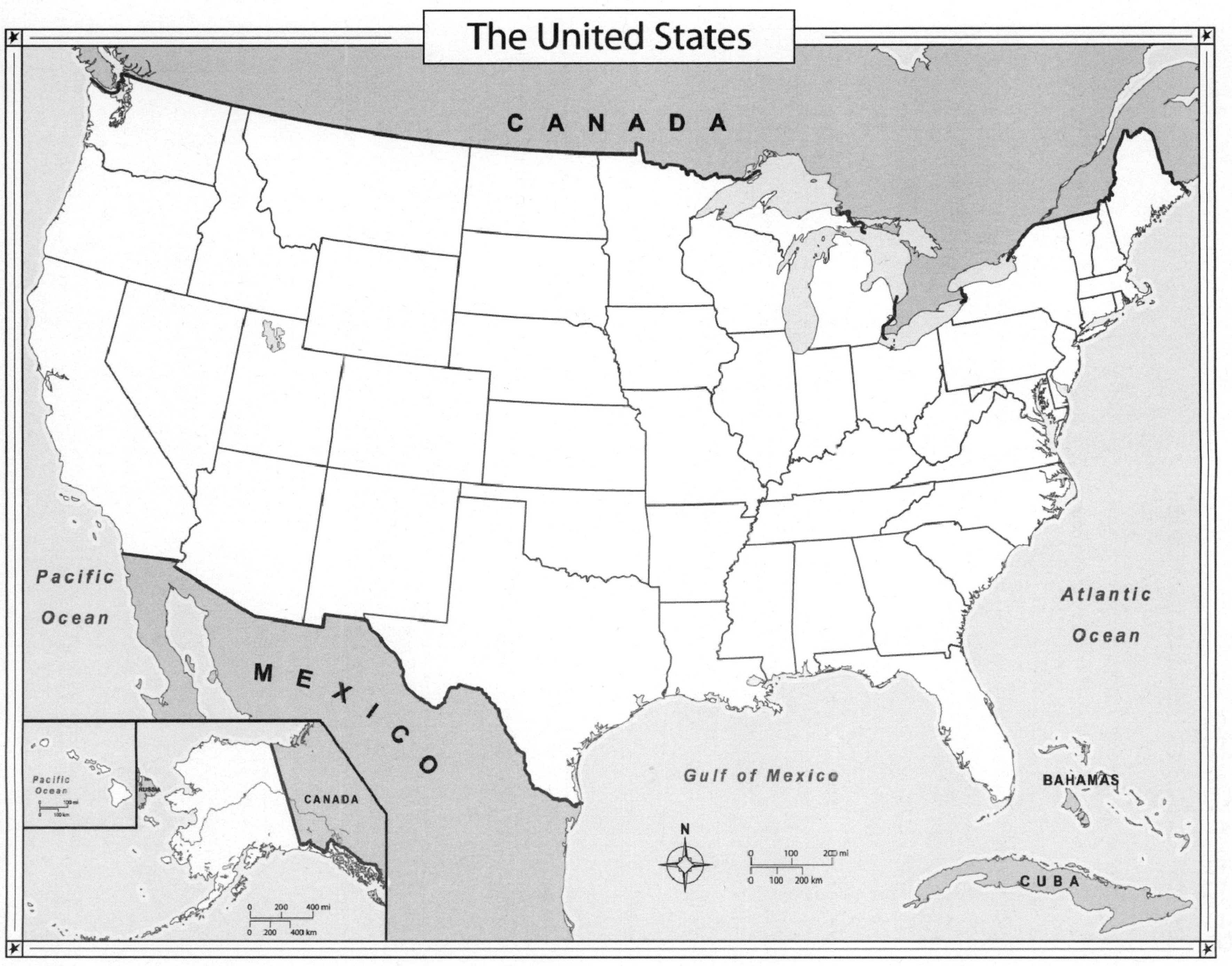
The United States
CANADA
Pacific Ocean
Atlantic Ocean
MEXICO
Gulf of Mexico
BAHAMAS
CUBA
N
0 100 200 mi
0 100 200 km
Pacific Ocean
RUSSIA
CANADA
0 200 400 mi
0 200 400 km

Student Guide
Lesson 4: Grave Decisions

In March 2003, a U.S.-led force invaded Iraq. Iraq's dictator, Saddam Hussein, had failed to cooperate with UN inspectors who were looking for weapons of mass destruction. President George W. Bush and his administration viewed Iraq as a major threat to the world.

While many Americans supported the war, some did not. Both sides had arguments to support their positions. Learn what these arguments were and why the war did not end as quickly as expected.

Lesson Objectives

- Identify reasons for the U.S. invasion of Iraq in 2003.
- Describe possible arguments for and against the military action.
- Explain why the Iraq War did not end as quickly as expected.

PREPARE

Approximate lesson time is 60 minutes.

Materials

For the Student

A History of US (Concise Edition), Volume D (1929 to Present) by Joy Hakim

History Journal

LEARN

Activity 1: War in Iraq *(Offline)*

Instructions

A. Read *(Chapter 66, pages 300–303)*

As you read, answer the following questions.

1. Who was Saddam Hussein? What about his personality and behavior made people fear and distrust him?
2. Even though Osama bin Laden was still at large, why did President Bush turn his attention to Iraq?
3. What challenge did President Bush propose to Saddam Hussein? What was the outcome of that challenge?
4. Describe some of the events that eventually led to Saddam Hussein's capture.
5. On May 1, 2003, President Bush announced that the war in Iraq was over. U.S. troops couldn't find any WMDs. So why did U.S. troops and other allies remain in Iraq?
6. While in Iraq, U.S. and coalition forces made some bad mistakes. What were the reasons for these mistakes?

Use the War in Iraq map to answer the following questions.

1. From what two Middle Eastern countries did coalition troop movements originate?
2. What two religious/ethnic groups lived in the region to the east of Iraq's capital?
3. Do you think troops moving south from the Turkey-Iraq border were helped or hindered by the local inhabitants of that region? Explain your answer.

B. Discuss

One of the main reasons for the U.S. invasion of Iraq in 2003 was that U.S. officials believed Saddam Hussein was actively seeking to acquire or manufacture weapons of mass destruction. Other reasons include:

- Bush believed a free, stable, and democratic Iraq was vital to American foreign policy interests.
- Intelligence reports appeared to indicate that Saddam Hussein had aided and harbored terrorist groups.
- The administration did not want the United States to appear to be weak on terrorism.

Discuss with your Learning Coach or other adult possible arguments that could have been made against invading Iraq.

ASSESS

Lesson Assessment: Grave Decisions (*Online*)

You will complete an online assessment covering the main goals of this lesson. Your assessment will be scored by the computer.

Student Guide
Lesson 5: Natural Disaster

In August 2005, a hurricane formed over the Bahama Islands. Named Katrina, it moved over Florida as a moderate Category 1 hurricane, causing some flooding but few deaths. After leaving Florida, Katrina headed across the Gulf of Mexico, gaining tremendous strength. The hurricane hit Gulf Coast communities east of New Orleans early on Monday, August 29. At 9 a.m., the eye passed slightly to the east of New Orleans. By Tuesday, floodwaters covered 80 percent of New Orleans.

Lesson Objectives

- Identify New Orleans on a map.
- Explain why a severe hurricane in New Orleans could cause so much flooding.
- Summarize the criticisms of government response to Katrina.
- Explore the role of FEMA.

PREPARE

Approximate lesson time is 60 minutes.

Materials

For the Student

A History of US (Concise Edition), Volume D (1929 to Present) by Joy Hakim

History Journal

LEARN

Activity 1: The Fury of Katrina *(Online)*

Instructions

A. Read *(Chapter 67, pages 304–307)*

As you read, answer the following questions and compare the answers to those in the Lesson Answer Key.

1. As Katrina became a Category 5, more than a million people left New Orleans. Why did others remain in New Orleans?
2. Explain why a severe hurricane in New Orleans could cause so much flooding.
3. What was the result of the slow government response to Katrina at the local, state, and national level?

B. Use What You Know

Create a time line of important events involving Hurricane Katrina and its effects on New Orleans. You can create your time line on paper, poster board, or online, using presentation software such as PowerPoint.

- Make the first entry on the time line be August 23, 2005—Tropical Depression 12 forms over the Bahamas; it will eventually strengthen and become Hurricane Katrina.

- Make the last entry on the time line be September 6, 2005—Congress returns to Washington and begins hearings on the Bush administration's handling of the disaster.

- Include five to eight entries in-between. The entries should describe important events of the hurricane, focusing on its landfall and effects on New Orleans.

- Use the Internet to conduct research and find five to eight suitable events for your time line. One good source can be found at the National Geographic website where you can view video clips titled Katrina Day by Day and Doomed New Orleans. The second video clip automatically plays after the first video ends.

C. Explore

Explore online the roles of FEMA and the Army Corps of Engineers.

ASSESS

Lesson Assessment: Natural Disaster (*Online*)

You will complete an online assessment covering the main goals of this lesson. Your assessment will be scored by the computer.

Student Guide
Lesson 6: Election Firsts

The presidential election of 2008 was a historic and groundbreaking election. For the first time in more than 50 years, neither an incumbent president nor a sitting vice president would be a candidate. The candidates who did emerge came from a greater variety of backgrounds than ever before.

In the end, the Republicans nominated Senator John McCain; the Democrats, Senator Barack Obama. One of the central themes of the election was experience versus change.

Lesson Objectives

- Identify ways in which the election of 2008 was unique in American history.

PREPARE

Approximate lesson time is 60 minutes.

Materials

For the Student

- Presidential Time Line
- Profile
- A History of US (Concise Edition), Volume D (1929 to Present) by Joy Hakim
- History Journal

LEARN

Activity 1: The Election of 2008 *(Offline)*

Instructions

A. Read *(Chapter 69, pages 310–314)*

As you read, answer the following questions. When you have finished, compare your answers with those in the Lesson Answer Key.

1. What made the race for the Democratic nomination in 2008 unique?
2. What modern technology did Obama's campaign staff use to raise money from a broad swath of Americans?
3. What was Obama's catchphrase that inspired his followers?
4. Who was the Republican candidate in the 2008 election?
5. Who is Sarah Palin and what did she add to the election campaign?
6. Who is Sonia Sotomayor?

B. Research

President Barack Obama

Research online President Barack Obama. Collect information from *The New Book of Knowledge*, Grolier's online encyclopedia, and from other websites (A good source would be the White House website).

Complete a Presidential Time Line sheet for President Obama. Be sure to include the following information:

- Personal Characteristics/Background
- Major Contributions
- Major Failures/Problems
- Domestic Policies/Activities
- Foreign Policies/Activities

If you need more space to write, you may use extra paper or the back of the Presidential Time Line sheet.

Hillary Clinton

The former First Lady and U.S. senator from New York, Hillary Clinton, lost the Democratic nomination to Barack Obama. Many expected, and hoped, that she would become the first woman president. She deserves to be included in the Profiles in American History in your History Journal. Write a summary about her by completing the Profile of Courage sheet. Collect information from *The New Book of Knowledge*, Grolier's online encyclopedia, and from other websites.

ASSESS

Lesson Assessment: Election Firsts (*Online*)

You will complete an online assessment covering the main goals of this lesson. Your assessment will be scored by the computer.

Name _______________________________ Date _______________________________

Presidential Time Line

If you can find a picture of this president, attach it here.

Name: ______________________

Years in Office: ______ – ______

Number of Terms: ______

Vice president: ______________________

First Lady: ______________________

______ President

☆☆☆☆☆☆☆☆☆☆☆☆☆☆☆☆☆

Name Date

Profile of

Place Picture Here

Student Guide
Lesson 7: Then and Now, Part 1

Two wars and a natural disaster are major events that plagued the United States in the 21st century. In this lesson you will begin researching the current situation for one of these events.

Lesson Objectives

- Conduct research to update recent historical events.

PREPARE

Approximate lesson time is 60 minutes.

Materials

For the Student

Preparing to Write

A History of US: All the People (Book 10) by Joy Hakim

History Journal

LEARN

Activity 1: Research *(Offline)*

Instructions

At the beginning of the twenty-first century, the United States experienced two wars, Afghanistan and Iraq, and a natural disaster (Hurricane Katrina) in New Orleans. You will choose one of these events and summarize the changes that have occurred since the beginning of the event.

- Create a Then and Now poster.
- Use the Internet, newspaper articles, and news magazine articles to find current information.
- When possible, incorporate pictures with your content.

You will begin your research today, but you will have two additional days to complete your visual essay (poster).

Name Date

Preparing to Write

Part 1: Read and Analyze the Essay Question

1. Read the following essay question to yourself. Read it again aloud. Highlight important words in the question.

   How successful were the equal rights movements of the 1950s and 1960s?

2. What does the question ask you to do? (Circle one or more items below.)
   - Compare and contrast?
   - Explain?
   - Describe?
   - Agree or disagree with a statement?
   - Prove something?

3. Rewrite the question as a sentence that shows your understanding of what the question is asking. Start with "I will ____________________."

   I will ____

   ____

   ____

   ____

4. Show your sentence to an adult and discuss the meaning of the question.

Part 2: Record What You Know

1. Use the chart on the next page to organize information about two important equal rights movements from the '50s and '60s.

   Information can come from:
   - Knowledge you already have
   - Time Line: 1945–1969
   - Sheets in your History Journal with relevant content

2. You may have more information in some columns than in others and you shouldn't try to list everything about the movements. An example has been provided for you.

Information on Movements

Movement	The People	The Ideas	The Events	The Results
Equal Rights for African Americans				
Equal Rights for Women	Example: Betty Friedan	Women want choice and opportunities to develop talents.	Founded NOW, wrote *Feminine Mystique*	NOW unable to get ERA passed; raised new ideas and changed stereotypes about women

Student Guide
Lesson 8: Then and Now, Part 2

Continue to do research for your Then and Now poster.

Lesson Objectives

- Conduct research to update recent historical events.

PREPARE

Approximate lesson time is 60 minutes.

Student Guide
Lesson 9: (Optional) Your Choice

You may use today's lesson time to do one or more of the following:

- Complete work in progress.
- Locate and identify the 50 states in the game
  U.S. Map Puzzle
  or print the outline map and see how many of the 50 states you can identify.
- Go on to the next lesson.

Please mark this lesson complete in order to proceed to the next lesson in the course.

Lesson Objectives

- Explore knowledge and skills taught in this course.

PREPARE

Approximate lesson time is 60 minutes.

Materials

For the Student

Map of the United States

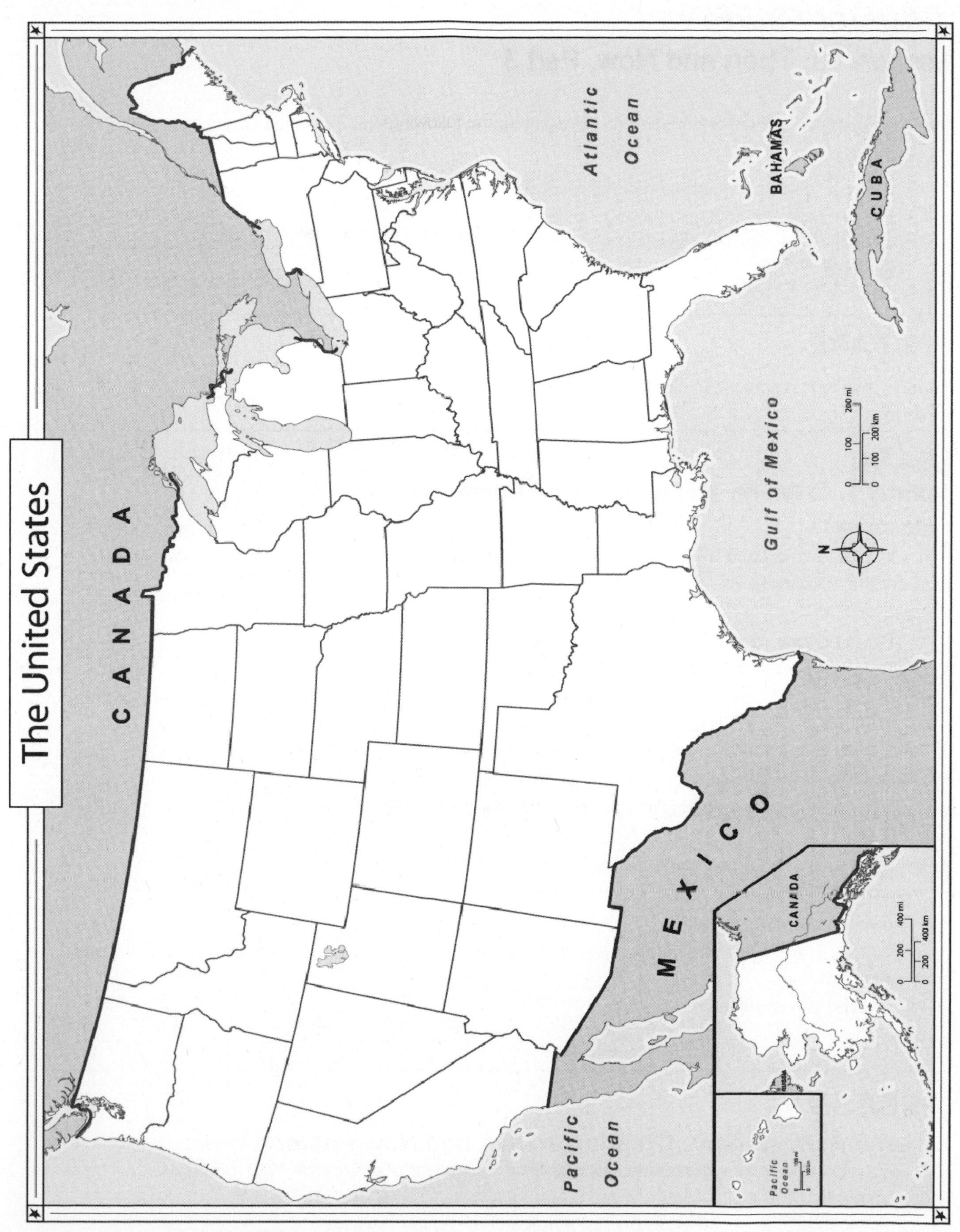
The United States
CANADA
Atlantic Ocean
BAHAMAS
CUBA
Gulf of Mexico
MEXICO
Pacific Ocean
CANADA
Pacific Ocean

Student Guide
Lesson 10: Then and Now, Part 3

You've researched current information on the event that you chose. Now it's time to create your poster.

Lesson Objectives

- Conduct research to update recent historical events.
- Present research findings in a visual essay.
- Write a well-constructed expository essay supported by primary sources in response to an essay question.

PREPARE

Approximate lesson time is 60 minutes.

LEARN

Activity 1: Creating a Then and Now Poster *(Offline)*

Instructions

You will create a Then and Now poster of the event that you chose to research. While creating your poster, consider the following.

- Organize your research into a "Then" section and a "Now" section.
- Title your poster including the name of the event that you chose.
- Include in your Then section accurate historical background information, reasons or causes for the event, or events leading up to the major event, and consequences of the event.
- Include in the Now section any major changes that have occurred, status of the people or economy or so on; and any new laws or regulations created as a result of the event.
- Include, when possible, any images that help support your content.

An adult will assess your poster. Items that you will be assessed on include:

- Assignment is completed.
- Content is well developed and organized; ideas are clear; and information is accurate, relevant, and complete.
- Spelling, punctuation, and grammar

ASSESS

Lesson Assessment: Creating a Then and Now Poster *(Online)*

You will complete an online assessment covering the main points of this lesson. Your assessment will be scored by the computer.

Student Guide
Lesson 11: Unit Review

You have finished the unit. It's time to review what you've learned. You will take the Unit Assessment in the next lesson.

Lesson Objectives

- Demonstrate mastery of important knowledge and skills in this unit.

PREPARE

Approximate lesson time is 60 minutes.

Materials

For the Student

A History of US (Concise Edition), Volume D (1929 to Present) by Joy Hakim

History Journal

LEARN

Activity 1: A Look Back *(Offline)*

Instructions

History Journal Review

Review what you learned in this unit by going through your History Journal. You should:

- Look at activity sheets you completed for this unit.
- Review unit Keywords.
- Read through any writing assignments you did during the unit.
- Review the assessments you took.

Don't rush through. Take your time. Your History Journal is a great resource for a unit review.

Student Guide
Lesson 12: Unit Assessment

You've finished the unit! Take the Unit Assessment.

Lesson Objectives

- Explain the presidential election process in the United States.
- Assess the impact of the Electoral College system on the election of 2000.
- Trace the events of 9/11/01.
- Identify Osama bin Laden and al-Qaeda as those responsible for the attacks.
- Recognize al-Qaeda's distorted beliefs.
- Identify Afghanistan on a map and the reasons for the U.S. attack.
- Identify reasons for the U.S. invasion of Iraq in 2003.
- Describe possible arguments for and against the military action.
- Explain why the Iraq War did not end as quickly as expected.
- Identify New Orleans on a map.
- Explain why a severe hurricane in New Orleans could cause so much flooding.
- Summarize the criticisms of government response to Katrina.
- Explore the role of FEMA.
- Identify ways in which the election of 2008 was unique in American history.

PREPARE

Approximate lesson time is 60 minutes.

ASSESS

Unit Assessment: Into the Twenty-First Century (*Online*)

You will complete an online assessment covering the main points of this unit. Your assessment will be scored by the computer.

Student Guide
Lesson 13: End-of-Course Review: Units 1–3

You've finished! Now it's time to pull together what you have learned this year. You've learned a lot, so we'll review it unit by unit. Let's start by taking a quick look at the first three units. Ready?

Lesson Objectives

- Demonstrate mastery of important knowledge and skills taught in the Changing and Growing unit.
- Demonstrate mastery of important knowledge and skills taught in the Politics, Power, and the People unit.
- Demonstrate mastery of important knowledge and skills taught in the Reformers, Newcomers, and Innovators unit.

PREPARE

Approximate lesson time is 60 minutes.

Materials

For the Student

Unit Snapshot

A History of US (Concise Edition), Volume C (1865-1932) by Joy Hakim

History Journal

LEARN

Activity 1: Units 1–3 *(Online)*

Instructions

Let's review! Study your work from Units 1–3. As you review the units, complete the Unit Snapshot sheets. When you have finished your offline review, complete the online interactive review.

Name Date

Unit Snapshot

Categorize important information from this unit.

Significant People	Significant Events

Significant Places	Symbols of the Period
	(What do you associate with this time period? Example: 1840s—covered wagons)

What was your favorite lesson? Why?

Name Date

Unit Snapshot

Categorize important information from this unit.

Significant People	Significant Events

Significant Places	Symbols of the Period
	(What do you associate with this time period? Example: 1840s—covered wagons)

What was your favorite lesson? Why?

Name Date

Unit Snapshot

Categorize important information from this unit.

Significant People	Significant Events

Significant Places	Symbols of the Period
	(What do you associate with this time period? Example: 1840s—covered wagons)

What was your favorite lesson? Why?

Name Date

Unit Snapshot

Categorize important information from this unit.

Significant People	Significant Events

Significant Places	Symbols of the Period
	(What do you associate with this time period? Example: 1840s—covered wagons)

What was your favorite lesson? Why?

Student Guide
Lesson 14: End-of-Course Review: Units 4, 6, and 7

Let's review the next three units.

Lesson Objectives

- Demonstrate mastery of important knowledge and skills taught in the Making Things Better unit.
- Demonstrate mastery of important knowledge and skills taught in the Entering a New Century unit.
- Demonstrate mastery of important knowledge and skills taught in the A Fascinating Era unit.

PREPARE

Approximate lesson time is 60 minutes.

Materials

For the Student

Unit Snapshot

A History of US (Concise Edition), Volume C (1865-1932) by Joy Hakim

History Journal

LEARN

Activity 1: Units 4, 6, and 7 *(Online)*

Instructions

Let's review! Study your work from Units 4, 6, and 7. As you review the units, complete the Unit Snapshot sheets. When you have finished your offline review, complete the online interactive review.

Name Date

Unit Snapshot

Categorize important information from this unit.

Significant People	Significant Events

Significant Places	Symbols of the Period
	(What do you associate with this time period? Example: 1840s—covered wagons)

What was your favorite lesson? Why?

Name Date

Unit Snapshot

Categorize important information from this unit.

Significant People	Significant Events

Significant Places	Symbols of the Period
	(What do you associate with this time period? Example: 1840s—covered wagons)

What was your favorite lesson? Why?

Name Date

Unit Snapshot

Categorize important information from this unit.

Significant People	Significant Events

Significant Places	Symbols of the Period
	(What do you associate with this time period? Example: 1840s—covered wagons)

What was your favorite lesson? Why?

Student Guide
Lesson 15: End-of-Course Review: Units 8–10

Let's review the next three units.

Lesson Objectives

- Demonstrate mastery of important knowledge and skills taught in the Hard Times unit.
- Demonstrate mastery of important knowledge and skills taught in The Second World War unit.
- Demonstrate mastery of important knowledge and skills taught in the Recovery, Reaction, Reform unit.

PREPARE

Approximate lesson time is 60 minutes.

Materials

For the Student

Unit Snapshot

A History of US (Concise Edition), Volume D (1929 to Present) by Joy Hakim

History Journal

LEARN

Activity 1: Units 8–10 *(Online)*

Instructions

Let's see what you remember from these three units in this course: Hard Times; The Second World War; and Recovery, Reaction, Reform. But first, print the three Unit Snapshot sheets to use during your review.

Name Date

Unit Snapshot

Categorize important information from this unit.

Significant People	**Significant Events**

Significant Places	**Symbols of the Period**
	(What do you associate with this time period? Example: 1840s—covered wagons)

What was your favorite lesson? Why?

Name Date

Unit Snapshot

Categorize important information from this unit.

Significant People	Significant Events

Significant Places	Symbols of the Period
	(What do you associate with this time period? Example: 1840s—covered wagons)

What was your favorite lesson? Why?

Student Guide
Lesson 16: End-of-Course Review: Units 11–13

Let's review the final three units: A Turbulent Time, Not So Long Ago, and Into the Twenty-First Century.

Lesson Objectives

- Demonstrate mastery of important knowledge and skills taught in the A Turbulent Time unit.
- Demonstrate mastery of important knowledge and skills taught in the Not So Long Ago unit.
- Demonstrate mastery of important knowledge and skills taught in the Into the Twenty-First Century unit.

PREPARE

Approximate lesson time is 60 minutes.

Materials

For the Student

Unit Snapshot

A History of US (Concise Edition), Volume D (1929 to Present) by Joy Hakim

History Journal

LEARN

Activity 1: Units 11–13 *(Online)*

Instructions

Let's review! Study your work from the final three units: A Turbulent Time, Not So Long Ago, and Into the Twenty-First Century. But first, print three Unit Snapshots to use during your review.

Name Date

Unit Snapshot

Categorize important information from this unit.

Significant People	Significant Events

Significant Places	Symbols of the Period
	(What do you associate with this time period? Example: 1840s—covered wagons)

What was your favorite lesson? Why?

Name Date

Unit Snapshot

Categorize important information from this unit.

Significant People	Significant Events

Significant Places	Symbols of the Period
	(What do you associate with this time period? Example: 1840s—covered wagons)

What was your favorite lesson? Why?

Student Guide
Lesson 17: State Capitals Review and Assessment

Lesson Objectives
- Demonstrate mastery of important knowledge and skills taught in the second semester.
- Identify the state capitals of the 50 U.S. states.

PREPARE

Approximate lesson time is 60 minutes.

Materials

For the Student

Map of the United States

ASSESS

Lesson Assessment: State Capitals *(Online)*

You will complete an online assessment covering the main points of this lesson. Your assessment will be scored by the computer.

Student Guide
Lesson 18: End-of-Course Assessment

You've reviewed all the units! You're ready for the End-of-Course Assessment. Take the assessment, and then take a well-deserved break! You've learned a lot this year!

Lesson Objectives

- Explain that Native Americans and homesteaders had incompatible ways of life.
- Identify the major reasons for the move to restrict immigration.
- Identify the challenges and impacts of building a transcontinental railroad.
- Define *monopoly, trust, command economy, market economy, hybrid economy,* and *corporation.*
- Describe the ways the nation was changing in the late 1800s.
- Describe the amendment process under the Constitution.
- Recognize similarities between the Red Scare of the 1950s and reactions to fears in other time periods.
- Demonstrate mastery of important knowledge and skills taught in the Hard Times unit.
- Demonstrate mastery of important knowledge and skills taught in the A Turbulent Time unit.
- Demonstrate mastery of important knowledge and skills taught in the Recovery, Reaction, Reform unit.
- Demonstrate mastery of important knowledge and skills taught in the The Second World War unit.
- Demonstrate mastery of important knowledge and skills taught in the Not So Long Ago unit.
- Describe Woodrow Wilson's plan for world peace and the reasons for the plan's failure.
- Compare democratic and totalitarian governments in terms of the value of the individual citizen.
- Explain the presidential election process in the United States.
- Trace the events of 9/11/01.
- Identify Osama bin Laden and al-Qaeda as those responsible for the attacks.
- Recognize al-Qaeda's distorted beliefs.
- Explain why the Iraq War did not end as quickly as expected.
- Explain why a severe hurricane in New Orleans could cause so much flooding.
- Identify ways in which the election of 2008 was unique in American history.

PREPARE

Approximate lesson time is 60 minutes.

ASSESS

Course Assessment: MS American History Since 1865 Assessment *(Online)*

You will complete an online assessment covering the main points of this course. Your assessment will be scored by the computer.